Dec. 2009

Lisa ~

May you have
peace in your heart.
I'M truly grateful
for all you've been to
me during our decades
of friendship.
  Love.
  Margaret Cowie

No Regrets, My Love

Margaret Cowie

authorHOUSE®

AuthorHouse™
1663 Liberty Drive
Bloomington, IN 47403
www.authorhouse.com
Phone: 1-800-839-8640

First published by AuthorHouse 11/19/2009

ISBN: 978-1-4490-3180-0 (e)
ISBN: 978-1-4490-3178-7 (sc)
ISBN: 978-1-4490-3179-4 (hc)

Library of Congress Control Number: 2009910770

Printed in the United States of America
Bloomington, Indiana
This book is printed on acid-free paper.

Dedication

To Will, the love of my life.
You gave me so many magical yesterdays.

Table of Contents

Part One

Part Two

Part Three

Introduction

This story is about two ordinary people that met by chance and became an extraordinary married couple. At times, it seemed as if we lived a fairytale life, but we were quite acquainted with pain as well. We triumphed over incredible hurdles through our life together, and enjoyed samples of the finer things in life. We finally found the peace our souls craved at our homestead nestled in the White Mountains of New Hampshire in 1998. Like anyone else, we thought we would live to a ripe old age, sharing abundant laughter and a simpler life, just the two of us. Suddenly, over twenty one years after we met life as we knew it would change forever.

I was raised an army brat, the oldest child of four, with two sisters and a brother. Our family traveled across America and Germany during the first seventeen years of my life. Military life is both a blessing and a curse. You get see the world, but are constantly uprooted and any social life you have established is abruptly cancelled. I made many great childhood friends and am still in contact with a few of them.

As a young person I lacked self confidence and was ashamed of what some call my stunning looks. I preferred to blend with the wallpaper and be left alone. Life as a child was not chipper. Although my mother tried to keep the family unit together and functional, I lived in constant fear of my father. He was a violent abuser, and at age seventeen I took an escape route through marriage.

I was married for less than a year when my mother's world caved in and she left my father. She and my siblings drove three thousand miles and landed in her hometown in Massachusetts. I graduated from high school that year and then by chance I began a career in dentistry.

My marriage ended in disaster. He was a master at manipulation throwing false accusations at me, and in the end was in complete control of my life. Things were so bad that I prayed for God to end my life so I could be relieved of my misery. I was young and afraid and kept hearing the vow *for better or worse* in my head and pushed to try to make things better. I figured I made my bed and now I had to lay in it. Finally, a friend steered me to her minister for some counsel. He dug deep, not only into my marriage, but into my childhood and the marriage I witnessed at home. He felt I was living my vows in the shadows of the bad marriage of my parents. He told me I could be set free if I was willing to walk away. With that I felt like I received divine permission.

After living in my cocoon of hell for eight years I got the courage to leave my ex-husband. I packed my bags, loaded my car and I drove from Washington State to Massachusetts, just me and my cat. The three and a half day trek across country turned out to be therapeutic and I felt immediate jubilation leaving my shackles behind.

I was an insecure woman after that ordeal of mental battery, and was not sure I'd risk loving or being loved again. I was in the stage of building a new life for myself without being told what I could or couldn't do and rather enjoying it. In Massachusetts I tested the waters of dating, but it was discouraging at first. Because of my past it was difficult to trust. I was twenty-five years old, and one night in my new found freedom I met Will and my life changed forever.

William Cowie, "Will" was raised in Burlington, Massachusetts. He was the first born son of four children with an older sister, a younger sister and brother. He came from a blue collar family fortunate enough to stay in one place and established deep roots with all his relatives.

As a child he enjoyed family vacations to the ocean in the summertime. During his years in high school he was involved in the performing arts and played the role of Sky Masterson in Guys and Dolls, and he also had the honor to sing in the district choir. He graduated from high school and then began to attend college, but soon felt a calling to join the United States Air Force. He had a strong desire to serve his country and perhaps see the world. He spent just over four years in the service and traveled to eight countries around the globe. With that he was a very patriotic American for the rest of his life.

During active duty in the Air Force he married an English woman while stationed in England. The marriage crumbled immediately and when his enlistment with the military ended he returned to the United States a single man. Shortly thereafter I met him and he showed me his world.

When we met I was working in the dental field and Will was an employed carpenter. He had a very strong work ethic and gave one hundred and ten percent to any task given to him. I am of the same mentality and I admired that in him, knowing it was a rare quality.

Will had a happy energy about him at all times. He could enter a room of gloom and instantly livened things up with his humor and wit. He was the life of the party, in a good way. He was a man of integrity; he was intelligent, ambitious, caring and generous, and had a strong sense of family. He was always willing to do for somebody else. He had the striking looks of John F. Kennedy Jr., and was male model material. With all his positive qualities and his willingness to love me and take me by the hand to show me the world, I was mesmerized and fell in love immediately. He was so different from the man I left behind and I was driven to drink from the fountain of richness he was offering me.

I think Will could see the hurt inside of me and wanted to show me life didn't have to be sour. He made me feel the excitement of a child wearing her favorite dress, anxiously waiting to go to a birthday party. In time, he would take me like a bird, heal my broken wing, and nurse me to the point of accepting his unconditional love and admiration for me. With that ability Will gave me an amazing gift, showing me how to have fun and find joy in living with him by my side.

Part One

No More Magic

Today I became a widow. It is August 26, 2008, just ten days after my birthday; I had celebrated so wonderfully with my husband. The key word there is with. I imagined so many things in my life, but never that I would lose my husband and best friend. Not now. We had our life planned out. How could this be possible? He was healthy and only forty-four years old. He was fine yesterday as he left me to go to work with his life loving, charming smile that suggested pure adoration for me. Somehow we experienced a remarkable past six months and were feeling like newlyweds again. Life has been cut short.

My husband Will left for work to test high voltage transformers on several assigned sites in upstate New York Monday, yesterday, just like he did every week. He took me to pick up his truck after having a brake job required to pass the state vehicle inspection and left for work from there. He was supposed to be on vacation, but his boss forgot to record the time off. She had him scheduled to be out of state for the week. Being a loyal and dependable person, Will agreed to work since we didn't have any formal plans for his time off. He owned his own company in the past and knew what it was like to be short handed.

At the repair shop, he kissed me goodbye and started to head out the door, but hesitated. He was concerned about me; he didn't want to leave me. We had the kind of relationship where we did everything together, including grocery shopping and laundry, and loved it. Never exiting the door, he came back to me, hugged and kissed me again, and then he began to leave, but stopped at the door again. He asked me if I was sure I was okay. I told him I was fine and to go ahead since he had a very long drive ahead of him.

Recent summer events created a passionate flame in our hearts that nothing could extinguish. He then repeated his motions for a third time. We said goodbye, and he went to the door hesitating. I chuckled at his cuteness and concern and confirmed I was going to be okay. He seemed uneasy about going, only because I thought he knew how much I was going to miss him since I was disappointed he didn't get the week off. He held the door open, and looked back at me over his shoulder with his fabulous smile and a sparkle in his eyes. As he looked at me I reassured him that I would be alright and would see him in a couple of days. Still standing at the door, he gave me a little wiggle of his butt, an inside joke of ours he got from an episode of Friends.

I felt giddy like a school girl, and in that moment in my mind I was already making plans for his return home Friday and could barely wait. Although difficult, we said goodbye knowing we would see each other in a few days, we had no reason to think we wouldn't. Tomorrow always came for us in the past.

He drove for about eight or nine hours. Around nine o'clock that night he called me to announce his safe arrival so I wouldn't worry. I was always concerned about a car accident with all the driving he did for work. He told me he had just arrived to the hotel and had not eaten any dinner yet and was tired. We usually talked briefly and then arranged a time to chat live using Instant Messenger on the computer. He was so tired and had to get directions to the work site, eat dinner and get washed, he asked if it was okay to skip our session that particular evening. I completely understood his exhaustion and told him it was perfectly fine and that we'd talk the next day. He called me a couple of times a day to check in so I figured we'd catch up then. We told each other, "I love you" and then said goodnight.

I watched a bit of a DVD and went to bed as usual that evening. I woke up the next morning and went about my daily chores. I decided that particular morning to go to the supermarket and buy groceries instead of doing torturous yard work in the hot August sun. We lived in the country and the store was just over twenty miles away. While I was there I did my other errands as well to free up our upcoming weekend time together.

I finished my running around in town and was almost home. As I drove down the hill into the village where we lived I saw the town hall. In an instant I realized I could stop in and do an errand for Will. He was running for New Hampshire State Representative on the Democrat ticket and the voting primaries were in a week or so. He went to the town hall that Monday to get an absentee ballot, but they were closed. He asked me if I wouldn't mind picking one up for him during the week, and of course I agreed to do so.

As I pulled into the parking lot of the town hall I noticed a state police car parked there and thought it strange. Our village's population was only about five hundred. I became curious about what type of an occurrence would require the state police and assumed the town clerk would fill me in since we were friends. The elementary school was across the street and the kids were outside playing during recess.

I parked my car and proceeded to go into the town hall, but before I got to the door the state trooper came outside and approached me as the town clerk followed behind him.

He said to me, "Are you Mrs. Cowie?"

I said, "Yes." I immediately got a sick feeling in my stomach wondering if I was being arrested or if my house burned down. I had not committed a crime, but one never knows about mistaken identity.

The police officer said to me, "I have bad news about Mr. Cowie."

I said, "Oh was he hurt?"

He said, "Mr. Cowie was killed in an accident at approximately seven a.m. today."

I did not believe what I just heard. My brain could not compute that message. I said, "What?"

The police officer repeated his message and I had heard him correctly. It couldn't be so, I just saw him yesterday. I saw his larger than life smile and felt his arms securely around me hugging me. I spoke to him on the phone, but he was too tired to talk. I was only stopping at the town hall for an absentee ballot, this couldn't be so. I fell to my knees in the parking lot and began to sob. Life as I knew it was over, my husband was killed. We were too happy for this tragedy to occur. I begged the officer to tell me it wasn't so.

Thinking back now, I think he probably felt helpless. The town clerk, my friend, picked me up and walked me into the town hall, I was numb. My mind was spinning so fast trying to figure out a way to erase what just happened so I could go home to my simple, little life. There, I could wait for Will to come home Friday like he always did.

They tried to calm me down. I couldn't stop crying and I was feeling nauseas from the shock. I asked if this was some kind of joke, begging them to tell me it was. It would mean Will was okay and I was indeed not a widow, lost in this world all alone. It would mean the love of my life would be home Friday, just like always. I so badly wanted it to be so and I could not grasp the news I was just given. It wasn't supposed to happen that way; we planned on living together forever. We actually thought we'd perish together in a car crash with our dogs and all die together, painlessly. Most importantly, we would be together for eternity.

I don't recall just how long I was at the town hall, if I had to guess, I'd say twenty minutes. I was falling apart, in shock, and all I could feel was my heart racing and the weakness in my limbs. I tried to pull it all together so they would think I was okay and let me go home. In all other situations I was always the stoic one who had great control and advice, but had neither in my moment of need. I wanted to go home and just try to grasp all of it. I needed to have my nervous breakdown in private, in my house with all of our things, our memories and our dogs. I wanted to curl up and lie on the floor and cry until I died.

The town clerk's son was at the town hall when all of this transpired. After I seemed to settle down some, his mother, asked him to take me home. I had to take my car because I had it loaded with groceries that needed to be refrigerated, so he rode with me. I only lived one mile away, there were no turns involved, and I could get there on autopilot. She closed the town hall and came to my house shortly afterward.

She and I sat at the table in my kitchen, I was in shock and numb and my body was shaking. I could not believe this was happening; I didn't want to believe it. During this bodily shutdown forced on by trauma to my brain I was wondering who to call first. I tried to sort out the idea of getting my husband's body back home since he was in New York. The state trooper had provided names and numbers to the New York State Police and the Coroner of the district in which he was killed. I was usually so organized, but my head was spinning, I was shattered and couldn't think straight. My friend sitting in my kitchen with me helped me with some of those thoughts. She had experienced death before and I never had. I let her guide me through the dark, turbulent waters I was wading in, feeling as if I was about to drown at any moment. The mind has incredible power in circumstances such as this; I was shutting down and became a zombie. She recommended a funeral director, but I could not fathom the thought of it. This was it; I had to engage in my new reality and make myself do it.

Our families needed to know what happened; I decided to call my mother first. I dialed the phone, and rehearsed what I was going to say while it rang. When my mom answered, I took a deep breath, and told her I had some very bad news. Just like in the movies, I told her to sit down for what I was about to say, and told her Will was killed today at work by electrocution. She screamed, "NO!" I began to cry uncontrollably again, yelling in my own head, No, is right. Will was larger than life and my mother loved him like her very own son, this couldn't be possible.

In response to my news, my mother wanted to immediately drive to my house and be with me, to mother me. However, I lived one hundred eighty miles from her house and did not want her to drive alone, upset. My friend's husband who was sitting with me offered to drive to Massachusetts to pick her up and I told her. She thought instead she'd ask my brother, who was also close to Will to bring her up here. We hung up from each other and I waited for her to call me back with the outcome. She finally called back and indeed my brother would be the one to drive her up to my house.

I had more phone calls to make in the meantime. The town clerk was still with me, she was wonderful. I had to decide who to call next. Will's family needed to hear the news. His mother was recovering from a heart condition so I was afraid to call her and give her the devastating news while she was alone. I couldn't bear being the cause of a disaster with her health. I pulled a name from my head and decided to call

Will's older sister. She was level headed and very good at making decisions and handling family matters.

With my heart beating out of my chest, I dialed her cell phone number. As it rang, I felt weak and nauseas. His sister answered and I asked her where she was. She told me she was walking her dog. I told her I had very bad news regarding her brother and asked if I could tell her now. She agreed it would be alright and then I told her Will was killed on the job today. She went silent and I was worried she collapsed to the ground with such a jolt of horrific information. I called out to her and she answered and then asked me how it happened. I told her he was electrocuted by the high voltage transformer he was working on at the ski resort in New York that morning. He died instantly by massive coronary since he was hit by 30,000 volts of electricity in his head. She was feeling the effects of this devastating, impossible news and asked if she could call me back when she got back to her house.

Will's sister called me back a few minutes later and we discussed how to tell the rest of her family. I offered to make the calls, but she eased me of the burden and offered to do it for me. She wanted to be sure her mother was in condition to hear such horrible news. As I presumed, she wisely contacted her mother's physician and asked his advice on how to handle the news. He recommended giving her some tranquilizers first to avoid triggering another heart attack, and she did. In the meantime, she made the call to Will's brother and other family members. It was a time of crisis and I was pacing like a caged animal not knowing how to escape. The gears in my head were turning, trying to reverse time, changing my new reality back to the past so I could move on and be normal.

I was at my house with the town clerk feeling so sad wondering what I had to live for. Life as I knew it ended in a blink of an eye. All I could do was continually recall the phone conversation we had just the night before and how we planned to talk tomorrow. Tomorrow would never come now, just the thought of that was killing me. I was crying and could barely breathe as the muscles in my chest and stomach tightened from the stress of such shock.

We just had the most magical summer and I basked in the memories of the fabulous vacation we had just taken to Boston in July. We spent three glorious days walking hand in hand, gazing into each others eyes, siteseeing, and doing the tourist thing there. Boston was special to us because while we dated we spent so much time there. We relived those days that July. I was trapped in the thoughts that there would be no more trips to Boston or to anywhere for that matter. We'd have no more conversations, trips for coffee, or rides on country roads. We'd have no more ANYTHING! It wasn't fair.

Romance In Boston

In the summer of 2008, like many other American's, we received a sum of money in the form of an economic stimulus package. It was presented by President George W. Bush, in hopes of pulling our country out of a sure recession. Will and I determined just how to put that money back into the economy too. We decided instead of paying bills or doing home improvements, we'd go to our favorite city for a vacation, Boston, Massachusetts. We hadn't taken a vacation alone without our dogs since 1992. Boston was significant because while we lived in Arlington we spent every weekend in that city. Faneuil Hall was the place to be on weekend nights. Those early years together in Boston created the fondest of memories for us.

My mother agreed to come to our house and stay with our dogs while we went away. We splurged and reserved a hotel right in the heart of downtown so we'd have quick access to all the places we wanted to see. We got up early in the morning, packed our luggage into our truck and made the four hour drive to Boston. Upon our arrival to the hotel, the valet took our truck and parked it for us. We checked in at the hotel desk and went to our room to freshen up a bit.

Shortly thereafter, we put our walking shoes on and went out to explore the city and took a tour down memory lane. It wasn't foreign to us at all; we knew the city like the backs of our hands. As we walked we looked at all the history around us in the architecture and buildings. The city has a wealth of history everywhere you look. You can almost travel back in time and get a sense of what life was like for the pioneers before us.

We walked to the Boston Public Gardens, an impeccably groomed park in the middle of the city. There are hundreds of trees displaying labels indicating what species they are and where they came from, as well as extravagant flower gardens including many varieties of roses in an array colors. There are famous sculptures, bronze statues and spectacular fountains throughout the park. There are walkways going through the center of the park and all around the perimeter of it as well, giving vantage to the city skyline. The state capital building, apartments and five star hotels that house the rich and famous, the Bullfinch Pub, also known as Cheers surround the park. It's a special place and tourists from all over the world visit it.

In the middle of the park is a pond where the famous Swan Boats float and offer rides through it. In the center of the pond is an island with a history for Will and me from our dating days. One frozen evening in winter, after a bit too much to drink at Cheers, we made love there. As we walked by the island holding hands on our trip, we both looked at each other simultaneously, and mentioned that night. Suddenly with the memory of it we felt a silly, heart fluttering feeling inside. Will squeezed my hand three times then, that was our code for "I love you." Will and I had many fond memories of that park. They were rising up inside of me as we walked hand in hand and sometimes arms around each other. It was just the most romantic time we had shared in a long time and reminiscing was bringing us such joy. We took that trip thinking money was no object since the government threw it to us. We spent the entire weekend touring the city on foot. We ate good food and shared the best of company between the two of us. In a city of thousands we were lost in our own world, oblivious once again to anyone around us. We seemed to experience that sensation frequently and I suppose that ability gave us the best quality time possible to each other.

After the stroll through the park we ventured toward Faneuil Hall. We noticed a Starbucks coffee house in our path and felt the urge to treat ourselves to a favorite, unavailable to us at home. Will ordered his traditional hot coffee; black no sugar and an iced coffee with a dash of skim milk for me. We continued our stroll through the city streets toward Faneuil Hall with our coffees in hand and our full attention toward each other.

We reached Faneuil Hall, a historical place known by many tourists and locals which was bulging with excitement. The visual stimulation to my brain was so grand, I wanted to absorb each bit of it and carry it with me for the rest of my life. The visit was logging more magical moments into my memory banks. I knew we'd share and laugh about them together when we were old and gray. Will and I walked holding hands like young lovers do for the entire three days and I think we were experiencing what is called a second honeymoon. Even though we were so familiar with the city, somehow it was still adventurous. We witnessed many of the street performances there, shopped at the stores and pushcarts, and dined a la cart at the food court. When we felt like relaxing we sat on a park bench. We took in all the sounds of the city and we watched musicians perform in hopes of earning their days wage or better, as passersby dropped money in a guitar case at their feet.

I remember as we watched a team of young female dancers perform, Will told me he was going to get a frozen fruit cup from a vender just up the way. The cups were filled with assorted melon chunks and grapes and were very refreshing on that hot July day. He asked me if I wanted one, I didn't, but instead I asked him to get me some fresh squeezed lemonade, also available at a push cart vendor. I remained standing where he left me and watched the dance troupe perform until he came back with the cool delights. He returned with a gleaming smile on his face that revealed he had a surprise he could not conceal. He then exposed the hand he had hidden behind his back and presented me with a long stem, yellow rose with fern and baby's breath. I felt a warm rush go through my body at that moment. I could see through his body language that he was so proud of himself and I knew exactly why. He remembered the old days when we courted of almost twenty years ago, how he bought me flowers at Faneuil Hall when we went there. He repeated that loving gesture that day and it reminded me that he was a romantic guy. Those thoughtful little things he did for me are why I loved him so much, he cared.

As we had done many times before, we ventured to the Charlestown Navy Shipyard to see the USS Constitution, or Old Ironsides as she is fondly known. I had discovered a water taxi offered from downtown to the shipyard during a previous visit to Boston, and thought it would be fun to take Will on it. The fee for the taxi was only $1.50 each way. We took the mini cruise offered by the Massachusetts Bay Transportation Authority; we got to see the city skyline and enjoyed the ocean breeze that cooled us off at the same time.

The boat delivered us to the naval shipyard and to our surprise Old Ironsides was under heavy maintenance. Luckily, we noticed adjacent to her was the destroyer USS Cassin Young and tours were free so we indulged. Will was in his glory seeing the ship, he loved history. As we toured the lower half of the ship we noticed people touring the upper level, but all the entrances were roped off. We could not locate an opening so I finally inquired and was told it was a private tour. However, one of the park rangers looked at his watch and told us he had time to give us a tour. He gave us an in depth tour of the entire ship and complete history lesson that lasted about two hours. He even took us down to see the steam engine room and explained how the steam was made from sea water and powered the ship. Afterward, Will and I were so excited about all we had learned and grateful for the ranger's efforts. We also felt honored to have gotten a tour in such detail.

We took the water taxi back to the docks near the New England Aquarium and downtown. We felt refreshed from the ocean breeze and we still had energy of a teenager and continued to take in more history along the Freedom Trail around Boston. There is a red line painted on the sidewalks around the city leading people on a fascinating tour around all the historical sites, either by professional guide or just you.

Eventually, we decided to head back toward our hotel to freshen up and perhaps rest in the air conditioned room before we tackled more fun in the city for the evening. On our way we went through the outdoor market open in the streets on weekends and bought the freshest peaches for only twenty fives cents each. They were so ripe that the juices dripped down from our hands to our elbows as we indulged in each bite of the fruit. We ate our peaches as we walked through the weekend crowds of Boston in summertime toward our hotel. We got to the hotel and reclined on our bed and turned on the television to rest. As we laid there we soothed our warm bodies from the humidity of a summer day found in Boston in the cool, air conditioned room. We didn't stay long due to excitement and awareness of more to do and see in our fair city in such a short time. We were bitten by the bug of anticipation, like that of a child waiting for Santa to arrive. We cooled off and felt rejuvenated and off we went to take in as much as we could.

Our three days in Boston allowed us to fall more deeply in love with each other, if it was even possible. Somehow, the flame we had in our hearts became a roaring bonfire. We could not stop gazing into each others eyes and we had to be holding hands constantly, we shared a kiss every so often for no particular reason at all. If people on the streets witnessed our affection toward one another then, they would've thought we were not a married couple by the way we behaved. We thoroughly enjoyed that vacation and all the romance in it, and were equipped to carry that feeling in our hearts for another decade before we'd take a trip like it again.

Our second honeymoon ended, but we took home with us new memories and the excitement of being together alone. We retained a gift in our hearts from that trip, a bond strengthened yet again. We felt like no one or no thing could ever break it or take it away from us. We talked about our vacation daily while we recalled to our minds all the magnificent new memories we had just made.

It was my sweet escape into denial now, hoping he indeed was not gone.

Farewell And A Funeral

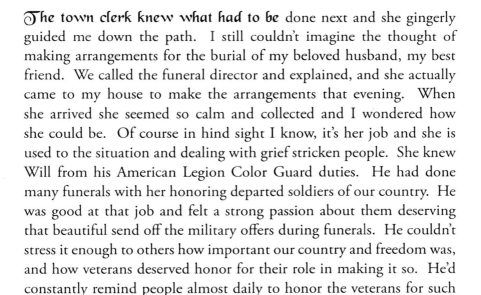

The town clerk knew what had to be done next and she gingerly guided me down the path. I still couldn't imagine the thought of making arrangements for the burial of my beloved husband, my best friend. We called the funeral director and explained, and she actually came to my house to make the arrangements that evening. When she arrived she seemed so calm and collected and I wondered how she could be. Of course in hind sight I know, it's her job and she is used to the situation and dealing with grief stricken people. She knew Will from his American Legion Color Guard duties. He had done many funerals with her honoring departed soldiers of our country. He was good at that job and felt a strong passion about them deserving that beautiful send off the military offers during funerals. He couldn't stress it enough to others how important our country and freedom was, and how veterans deserved honor for their role in making it so. He'd constantly remind people almost daily to honor the veterans for such a gift.

It was my turn now to have my husband, a veteran, honored. All the planning was surreal and I just followed the funeral directors queue. She asked all the questions, I gave the answers, and if I didn't have them I looked them up in a file cabinet. It was quite amazing how smoothly it all went and I was grateful for her professional expertise in my time of crisis.

The arrangements for the funeral were set and the funeral director went to New York and retrieved Will's body. Once she brought him home she made all the arrangements for a viewing. Will and I had discussed in great length, our wishes upon dying. This time though, it wasn't just casual talk at the dinner table, nor was it a rehearsal, it was very real. I was grateful for those talks we had, it made the steps of planning his funeral so much easier.

I knew exactly what my husband's wishes were. He wanted a viewing or a wake as they call them in New England. He wanted to wear his United States Air Force dress blues for a viewing in the casket, and then military honors at the funeral, to include the twenty-one gun salute and the playing of Taps. He wanted a Catholic Mass service and to be cremated and have his ashes divided up. He wanted some to be scattered here on the trails of our twenty-seven acre homestead, some to keep for myself and he was adamant about having some placed at the New Hampshire State Veterans Cemetery in Boscawen. He had been there for some MIA/POW vigils in the past and thought it was a beautiful place. Every time we'd drive by the exit for it on the highway, he'd tell me we needed to go there so I could see the cemetery and how beautiful it is, but we never made that trip. He also wanted me to be sure he got his bronze plaque which was one of his veteran's benefits so I made certain of that as well.

After the funeral director left I had to find all those things Will wanted to wear while ritualistically displayed in his casket for all to come and say their goodbyes. I had a little bit of time since I had postponed rushing the funeral. I knew it would be difficult for some to get here on such short notice and I wasn't ready for it either. My brain was so overwhelmed it was short circuiting and I couldn't remember anything let alone think for myself.

It was dark and my mother and brother arrived from Massachusetts. My friends, the town clerk and her husband were still with me trying to get some food in my stomach. He had even gone home and put a tray of finger sandwiches together, God love him. I tried to eat, but couldn't get more than two bites of my sandwich or even any soda to go down. I wanted to lie down and die myself in reality. My soul mate, who was also my best friend, husband, and hero in my eyes, was gone. GONE! How was it possible, how could my life go on?

My head was swirling. I felt like I was in the Calgon television commercial from three decades ago. It shows a woman with all these scenes playing out in her head; from cooking dinner, to the dog, to the kids wanting her, etc., landing her in complete confusion and she says, "Calgon, take me away." So many thoughts of our past, present, and future were hitting me as fast as light flashes and now had me in complete confusion. I was breathing, walking, and crying, but that was all I could do on auto-pilot.

The phone was ringing off the hook by the next day and for days after that. Will knew so many people from all walks of life. He was very involved in community, veteran's affairs, the American Legion and other military based programs, as well as politics. Will was one of those guys many people met once and would never forget. He just treated everyone he encountered equally. I think many were aware of that trait and were pleased to be a friend to him for that reason. He had this charm and sparkle about him that became apparent whenever he entered a room. People would stop what they were doing and come from all around to visit with him, similar to the attraction to an admired celebrity.

In the next few days many friends and family members came to see me and express their sorrow. I think they just had to come all the way up to our little house in the country partly to truly see with their own eyes how I was doing. I was in shock and denial and I was doing fine. It hadn't truly hit me that Will was gone forever. I knew he was gone, but I just couldn't grasp the real concept of it, it hadn't had enough time to sink in.

I had to find the clothes the funeral director needed for the viewing. I knew what I was looking for. I went upstairs and opened Will's closet and found everything neatly hung there as if it had all been placed there intentionally for this day. I remember asking the funeral director if I needed to give her Will's shoes. I figured no one was going to see his feet while in a casket. She said they weren't necessary unless I thought so. As I was looking for everything, I saw his shoes neatly placed right there with everything else. It was odd, but I decided Will was a perfectionist and he wouldn't feel right in that casket without his shoes. I polished them to a military high-shine to honor him, and included them and his military ribbons for his uniform with the rest of the clothing I gathered up.

I wanted to give him one last love note from me. We exchanged them frequently and he had just left me a wonderful one on our chalkboard. I wrote it on one of his monogrammed handkerchiefs with black permanent marker. Then I strategically tucked it into the inside, left, breast pocket of his dress blues knowing it would be close to his heart there. I wanted him to have something so he would know how much I loved him and know it also in the afterlife, if that is even possible. In times like this we all perform rituals and have to believe in something. I also wrote a goodbye letter from our dogs and placed that with him in the casket.

The funeral director let me see Will a couple of days prior to the viewing. I hadn't seen him in the morgue, in a hospital, or in my own living room for that matter. It was not real until I saw him dead. It broke my heart to see him lying there in a casket, and made it all seem so real and final now. As I looked at him, I spoke to him and said goodbye, and told him how much I loved and adored him. I touched his hand, it was cold and rigid, and he felt like a mannequin.

I brought the dogs with me on the funeral directors suggestion so they could say goodbye. They went right up to him and stood on the kneeler in front of the casket. They sniffed his chest and proceeded upward until they got to his hair. Their tails started wagging as if they finally recognized him and they licked his face and ears with extreme joy. Their reaction then was the identical greeting they gave to him whenever he returned from work. Almost as quickly as they went up to him they got down and wandered off. It was as if they had the closure they needed and knew that he was gone forever.

I put our dogs back into the truck and went inside to say goodbye one last time. I laid my head on Will's chest as if to hug him while tears slowly flowed from my eyes. Then I told him I loved him and said, "Goodbye my love."

Since I took our dogs to that visit they have never gone looking for him. One of our dogs in particular, Isabella, almost always knew instinctively, like clockwork, when Will was due to pull into the driveway on Friday. Neither she, nor the others have gone to the window looking for him. I wonder if they somehow can realize and accept death easier than we humans can.

Will's older sister asked me if I wanted her to order any flowers for me with her order. I had no idea what I wanted. I was so focused on creating picture boards to be displayed at the wake to tell the story of Will's grand life, I hadn't even thought about flowers. It only took me a second to decide and I asked her to order a single white, long-stem rose and have it placed on Will's chest, pure and simple. I got to the funeral home the night of the viewing and noticed all the floral arrangements, but it was a blur. Then I saw my single rose with fern and white ribbon embellishing it lying on his chest. The symbolism in that one flower elegantly expressed my love for him and the simplicity of our lives together. I know he would have known why I selected it if he was there to see it.

The night of the wake was busy with what seemed like hundreds appearing to pay their respects. I don't think my husband knew just how many lives he touched. Though the viewing lasted three hours, there were many faces I had seen standing in the receiving line that I never got the chance to speak to. I had taken some anti-anxiety medication to get through the days events because my body was trembling, I was a complete wreck. The American Legionnaires came to the wake from all over the state and gave a beautiful tribute to Will. Will worked very hard for that organization and served as District Commander and would've been pleased witnessing the honor the send off signified.

Before leaving the funeral home I went to say goodbye to Will in the casket, I felt numb. I experienced a peculiar emotion when I went to the casket, I noticed another long-stem rose lying on Will's chest, but it was red. That was my tribute and I was upset by the second flower. I wondered who would copy me and take the loving passion sent with that white rose away. I didn't speak of it for a few days, but it was weighing on my mind. Finally, out of the blue I mentioned it to my mother. She half laughed and explained the rose was from Will's grandmother. She was crying and at the last minute the flower was ordered by the funeral director. In her sadness she hadn't realized she already had an arrangement sent to the funeral home. I felt relief from the story about the mystery flower; it confirmed Will didn't have a secret admirer.

The morning of the funeral, the family and pall bearers met at the funeral home. Before we left for the church, Will's cousin presented a slideshow video to music he put on a DVD with some photos he got from me and his mother. He played it for us on a small television and immediately the tears began to flow uncontrollably. The photos were highlights of Will's life with Lee Greenwood singing; *God Bless the USA* playing in the background. One of the lines in the lyrics is; *I'm proud to be an American* and it struck a chord, it was so powerful. It appropriately described Will to anyone who didn't know him as well as to those who did. He was a loyal American, a true patriot and veteran, and politician. After the presentation, inducing fond memories and tears, I was given a copy of the video to keep.

The funeral director requested a copy as well to download onto the funeral home website, but he declined at first. She insisted, because it was just so powerful and ought to be shared with all who cared about Will. He understood her rationale and plea and he finally agreed. The next thing I knew, I was e-mailing friends from all over the country to let them know the web address and how to view that video.

We collected ourselves and went to the Catholic church. There, all the pall bearers and the American Legion Color Guard were standing at attention with the casket draped with the American flag. My beloved husband, my best friend was inside of it, but it still didn't seem real to me. Oh my God, this was it, but I so badly didn't want it to be so. I somberly walked past the coffin and into the church, shaking like a leaf, fighting back my tears while focusing on getting to the front pew. As I entered the church I saw people seated there. I only had enough energy to concentrate on getting myself seated, so I looked straight ahead and walked down the aisle on autopilot.

We selected perfect readings and music for the day. Everything was going to be exactly as Will would have had it if he planned it all himself. I wore a simple, black dress with short sleeves and a single strand of pearls around my neck, as well as Will's American flag lapel pin in his honor. He wore it to many occasions on the left lapel of his jacket, even if only to make a statement in a crowd that took our freedom as Americans for granted.

My entire body continued to shake while sitting in the pew and I was feeling weak and queasy. I had prepared a speech to read, but I didn't know if I could do it due to my nerves. I asked my sister in-law if she would do it for me if at the last minute I decided I couldn't. I knew in my heart I really wanted to do it myself, to honor Will and to show him how strong I could be. Coming from me, the congregation would understand fully who and what we were, and why our life was as it was.

I engaged many family members to do readings, be pall bearers, and also perform Eucharistic duty and help with Communion. Will's brother agreed to do a biblical reading at the service. As he took position at the pulpit he stood frozen in silence. I could see he was struggling, he lost his big brother. I asked his wife if she would go up and help him if she thought he needed it. Just as she started to exit the pew he found the strength and began to read.

I continued to breathe as I sat in the pew and asked for a helping hand from God to help me deliver my heartfelt message in a few moments. He answered yes to my prayers and in the last second I pulled it all together "on eagle's wings…" I walked up there, my tears dried and I felt a sudden calmness. I was a proud widow about to honor my husband. I looked out at the congregation recognizing few and I began to read my tribute to Will and our life. Hoping Will was there to witness the day I included some details only he would understand.

By Chance
August 2008

*"Will and I met **by chance**! God reached down and guided us at the fork in the road in 1987 and put us on the journey He planned for us so that we would meet.*

Meet we did! We met under curious circumstances that we always laughed about later, but it was God's hand putting it all into place. I have no doubt about that. We immediately became best friends. We could count on each other for anything. We always knew what the other was thinking and could anticipate the next move. It was as if we were of the same flesh. Will completed me.

It seems just like it was yesterday that we married. We had a creative wedding and it was sealed with our signature. I can still see my grooms face vividly as I walked down the aisle. In that moment his face told me I was his princess. He placed me high upon a pedestal like a fine crystal figurine.

We shared a sense of adventure. Will preferred to step outside the box and I loved that about him and was willing to follow his lead. Always doing what we thought was 'us' and not to impress anyone else. That was just the beginning of our journey with all the 'bumpy roads in life.' We did encounter many of those bumps, some larger than others. I am sure when his brother, our best man, toasted us with such simple, but wise words had no idea the power behind them. We had that toast memorized and it did indeed get us through turbulent times. It allowed us to forget those 'bumps' and celebrate the happiness we shared day to day.

Eventually, we ended up with a large family of four legged furry children, our dogs. Because we believed in spoiling them they kept us active and introduced us to beautiful northern New Hampshire. We turned 180 degrees and instead of spending all our free time in Boston while living in Massachusetts we were drawn to peace in the woods of the White Mountains. Between dog sledding in winter and all the hiking I thought I would never survive, we decided we had to relocate to the area.

By chance, we found the perfect home for us and we moved in almost ten years ago. We spent many hours doing home improvements and maintenance on the property so we could enjoy its splendor. I loved all our walks side by side around the trails he created. I will cherish those days as I walk the trails now. We enjoyed a great simple life here.

By chance, Will got involved in politics, community efforts and organizations. It was like the Life Cereal's slogan became his; 'give it to Mikey he'll eat it.' Anyone could ask him to help out and he'd do his absolute best to get it done. He made many friends along the way. He was so passionate about making his voice be heard. Not all were willing to listen, but afterward, they seemed to come around and join his team. It seems now that voice has made quite an imprint that isn't likely to be forgotten. I am proud of all he accomplished.

I will cherish many memories of us. The events in the last few months will give me a smile when I need one. We really did have it all. We were happy being simple people frequenting the flea market or getting a local cup of coffee, or just plain working hard on our land. Then on the other side of the coin we enjoyed elegant parties and gala events in a tuxedo and gown with the other half of the world. I feel like we lived a fairytale life.

I used to blush when he would introduce me as his lovely bride even after over eighteen years of marriage. I finally got used to it and realized the compliment in it. I thank you for that, my love. I am ever so grateful for his love and respect for me. I always could feel how deeply he loved me whether we were together or apart. It was all the little things he did that touched me everyday. He made me sparkle and I told him so. Our marriage was a gift. I too, would marry you ten times over.

Will, **by chance** you left this world last week. All of what we shared and were passionate about is what will carry me through the remainder of my journey, along with Gods guidance. I am grateful for what you did for me so I can be strong. It won't be easy, but you gave me confidence. I will continue to work toward our goals and try to complete the plan at our beautiful spot in the world. It's our little piece of heaven. I feel at peace there and know you did too. I stand in our yard and see the beauty surrounding me and feel it is like an oil canvas depicting the love we shared. I will miss you deeply. I have no regrets and wish you peace. Be at peace with God now and do His work. I love the love we had.

I love you forever and miss you, your adoring wife,

Margaret"

The service continued and others were invited to speak, a close friend of Will's spoke and I was grateful. The priest continued with the ritual for funeral and we finished up the Mass and celebrated Communion and song.

We were led out of the church to go back to the funeral home just a couple of blocks away for the remaining military honors, the twenty one gun salute and Taps. I stood there in pain and grief barely able to breathe listening to a prayer, watching servicemen remove the American flag from the casket and carefully fold it. I stood at attention while listening to Taps being played on the bugle and thought of Will's military service. Suddenly, I heard the commands to shoot, and each shot made me jump as they echoed through my head and rang with finality. He was being honored in only a way dead veterans are honored so it had to mean he truly was dead. Will's nephew is in the Army National Guard and he presented me with the flag. I have a photo of that moment taken via cellular phone and you can literally see the pain in my face, neck and posture.

After the funeral I kept having a recurring dream that Will was still alive for eight nights consecutively. In the dream, I was at the site of the accident and found him there alive crouched in the bushes. Excitedly, I said to him; my honey you're still alive. He said; yes, I was hit by the electricity, but it only threw me and didn't kill me. He proceeded to tell me one news reporter got the accident information right and recorded it on video. He showed it to me on his laptop computer and it revealed he was thrown into the bushes just like he said. I was thrilled he was alive and told him he had to come home with me, but he said he couldn't. I was confused by his reply and asked him why. He told me I had already buried him and he can't come back.

Shock and grief controlled my mind allowing me to reconstruct things by using my imagination giving me a happy outcome of such a tragedy. With my heart fighting my logic brain, this journey was making me wonder how I could possibly survive it. Through my insanity I kept replaying the magical memories of our trip to Boston in July in my head. They soothed me and my salty tears had some sense of joy to them then. I am grateful for the events that took place just weeks and days before my husband's death. But it still breaks my heart to think about how in love we were and suddenly it was just ripped out of my hands forever.

In the next few weeks I had a lot of phone calls to make to take care of the things death brings to those left behind. I had a date of which Will's ashes would be returned to the funeral home so I scheduled the interment first. Over the phone the secretary gently guided me through the process and reserved an appointment for interment services on September 26, 2008.

Later, I received an envelope with rules and regulations to follow upon visiting the cemetery. It also had information about leaving flowers as well as how frequently things left at the graves are cleaned up to keep a stately appearance to the grounds. In the same envelope there was a form to fill out. I had to write the message I wanted engraved on the military bronze plaque. It would be placed on the columbarium vault that would hold Will's remains. They had already completed the section of his name, life span dates and military rank. I was to choose his religion, if any, and a message of a certain number of characters. I struggled with trying to find the best descriptive words. I hoped to perhaps establish his legacy for a stranger who may read the plaque, as well as something coming straight from my heart to honor my husband. After a few days of working it all out on scratch paper I achieved my goal. The final plaque reads; William J. Cowie -- A1C US Air Force – Lebanon – November 23, 1963 – August 26, 2008 – A cross for his religion signifying Christian – Best Friend – Husband – Hero – Forever held in my heart.

I still had to contact social security, our home mortgage company, and life insurance companies. An agent from workers compensation called me just two days after he died and explained I was eligible for widow's benefits. As instructed I called her back to get the ball rolling since I had no form of income. I had received many condolence cards containing monetary gifts, and could get by for a couple of months on that. It was difficult to accept them, but it was my reality and I had to. Someone reminded me how wonderful it feels to give. I was a great giver; I thoroughly enjoyed the gift of giving, I just hadn't learned the art of receiving. It dawned on me that it may be one of my lessons to learn during my journey here on this earth.

Trying to make all the necessary phone calls wasn't easy, there wasn't a manual on what to do or expect. I was put on hold and then transferred. I had to wait for applications to come in the mail and then complete and return them with original death certificates attached. Some would be lost in the mail and I would have to repeat the steps again. I had experience dealing with insurance companies and I knew ahead of time what questions I needed to be prepared to answer. My wisdom in that department did make things go more smoothly. I kept a log and recorded all the phone calls I made and names of personnel in it, in case I had to refer to it later, and I did.

I read the condolence cards all over again and cried as I realized all the love that was sent along with them. There were well over a hundred of them, I had no idea so many people cared. I started writing thank you cards in response to all of them with personal notes for marathon sessions. I wanted to express gratitude from my heart to everyone who reached out to me. The project kept my mind busy and the tear ducts dry for a few moments.

The Interment

Will's ashes were returned and I met with the funeral director to finally select an urn. She had given me some catalogs to look through, but it was the most difficult thing for me to do during the entire process. Will and I had spoken candidly many times about our wishes if our death should occur, but we overlooked the urn. It was like selecting the perfect tuxedo for him to wear at our wedding. I scanned the pages of catalogs for two weeks, but still could not decide.

Finally, while at the funeral home to put in the order, I realized I kept looking at one in particular, it had to be the one. It was solid pewter, polished to a high shine with the smooth curves of a traditional urn. It was simple yet elegant, just like my husband was in personality. The design included a noble roping around the base, the edge of the lid, and around the body of the urn itself just above the engraving where Will's name and life span dates were placed. I thought of his military duty when I realized the urn was called *Arlington*. It signified both honor for his proud service to his country and our life together. I ordered it, but I still felt as if there was a chance he could come back to me somehow, I was still in denial created by my shock. A few days after I placed my order, the urn was ready to be placed in the columbarium at the veteran's cemetery in Boscawen.

September twenty-sixth was a rainy day. I drove about two and a quarter hours to meet family and friends to witness Will's ashes placed into the final tomb. The interment service was to be held outside at a designated section where a vault was reserved for Will's urn and cremains. The inclement weather seemed to amplify the somber mood of things.

I looked for escape from my anxiety with an attempt to celebrate what we had together in life, so I listened to a favorite music CD of ours, mainly his, in my car while driving down the highway. It was a collection of greatest hits by Frank Sinatra. As song number three; *The Way You Look Tonight* began to play I instantly remembered how Will used to stop whatever he was doing, come and get me from whatever I was doing, and excitedly drag me to the living room. I say drag; because sometimes I had my hands in dishwater with suds on them, but he couldn't wait, he had to make me have some fun now. He swept me off my feet and he'd swing dance with me as if we were on the ballroom floor. That little inconvenience of being interrupted while doing something not very important after all, always made me smile, Will did that for me.

Those two minute adventures in the middle of the day, for no reason at all, made me grateful to have him and love him so much. That was his frequent gift to me because I had the tendency to be so serious at times. The memory now brought me tears of joy. I danced in the seat of my car while singing at the top of my lungs as if Will were in the car with me, distracting me from my pain and anxiety due to losing him.

At one point I turned off the CD since it played through twice already and listened to the radio instead. I hit the search button and began picking up a rock station. I heard a song I never heard before and have not heard again since called; *Life Is Beautiful* performed by Nikki Sixx. The lyrics at that moment said, "Will you swear on your life that no one will cry at my funeral." Wow, suddenly intense feelings of my husband talking to me from the Other Side through the radio jolted through my body. I always believed in life after death on the Other Side, but since experiencing my husband's death I needed to feel connected and seemed to believe even more now.

I arrived to the cemetery entrance and was reminded of my conversations with my husband to go see it some day. Will was absolutely right; I felt a confirmation in his taste with choosing a grand, meticulously landscaped, peaceful parcel of land on this earth and I sensed a heroic feel to it. It was a beautiful thought he could not communicate to me, except that I finally witnessed it then.

I began to think in slow motion as I pulled up to the main office. I really thought since I already had the church service and the honorable salute behind me, today was going to be easy. I parked my car, took a deep breath, and then noticed some familiar faces already there waiting for me. I said my hello's and then delivered the urn holding my husbands ashes, and the American flag from the service three weeks ago to the main office as instructed previously over the telephone. The flag was to be used for another military salute performed that day by the U.S. Air Force National Guard. Within minutes of my arrival many others arrived to pay their respects to my husband, their sibling, son, nephew or friend. We walked to the section where the ceremony would be performed and waited for the priest and the service to begin.

I was standing right up front in the position a widow takes at her husband's interment. The rain let up for the moment and I thought perhaps Will was making that happen. It was still damp and cold, typical for autumn in New England. I was wearing a pair of dark, wool slacks and a sweater with plenty of adrenaline running through my veins that I felt warm enough.

The priest arrived and began to recite what he had prepared for the days events. His words struck a chord and hit me hard in my heart. The thought of that song I heard on the radio and not crying that day came to mind. However, I could not retain my tears; the nerves were still too raw. My tears welled up in my eyes and I looked up to secretly catch them and hide them, then they gently poured over my lower eyelids and silently flowed down my cheeks, to my chin and to the ground. I cleared them off my face the best I could with my cold, bare hands since I had no tissues with me. It shocked me that I could not control my tears and emotions.

After the priests words there was a silence succumbing us. I sensed majestic peace as I heard the dry leaves of autumn rustling in the trees surrounding the cemetery as the wind softly blew through them. It reminded me of our walks in our woods at home.

In the silence, the U.S. Air Force National Guard's Color Guard team of three exited the office doors of the main building, and walked along the walkway toward the group gathered to pay respects to Will. My heart began to sink again. It was a beautiful ceremony, but yet another sign of finality and I didn't want it to be so. The men and woman of the color guard were impeccably dressed in their proper formal attire. Their hats, buckles, pleats, creases, and military ribbons were strategically placed on their uniforms and worn proudly. They walked in unison in a slow march toward the flag poles at the rotunda, where the State, the POW/MIA, and the American flags were flowing in the light winds of the day, and then they stopped and saluted them.

Each soldier carried a military symbol in their white glove adorned hands. One carried a neatly folded American flag, the other carried a bugle, and the soldier in the center of the three proudly carried the polished, pewter urn, containing Will's ashes. They resumed their silent march leaving one behind at the flag site. They placed the urn on a table draped with navy blue velvet in front of the selected vault in the columbarium. The two soldiers then began to unfold the American flag slowly and symbolically. Once the flag was open fully, the soldier positioned at the flag rotunda behind us began playing Taps on her bugle. With that, more tears began to flow down my face. After the music stopped, the two guardsmen ceremoniously folded the American flag tightly with precision, tucking the end into one of the flaps forming a traditional triangle. Once it was folded they presented it to me and saluted me in honor of Will's service as a soldier for the United States Air Force. I tried to keep my composure, but I was so sad, I never imagined I would experience this day.

The priest said some final words and then I stood and watched as they placed the urn into the vault, and the cover was secured over it. Some people came and expressed their condolences to me and we talked briefly, then it was time to leave. Will was in the resting place he so wisely and articulately chose. It was over.

People hugged me and said goodbye as they began to leave and I thanked them for coming. Will's family and I planned on having lunch after the interment and knew of a restaurant near by. We sat and broke bread together, shared conversation of normal life, and even shared some laughter.

After lunch I drove the long journey home and I listened to Frank Sinatra's greatest hits CD and when "our" song came on I hit the replay mode on the CD player. I listened to the same song for over two hours. It made me cry, but I remembered being in Will's arms and realized I was crying tears of joy.

Life Feels Empty

Since the day I discovered my husband was killed and taken from me, I have wandered around aimlessly. I feel like one of those little balls in the pinball machines at an arcade. The paddles in the game push the ball, me, around the board under glass to keep me in this life whether I want to be or not. I breathe, walk, and live on autopilot. I feel as if my soul has withdrawn to escape the pain, and has crawled into a dark corner of its human body and cries as I cry.

Early on in this so called journey of grief, I wondered if people knew I was a widow as they looked at me while I walked among them. It seemed as if they were pointing at me, whispering about how sad life must be for me. Once that sensation subsided, I then wondered why life did not stop for me and let me rest so I could acclimate to my new state of being, lost and numb. Everywhere I went I could feel the world rapidly passing by me like rush hour in a big city, and everyone knew their way except me, making me feel disoriented.

I was surrounded by many of my friends and family in the early stages, but I still somehow felt so alone and thought no one else could know my pain. I thought no one loved their husband as much as I loved mine. At times I would fight off the urge to cry. It wasn't in my nature to be so out of control of my emotional state and go into a complete meltdown. Oddly enough, the feeling of loss and despair left me when I allowed my body to shut down to cry what felt like rivers of tears, they offered me healing in the moment.

Nighttime was hardest for me; it became my ritual to pray to and to question God, and then hold a conversation with my departed husband hoping he could hear me. I wanted him to know I loved him so deeply and would tell him, "I have no regrets my love." The fact that he had been suddenly yanked away from me and the magical life we knew together with no warning, and without any choice in the matter was my only regret now. By the end of my self pity sessions and desire to talk to my husband one last time, tears soaked my pillow.

For months in search of comfort I laid there in my bed with one of Will's shirts still containing his scent. It allowed me to imagine I was in bed beside him holding him until I would fall asleep from sheer exhaustion from crying.

It seems now the only thing that gets me through my days without my husband are all the memories we created. I am grateful we shared so many hours together, and relish in remembering all the good, whether grand or small, as well as the bad ones. At least when I reflect on the bad days, there was a light at the end of the tunnel with a happy ending, he was here with me, making them less sad as my days are now.

Each day the memories come to me without warning, and are played out in my mind like a video tape recording of my life with my honey. I am hopeful as they flood out of my memory banks and I can visualize them like life itself. They will push me through my journey of grief and healing helping me to find a purpose to my life.

I hold on to all the wonderful memories we created together over the last twenty-one years. I am hopeful with each memory that comes to mind, the ever so giant hole in my heart will begin to heal and repair itself. The little tidbits of our story remind me of how and why we were so close. With all the smiles and tears through our years together we became inseparable. Will was my honey, the love of my life, and my best friend. I fall in love all over again reminiscing.

Part Two

We Met By Chance...

On December 10, 1987 I met Will. When we met I didn't know it, but it was the first day of the rest of my life. You know that old expression. I was twenty-five years old and had just moved to New England about six weeks prior to meeting him. I was going through a messy divorce. Circumstances were where I wanted out of the marriage, but he didn't. That is entirely another story though.

I was in the habit of stopping into a Ninety-Nine's restaurant in my neighborhood. It had a night club with a DJ for music and dancing certain nights of the week, known as the Greenhouse. I felt comfortable going in for one drink since I knew the bouncer and bartender, and felt they kept a watchful eye out for me. I was new in town and newly single as well. It was close enough to my house that I could make a quick exit and be home in just minutes.

That particular day, a Thursday, I was out shopping at the mall for an outfit to wear to my office Christmas party. Attire was supposed to be sort of festive dressy, but not formal. On the way home I drove by the nightclub and decided I would stop for one drink and then go home. It was a night the DJ was on, and I thought there would be no harm in having one drink and maybe a dance. I wasn't necessarily looking to meet anyone. I just enjoyed the social activity and dancing, and it was a form of stress release too. When I went there and danced, sometimes I'd be asked for my telephone number. I always made one up if it was someone asking I wouldn't be interested in hearing from, which was the case every time. I was the type to play it safe and had a good sense of character. I was getting a taste of the single life after marrying too young, and living through what seemed like hell with my oppressor for eight years. I was only interested in having fun.

At the club I sat myself right up at the bar. I knew the bartender that was on shift that night, I ordered a whiskey and coke and we chatted. It was full capacity that night, almost standing room only. It was payday and everyone had plenty of money to spend on the nightlife scene then. There were three guys sitting to the left of me at the bar and we began to talk to each other. We never met before that night.

The guy sitting closest to me asked me to dance and I accepted his invitation. I pretty much knew immediately that he wasn't my type once we hit the dance floor. I had already determined he was getting a fake phone number if he asked for one. We finished our dance and sat back at the bar, and then he went to the restroom.

The guy sitting on the other side of him scooted over one bar stool to sit next to mine, and we began to chat. I wasn't nervous in the least around him, he was warm and friendly. I usually played it real safe and kept my guard up when I met strangers, especially in the bar scene, if you know what I mean. For some reason that night I didn't feel that paranoia at all with this guy. Perhaps it was my woman's intuition. Perhaps it was something else, something much bigger.

The guy that sat closer to me was Will. He asked me to dance, we did, and I liked his style. He was a good dancer and we seemed to connect as if we had already known each other somehow. He was a gentleman and we hit if off immediately. All my guards were down with him and he swept me off my feet. We sat back at the bar and had another drink and talked and laughed more.

There was a third guy with Will and he decided he wanted to leave the club. The three guys arrived there together in one car, but Will hadn't driven. He told me his friends wanted to leave, but he would stay if I would give him a ride home. I asked him where he lived and he told me, Arlington. I was so new to the area I had no idea where Arlington even was. He explained to me it wasn't very far to go, and with that I surprised myself and agreed. That answer defied all the boundaries I set for myself. We were having a fantastic time, just like the lyrics say in the song; *Strangers in the Night* performed by Frank Sinatra.

After awhile we had enough of the party scene and I took Will home, rather, he took himself home by driving my car with me in it. He knew the way and we decided it would be easier if he drove. He took me through many strange city streets until we arrived to his apartment building. In my mind I was wondering how I was going to find my way back home. Let me remind you, I don't know what was guiding me to do this with a man I didn't know, it just happened. Was it fate?

We got to his apartment and he invited me in and once again I agreed. Wow, another surprise answer on my part. My logical brain must have gone on vacation at that point. I felt like I was being led by the hand down a path I was supposed to be on though. It was as if the Universe was leading me on a journey I had already studied the script for and rehearsed, and now the nervous jitters were absent and it was curtain time.

We went into his apartment. Will and I hung out for awhile and had a couple of drinks and listened to music. Will loaded the CD player tray with six discs and set it to play on random selections allowing it to play for what seemed like forever. I don't know if it was pheromones or raging hormones running about that night, but one thing led to another and I spent the night. Yes, you read that right. I don't know how it happened either. We slept in his twin size bed completely naked after an amazing sexual interlude. We slept with our bodies touching; my back leaned in tightly against his chest and his arms around me all night. It was transcending, I felt so relaxed with him. I can't stress enough that I had never done such a thing.

I went home early in the morning; I would say around five o'clock. I had to work and so did Will. I wrote my phone number on a marker board hanging on his kitchen wall. He was the lucky recipient of getting my actual phone number. I had not given it to anyone else.

When I got home the morning after such excitement, I paced in my bedroom wondering what the heck I was thinking and how it happened. He didn't hurt me. As a matter of fact, he couldn't have been more kindhearted and he seemed so genuine. I had fears because he had quite a few tattoos, eleven in total, which I hadn't noticed until we had gone to bed. After I left him I assumed he was some kind of bad boy, biker type or something even less appealing to me. I was conservative; I couldn't date someone with all those tattoos. How stereotypical of me. You have to remember it was 1987 and that I was very inexperienced. I could only wonder what kind of person he really was. I figured then, I would write it off as bad judgment and he would never call anyway. I assumed I was the product of a bar night pick up and perhaps a one night stand.

The day after I met Will I got home from work and he called me. What?! I wasn't prepared for that. He wanted to see me again. I was ecstatic and once again plunged into the unknown voyage that felt so right.

I went over to meet him that evening and we wandered around Boston and grabbed a bite to eat. Will was a native of the area and knew all the places to go and how to get there. I let him lead me and I gladly followed. I fully trusted him and we had a fabulous time. I was infatuated with him for some reason; it was love at first sight. I know that seems impossible, but I just felt a connection and couldn't explain it.

After a great time enjoying the city nightlife we returned to his apartment. Need I say more? The events from the night before were repeated and I stayed the night as well. I was completely flabbergasted by my behavior. Something about Will gave me tingles of excitement down my spine every time I was with him. I took the bait; hook, line and sinker and I would be his girl as long as he'd have me.

I think Will felt the same fascination with me as well. He called me everyday and we went out or I at least went to his apartment just about every night. He was good company, handsome, charming, and an all around fun guy, and with all that, he was respectful as well. He treated me like a lady even when his guy friends were around. What more can you ask for in a man? He was still a stranger, but I wasn't seeing any faults in him yet. Somehow he didn't feel like a stranger to me. I was completely at ease with him and I longed to be with him all day and night. We'd be together every evening after work and I went home late at night or the wee hours of the morning since we had to work the next day. Will must have had the same longing that I was experiencing, because he would call me at two or three o'clock in the morning and beg me to come over after I was already there and had gone home. I would go to him.

Instant Love Affair

Just a few weeks into our affair, Will called my house quite late one night and my brother answered the phone. I was temporarily living at home after relocating to New England with the clothes on my back to escape the manipulative grips of my soon to be ex-husband. Because he called so late my brother was being defensive thinking it was some creep looking for me. I was in bed anyway. My brother told me the next morning some guy named Will called. I felt my heart flutter with that announcement.

I contacted Will and we met after work again. I'm telling you we were breathing the same air. I could barely concentrate at work, I thought about him all day. I felt like I was head over heels in a school girl crush on someone who was two grades higher than me.

Our relationship blossomed so fast. It was like creation in the Book of Genesis in the Bible. That kind of power through the Universe seemed to create an eternal love between the two of us. We were put together and meant to stay together. I can't explain it, it was just meant to be, I could feel it.

Will invited me to his office Christmas party to be held at an elegant restaurant given a five star status in Boston. I was thrilled he asked me and agreed on the spot to go with him. Our relationship was still so new, but the comfort I felt with him was equivalent to the feel of wearing a pair of well broken in slippers.

Will confided in me that he needed something to wear to his Christmas party. He asked me to go shopping with him to buy something acceptable to wear to it. He was freshly out of the Air Force and worked as a carpenter in civilian life. He didn't have much in his closet for going out to a fine restaurant.

We went to Lord and Taylor, sort of an upscale department store in our area. The shopping excursion revealed to me that he had exquisite taste. (I didn't figure that out by his choosing me to be his date…) He tried on some slacks and dress shirts. With my opinion he decided on the perfect outfit to buy. He got a pair of black wool, cuffed dress slacks with the perfect cut for his body type. He got a men's white dress shirt and a pale pink, crew neck, cotton sweater to wear with the slacks. He looked great in the outfit and the colors were perfect too. He also bought himself a beautiful, long, wool coat and a cashmere scarf. The coat was a very dark gray with thin, black, vertical pinstripes and a black, velvet collar. The scarf was cream colored with a fringe on each end.

He looked simply marvelous in it. Close your eyes and imagine the most handsome male celebrity in your mind walking the Hollywood Red Carpet at the Academy Awards. That was exactly how fabulous Will looked… He was six feet two inches tall and looked great in that long coat. He was the epitome of tall, dark and handsome. He was any girl's dream date. He had shiny, dark brown, almost black, curly hair cut shorter on the top and sides and then longer in the back, and it felt like silk to the touch. He was slender and he had amazing cheekbones and green eyes. He was my handsome Prince Charming with a heart to match even then. I hadn't realized it to the full extent just yet though. We had only just met a couple of weeks prior.

Will picked me up for the party at my mom's house. It was the first time she met him. He was full of energy and excitement. She was lured into his spell by his charm. My mom was never one to judge and she also has that ability to sense good character. She seemed to give me her blessings for my pursuit of a relationship with Will. I had this enormous need to be with him and I doubt anyone could've persuaded me he wasn't right for me.

We were all dressed up and ready to make a grand entrance at the party. The restaurant was on the waterfront in Boston. We arrived with every hair, piece of jewelry and make up in place. Will looked deliciously sexy and I couldn't keep my hands off him. It was cold out and he had his arm around me. I felt as if I was protected from all evils when he held me. I felt so smitten by his appearance, knowing I was the lucky woman with him and wasn't willing to share. I felt so glamorous on his arm while entering such a prestigious place.

We dined with the elite set of Boston that evening. Dinner included several courses as well as dessert and drinks. The company really gave their employees a party that was over the top. It gave us a glimpse of being a member of society's upper class. I was glad Will was comfortable taking me along his side. I remember all these details as if they just happened yesterday and I smile gratefully for the gift.

Once we left the party we went to his apartment and the nightly ritual played out. We were becoming best friends and I was already falling deeply in love. It seems impossible since we had only known each other a couple of weeks. It is difficult to explain how comfortable I was with him; we just went together like peanut butter and jelly. My insatiable thirst to drink him up was unquenchable.

We continued to date and have the time of our lives, you know, just like young lovers do. You have no worries because there isn't any room in your brain for them at that age. All you can think about is that special person you are falling in love with. The sheer joy of spending time together was enough fuel to make you survive any tragedy. If you didn't have to work you would be inseparable.

Will used to take me to so many places around the city of Boston. We liked eating out, so we invested in one of those city books with coupons to dine at just about every restaurant in Boston and the Metro area. They offered purchase of the first entrée; get the second one half price or free. That enticed us to try many different varieties of restaurants and cuisine. We even went to sports pubs to watch hockey on the big screen and ate appetizers and drank pitchers of beer. I was happy being with Will anywhere. I was on top of the world.

Family And The L-O-V-E Word

After a couple of months, Will told me he loved me on the phone. I didn't know how to respond, I was caught off guard and I wondered to myself if he meant it. I let it go for the moment even though I had deep feelings for him. I just wasn't prepared. I saw him the next day and I just had to ask if he meant what he said. He told me he knew I was going to ask him, as if he might have slipped saying that to me. Then he told me he did indeed mean it. I was thrilled. I think he felt put on the spot when I asked him, but he was brave enough to be honest with me. I appreciated that trait about him. We were starting a new chapter of our relationship now that the love word had been used.

We went on as usual, except now I was spending days and nights with him on weekends. We were kind of living together part time. I discovered on those weekend encounters that he was not only super model handsome and all the other good qualities I mentioned, but on top of that he was a good housekeeper too. I was impressed and gave him an all around ten in my ratings book.

Will took me to his parent's house and I met his mother and father shortly there after. While we were there I met his brother and nephew as well. I did not realize it then, but I think the visit was to display me and to get the nod of approval from his mother and father. It all seemed to go quite well.

Will talked to his mom and dad on the phone every day. I thought it was sweet that he called them so often to check in. He was so considerate that way. A couple of months later, I found out that his father was fighting a battle with cancer.

After the first cold visit to the family, Will tested the waters with other family members. We took a ride to New Hampshire to see his older sister. One of her children was having a birthday party. I met the rest of his immediate family that day, including his grandparents. I was made to feel like a part of the family. I sensed that Will assumed I was as comfortable around his family as he was, by his casual mannerisms there, and I was.

Will and I did just about everything together including going to the grocery store to fill his kitchen cupboards with food. We had similar sense of humors and were so giddy and in love that even that task was fun to do. We'd go to the mall just to walk around and window shop and then grab a bite to eat at the food court or at a restaurant near by.

One time we were at the mall and we passed a store that did ear piercing. He asked me what I thought about an earring in his ear. I told him it could be kind of fun, so he got his ear pierced right then and there. He never thought twice about it. I had a diamond earring without the mate and told him he could have it. He was chomping at the bit to get the initial healing stud out of that ear and put the diamond in. He couldn't wait and made the change earlier than it was directed. It healed fine though regardless.

We went to his parent's house again soon after the earring episode. He didn't say anything, but I noticed he was parading around the house trying to get someone to mention the earring. It was about a quarter carat and sparkled brightly when the light hit it. I don't know how anyone couldn't see it.

Finally, his mom spoke up about the earring. I think she noticed it, but was trying to avoid saying anything about it because she could sense he wanted her to so badly. He was kidding around with her and pretended he didn't know about any earring. He was always the funny guy; it came so naturally to him. His humor was dry at times and you

46

had to be able to read between the lines. But he knew in his heart he was just the funniest guy on the planet, and yes, he absolutely was.

I figured the talk around the fireplace later at his parent's house was how I must have been a bad influence on their son. In actuality it wasn't me that persuaded him to get an earring or anything else for that matter. However, because they knew we met in a bar I could only imagine the thoughts in their heads. Later, I would find out that Will's father liked me though.

Will had been honorably discharged from the Air Force only a few months and was enjoying a new found freedom from Uncle Sam. He was letting his hair grow longer and getting earrings. He was testing the waters and enjoying the ride. Will always had the best sense of adventure. It was contagious. Before we met I was cautious and not always willing to try anything and everything. His ability to do that allowed me to throw up my hands and give in, and agree to do just about anything too. I'm not sure I would jump off a bridge in a bungee jump though. So I'll say within a certain comfort radius I would be willing to join him on any adventure.

Moving In

Will's roommate had disappeared on some sort of walkabout retracing England from his Air Force days. They were in the same unit and stationed in England at the same time. He was gone for months and still had no date set to return.

By June Will was still paying the rent solo and I was looking for a place to live, so we decided to move in together. I was practically living there with him anyway. I remember when I moved in, Will was nervous about me changing things and redecorating the apartment. He had mentioned it casually once. I think his friends were putting ideas into his head. Perhaps they were a little jealous of the direction his life was turning. They may have feared he'd be too busy for them and leave them in the dust. Or perhaps they thought a woman would decorate with stuffed animals, lace curtains and puffy stuff all over the place. A few months later he asked me why I hadn't put a woman's touch on the apartment. I reminded him of his words. With that he insisted we decorate.

We went shopping together and picked out some things to make the bachelor pad a home for the two of us. No lace curtains or girly stuff was on the list. I wasn't into that anyway, I liked a cleaner, contemporary look. Although Will was proudly in touch with his sensitive side, as he called it, it surprised me what he would pick out and be okay with. Our bedroom did end up being quite feminine, but without lace and stuffed animals. We didn't change much in the living room area. We added some vases and throw pillows, drapes, and some scatter rugs to give the very dated apartment rejuvenation without a complete remodel. It was losing its bachelor pad look and was gradually being transformed into our first home together.

We tried to maintain a friendship with his friends. We would go to sports bars and watch hockey games on a big screen television and his buddies would come along. We even went to some Boston Red Sox games. I'm a people person and I was fine with all of it. None of his friends ever offended me or took advantage of me. We always had a tremendous amount of fun.

We found this hole in the wall bar in Revere that we'd all go to. They had live entertainment on weekend nights. The tables were set up banquet style where everyone sat on benches and drank and enjoyed the show. The same guy performed each week. He was a one man band and comedian with all kinds of silly props, whistles and bells. He sang familiar jingles, but changed the lyrics and asked for audience participation. We'd all be so drunk we would sing his silly songs with him and laugh all night long. I look back and think that atmosphere is only for the young. It was a grand time each time we went, and more memories were formed and have left an imprint on my mind and a smile on my face.

I constantly look back and as I do, the credit card advertisement comes to mind. It's the one where they go on to explain how buying certain things cost a certain dollar amount. Then they mention something that is very expensive, but would be such a joyous event or occasion, and for the dollar amount they say; "priceless." That was our history together -- priceless.

Eventually, Will and I began to do things that did not include his friends so much. I suppose things were more serious between us and we just grew out of his drinking buddies. It is unfortunate, but it happens to all of us as we mature and find our true love. We were eager to explore what the world had to offer us. We found ourselves in whatever it was the Universe had in mind for us to share together on this new journey.

We began doing more things with his family. We took more trips to his parent's house for coffee and donuts, or Sunday dinner. We wanted to stay in the loop and make a visit just because we cared. Will was such a generous, loving guy. He was always concerned about his family and I admired that. Occasionally on Sunday, Will and I would join his uncle and grandfather and go to a tiny diner in Arlington for breakfast. Gramps always loved his eggs sunny side up. They had to be prepared just so or he would send them back. Will's uncle and grandfather welcomed me into the family like I was born into it. I enjoyed that comfort they gave me.

Sometimes we would wake up Saturday morning and decide on a whim to go to Salisbury Beach for the day. Sometimes we would go to a Red Sox game or we'd take a drive to Faneuil Hall in Boston. That would become one of my favorite places to go to with Will. We just both enjoyed going where the winds would take us.

I remember going places with Will and if I was sitting beside him I would have my hand on his thigh while our legs touched. I just felt so compelled to always be touching him. He told me he liked it and enjoyed the admiration. We'd be at our apartment or at someone's house and I would find myself staring at him. He would see me from time to time and flash me a smile and a wink, with a twinkle in his eye. I was snared in his seductive, magical spell and I must say I loved it.

Our First Vacation

—————————— ∽∽) ——————————

The summer of 1988 we took our first vacation together. We decided to go to New York City, neither one of us had been there before. Will had an Air Force buddy he wanted to go see there, it would be a reunion. They planned it all out and he asked us to stay at his house in Brooklyn. We drove to the city on a hot summer day in August. Getting there was quite an adventure. Will was so great behind the wheel though, he could find his way out of any maze blindfolded, and we would arrive unscathed, I swear. I always admired that talent he had; it was not one I possessed.

We got to Brooklyn and found his friends house in a quiet neighborhood, neatly tucked in with many other brownstones lining the street with towering deciduous trees along the sidewalk. Will and his friend of course had their *guy* reunion and then he immediately introduced me to him.

The next day we went into New York City. We got the complete tour with our private guide, Will's friend's brother. He chauffeured us all over the city that day. We were tourists so we went sightseeing. We stopped at a park and got what was called a "dirty water dog" off a vendor. It was a hotdog on a bun, but it was apparently cooked in the same water as many hot dogs before it that day. It wasn't polluted in any way; the water just looked cloudy from all the fat drippings from all the hotdogs prepared earlier.

While we were in the city we did the biggest tourist thing of all, and that was going to the Statue of Liberty. We moseyed around the grounds and gift shop and then climbed to the top of "Lady Liberty." It was sweltering inside the massive structure. It was August and it was around 90 degrees Fahrenheit and felt like the humidity was eighty percent or higher. There were hundreds of other tourists inside the structure with no ventilation, and it felt like a sweat lodge in there. I can remember touching the hand rail along the spiral staircase going upward, and feeling it was wet from all the sweaty hands and bodies. It gave me a sort of sick feeling knowing each time I touched the rail there were swarms of germs on it. We proceeded to climb the steps inside the statue until we got to the crown. We had our cameras and took photos of each other and of the view which was obstructed by haze and pollution, but still quite amazing.

Later, Will's friend joined us and we went to see the aircraft carrier USS Intrepid. The guys were very excited and interested in seeing everything aboard. I like history myself, but I didn't have the same passion about the ship since I was never in the military. I took loads of photos that day to freeze our moment in time and cherish the memories sparked each time we'd look at them later on.

After the adventure on the ship we went for a bite to eat. We were outside Coney Island. We walked up to an outdoor take-out place and got deep fried frog legs. Yes, they tasted like chicken. Will was always up for trying foods he had never eaten before. There's that adventure thing again. I was usually game as well, but with some precautions. Throughout our life together I tasted many unusual foods. My motto is; try it and if you don't like it don't try it again.

After our take-out dining experience we ventured into the Coney Island amusement park. We walked along the board walk and took in the excitement and the history of the park. The two guys decided to take a risk and go aboard the old, rickety, wooden roller coaster there. I decided to take the miss since I'm not really into rides and I had never been on a roller coaster. It's just a fear of mine. Of course they tried to convince me to go along, but I told them I would be quite content waiting on a bench while they went for the ride of their lives. They were fully absorbed in the thrill and experience of riding with their hands in the air. I was surprised after all the food they ate that they didn't feel sick afterward.

The next day we once again went to explore the city. We took the subway just to experience it. It was absolutely not a scary way to travel, as television can depict, and was completely uneventful. Our guide took us through the theater district and to Harold Square, then to Macy's Department Store.

We went to the Empire State Building, but it was closed to visitors. There was a fire happening at that very moment. We couldn't get many details so we moved on. We ended up at the World Trade Center. We decided to take the elevator up to the observation deck.

There were two ways to observe. One deck was fully enclosed and you were surrounded by glass 360 degrees. On the glass were etched outlines of buildings in the cityscape. As you looked through the outlines you could find the points of interest in the city down below. The air quality was quite hazy and we couldn't see too far in the distance. However, if you looked down you could see so much.

There was a bench incorporated into the marble steps all along the wall of glass. Oh my God, we were so high up that I was getting a bit of a queasy stomach sitting there. In order to look down you had to lean into the glass which was angled outward a few degrees so you could see more. You could see cars down below that looked smaller than an ant. I am not a huge fan of heights so I had to take a look down in small doses.

Will on the other hand was really enjoying the scenic adventure. Our guide had brought us to the perfect place for a thrill. As if that wasn't enough we ventured to the top deck outside. We were contained by a railing set several feet from the edge of the building. The view was amazing, but still restricted by a haze of humidity and air pollution.

That was our last day in New York. We ate dinner with Will's friend that night at his house in Brooklyn. We spent the evening talking and the guys took that time to reminisce about old times in England. The next day we were on the road back home. Our first vacation was magical for me.

Discovery Tour

We lived together, we pretty much did everything together, and now we added to the portfolio that we took a great vacation together. Everything just came so natural to us.

Will's brother was engaged to be married in September 1988. Will was in the wedding party and I was invited to attend as his guest. I was in for the big family meeting because all the relatives were going to be there.

Will and I arrived separately since he had to be there early for pre-ceremonial itineraries. It was a lovely day for the big event. They had a traditional wedding and it was beautiful. I arrived to the reception and it was set up so elegantly. The bride and the establishment did a beautiful job in preparation for such an important day. I can't exactly remember who I sat with at the reception. Will was sitting at the head table with the rest of the wedding party so I was on my own.

I remember that I asked Will's father to dance that day. He and I got along so well. He was still undergoing cancer treatments and he didn't want to dance because he felt like he was too weak. The song the DJ was playing was called; *That's What Friends Are For,* performed by Dionne Warwick, Elton John and Stevie Wonder. That song would become significant later. With some prodding, I convinced Will's dad to dance with me even if it was only for thirty seconds. We danced and he did rather well I must say. I am so glad I was able to persuade him to do it. I think Will was proud of me and his dad too. He was such a sentimental guy.

After the bridal party performed the rituals done at a wedding reception, they were freed from their duty and joined their significant others, and enjoyed the remainder of the party. I was excited to finally get Will to myself. He led me around the reception hall and introduced me to his extended family members. I know he loved giving them all the chance to meet me and I wasn't shy about meeting them either.

Soon autumn arrived. Even though we lived in the city, the streets in the old neighborhoods were lined with enormous, deciduous trees that turned an array of fiery colors for their grand display of fall. We enjoyed drives along back roads to see the brilliant foliage. At times the trees would cross over the roadways and form an archway just like in a romantic dream.

We lived near Walden Pond. Each time we went there the scenery would be different. One day the water would be calm and it would sparkle as the sun hit it. Then another day it would be covered with a mist of fog rising off it. I felt peaceful at that place when beach season was over. I loved walking the loop at the pond especially in autumn, the scenery was quite breathtaking and it offered a serene feeling. I felt like a kid when I walked along the leaf covered trails and heard the thrashing and crunching under my feet.

During our travels we'd stop into small diners or places for ice cream or a quick bite and a cup of coffee. When I was with Will on those little, dreamy rides in the car, I felt like we were the only two people who existed. I would get lost in him. He took the reins and took me places I never knew existed. I felt like he knew everything. He had such a knack for sniffing his way around foreign places. He always found some enchanted place for us to stop for a break, as if he researched it and planned it all out ahead of time.

When we would have our friends over to the apartment we'd enjoy music, snacks and drinks, and play board games. Will liked and owned the game Trivial Pursuit. I played the game with him and tried to be a good sport, even though most of the questions I had no clue what the answer was. He possessed a wealth of knowledge and he'd always win the game. He knew the answers to almost all the questions. He would fill his round playing piece with all the designated pie wedges required to win, in what seemed like record time. I remember accusing him of cheating once. His response was; "What do you think, I study the cards?" It wasn't impossible. I accepted his argument and justification on the subject and let him take his prize with full pride.

It wasn't only physical attraction that drew me to him now; I was also attracted to his stupendous intelligence. He was both smart and beautiful. He not only had stunning looks, but he was also warmhearted. He was perfect in my eyes. If he was a con artist he would have been able to rob me of every cent I had and then some.

I was tired of losing on game night so eventually we bought a board game called Pictionary. I had played it in the past and considered it my game of choice. I had some artistic talent and was able to draw out my clue quick enough to beat the sand hourglass timer of two minutes. That frazzled Will's competitive spirit. Now the tables were turned and he accused me of cheating. I wasn't cheating I was just good at the game and it felt good to finally win. We continued to play both games when we entertained friends. He went on winning Trivial Pursuit in record time each grueling game and I won Pictionary with my partner every time we played that.

Eventually, Will did try to cheat at Pictionary. He wasn't accustomed to losing games. I caught him one night whispering the clue from the card he had drawn to his partner. He'd just start his drawing and within three seconds his partner would blurt out the answer and be right every time. I made my accusation and gave him my proof, but he denied any cheating was going on. The secret couldn't be concealed long and someone would laugh and break the straight faced lying that was happening at the game table. It was all in good fun.

Christmas Cheer

———————— ⌒⟩⟩⟩ ————————

𝒯he holidays were approaching. Even after dating for almost a year we were connected at the hips, doing everything together. We yearned to be together as if our souls were suffering when we were apart. That phenomenon would last throughout our lives.

Christmas was only a couple of weeks away. It was our first one living together and we decided to put up a fresh cut tree. We went to one of those farms where you select and cut down your own tree. It was exhilarating. Both of us were perfectionists. We searched together with a saw in hand and finally found the perfect tree. My strong and handsome escort cut it down like an experienced lumber jack. There wasn't anything Will couldn't do. We took it back to the car and loaded it up, and brought it home. We were like a sappy, romantic couple holding hands in one of those love story movies.

We set the tree in the stand and decorated it, but it was so large it needed more ornaments. The next day we ventured to a garden center turned holiday store in Lexington called Four Seasons. It was like a Christmas paradise inside and we spent a couple of hours wandering around in the store. They had the most gorgeous decorations and garnishing I had ever seen.

While we were there they had some sort of potpourri simmering and the place smelled divine. The scent stimulated our senses, but seemed to cloud our minds. We had so many ornaments in our basket we couldn't decide which ones to actually get, due to the confusion created by the luscious aroma wafting throughout the store. We finally narrowed it down to just a few items and made our purchase.

As we were leaving, we noticed some farm animals in a penned area outside the store. There were goats and brilliantly colored, unusual looking chickens. There was a coin operated machine to buy grain, identical to the kind one buys gumballs from. We put a quarter into it and bought some feed for the animals. We were intrigued by the birds with plumes of feathers around their feet. We hadn't seen anything like them before. We talked about how cool it would be to have some ourselves someday.

We returned to our apartment and made dinner for ourselves. Afterward, we put on some Christmas music and Will put on his holiday hat. It was a ski hat from Polaroid his uncle had given him one Christmas when he was a teenager. It was a sentimental thing with Will. We had some eggnog with nutmeg sprinkled on it, and proceeded to decorate the tree like an old married couple. We discussed placement of each ornament with each other so it would be a masterpiece when we were finished. Finally, the task was complete and the creation was perfect in our eyes. The only thing missing were the gifts. We would get to that next.

We went to the mall and tried to shop together for each other. That didn't work out so well. I'd always take longer looking around in the store trying to come up with the perfect gift for him. I am that way with each gift I buy. I have to analyze it from all angles. It has to be special and the recipient should feel that I put a lot of thought into it. I guess I am just a little bit particular or just too sentimental. Suddenly, I could feel Will looking over my shoulder with his bags in hand announcing he was ready to go. I hadn't gotten one gift yet, I needed more time. We decided to split up and set up a time and a place to meet in the mall. The pressure was off and our mission was accomplished.

We took the gifts home and of course made each other swear not to peek. We hid them until we could get to the wrapping stage of it all. I know this was nearly impossible for my sweet Will, for he loved Christmas like a child. I loved that about him. Eventually, the gifts were wrapped and placed under the Christmas tree. That's when the shaking of packages and the guessing game began, and continued all the way up to Christmas Eve. With that excitement we could have rewritten the lyrics to the song; *The Twelve Days of Christmas.*

We both had a sense of humor, and we'd sneak extra noise making items into the packages to try to trick each other of the contents. Will, being a carpenter, used to put screws and nails in the boxes. I was less clever, but more artistic and used sleigh bells or something that rattled.

I had enough patience to wait for Christmas to open any gifts, but poor Will couldn't wait. He would tell me he was kidding, but I believe in my heart he had great difficulty waiting for Santa to come. As it was, we had to open all our gifts on Christmas Eve. I was raised to only open one gift then and on Christmas Day we opened the rest. Will said his family always opened all their gifts on Christmas Eve. With much provocation he convinced me we should scoot the gift opening up a day to Christmas Eve. I figured it wouldn't hurt anything to do that, so we did.

We went to his aunt's house for a big, Italian Christmas Eve. As always, Will felt I was as comfortable as he was with his family and I was kind of in charge of fending for myself, which was fine. However, it was the food on the table I wasn't so comfortable with. Okay, now I am of Irish descent, keep that in mind. The menu on Christmas Eve at his aunt's house included many sea foods. There was no problem with that; I had eaten seafood in the past. Well, the seafood that night looked like sea creatures to me. We had spaghetti, I was fine with that. Who doesn't like spaghetti? They served me a plate and added a home made red sauce.

The next course was Maine lobsters. I was from the West Coast and had only eaten Alaskan King Crab legs. I didn't even know how to eat a lobster, or whether I even liked it. Will just said to me, "Come on my honey, it's really good." So I tried to eat a lobster.

I was a novice and I didn't know how to get the meat out of it. Will had to show me how to cut into the lobster to get the meat out. First, he broke the tail off from the body, and then this disgusting, green, pasty fluid, guts I thought, came out of the creature's body. I learned it was called the tomalley. Will said it was a great stuff. It sure didn't look very appetizing.

His family was probably noticing me wrinkle my nose being unsure of how to eat the delicacy. I would have laughed at myself if I was on the other side looking in with them. Okay, Will got the tail off for me, and then he removed the claws and explained how to use nutcrackers to open them. Then he sliced down the middle of the underside of the tail and bent the side's outward and poof, out came the tail meat in one solid piece. I thought that was quite impressive.

I tasted the green tomalley, but it tasted like dirty, salty, sea water. I decided to pass on the green stuff that oozed out of the lobster. Will scooped it up and ate it on some Italian scali bread. Good for him, I thought. I watched him eat his lobster so skillfully. He made certain to suck the meat out of all the tiny legs narrower than straws as well as the larger pieces of the crustacean. I ate the tail and claw meat and left it at that. It looked like way too much work to get small amounts of what remained in the tiny anatomical parts of the lobster. I am grateful for getting the chance to try all the strange foods he introduced me to.

After dinner we all mingled and laughed while stories of past Christmases were told. It was a full night by the end. Soon everyone was leaving the house one by one and we decided to leave as well. It was still Christmas Eve when we got home to our apartment and Will told me we had to open our gifts to each other. I agreed to go ahead and appease him. I appointed him director, which I think he gladly accepted, and he was in charge of passing out the gifts.

I sat on the couch until he divided up the gifts and placed them on the coffee table. Then we each opened one at a time, trading turns while we watched each other, waiting to see their reaction. That was Will's idea too; he was always quite clever. We would be our goofy selves and ooh-ah over each others gifts. Shortly after every package was opened we decided to go to bed. It was a full day and tomorrow would yet again be filled with travel to visit our families and eat more food.

We separated for the Christmas Day festivities knowing we'd meet up later in the day. I went to my mother's house and had dinner with her, my two sisters, and my brother. Will went to his mom and dad's house for dinner. It was hard for us to be apart, we were so used to being glued at the hip. It was important to see our families though. My family didn't do anything big Christmas Eve and that's why I went to Will's family gathering.

All the respectful obligations for the Christmas season were finished. We pleased everyone and we had some fun ourselves. It was a completely new experience for me to indulge in the Italian tradition. We had new gifts to try out and we had each other. Our bond was growing stronger and stronger. It was like a little Christmas magic sprinkled some more fairy dust on us that season.

Life's Surprises

———————————— ⟨⟩⟩⟩ ————————————

It was 1989 and the holidays were over and we resumed to our life as usual. I must say it was never hum-drum for Will and me. We were practicing each day living life to the fullest without even realizing it. We were open to spontaneity and it allowed us to live with such zest for life.

We each had full time jobs and our mornings were just like any other couple around the country. We had to determine how both could get ready without disrupting the routine of getting into the bathroom for the morning tasks of preparing to face the world. Let's see, there was showering, make up, drying hair, brushing teeth, etc. We managed to make it all work. Of course, just entering the second year of our love affair we just shared the bathroom. We had nothing to hide from each other. Hey, and if we had to share the shower to save some time, we did. Those showers gave us something to reflect on throughout the day too. Those were the days, young uninhibited love. Then off to work we went, but not before we said I love you and got a kiss, then said our goodbye.

I was living in a daydream state most of the time and work was still difficult to get through. I was still able to multi task and perform my job, but I was constantly thinking of being with Will after work. That giddiness in my heart was still lit like a roaring flame and it wasn't dwindling. I couldn't get enough of Will. We did ordinary things during the week just like anyone in any town USA, but we did them together.

In the evenings we sat slouched on the couch and his arm would be around my shoulders, and my hand would be on his leg. Or better yet, we would lie on the couch together. It seemed neither one of us could get enough physical contact. It was rare, but if we weren't sitting that close I would catch myself staring at him still. I would stare at him and study his face, almost like an artist preparing to paint on canvas or sculpt out of clay. I was magnetically drawn to do so. Sometimes he wouldn't notice. I would catch myself in the act and consciously pull my eyes from him. I wonder now if my soul had finally found its mate that it had searched for all those years before we met. I can at least think that it was so.

Many nights we'd go out for an appetizer plate at the Ninety-Nine's restaurant. Will loved to go out to eat just to be busy I think. We would go out and enjoy food, drinks and company. We'd gaze into each others eyes at the table and have philosophical conversation. I was so enamored by him. With that kind of attraction I don't think I could ever resist going anywhere with him.

We'd go visit Will's mom and dad often. His dad was enduring cancer treatments and you could see the toll it was taking on him. Will and I couldn't do much except to be there for him. I think mostly our visits made him happy just knowing we cared enough to do so, and it broke up the monotony. I could see he loved his son so much.

There were many memories and stories Will shared with his father. They were held in a vault and Will had the combination, and in time he would open it up and share with me. Sometimes we would stop and buy a custard pie for his dad on the way to his house, it was his favorite. I noticed his eyes light up and a smile came to his face when we brought a delightful treat. I was so happy we could make him forget his illness and pain for a few moments.

Will's dad had some medical emergencies related to his illness and had to go to the hospital. He was weak and got colds and then pneumonia easily. We would visit him every day at the hospital. Will wanted to give his dad the gift of love in return by dropping whatever he was doing and go see him. Will's dad would get well enough to be discharged from the hospital and be sent home, where his wife, Will's mom, took care of him. I can't imagine what life must have been like for her. She was required to be an on call nurse twenty four hours a day. I think visits from the family members gave her a break from time to time.

Will and I had discussed never marrying and just living together forever on more than one occasion. I think we were so comfortable we felt we didn't need a marriage certificate to improve our relationship or to glue it together. We both survived marriages that dissolved and were not ready to pursue that journey again.

The marriage subject came up frequently by now. We had a habit as I mentioned, of having philosophical conversations while dining in restaurants most of the time. We always gazed into each others eyes while we talked. Our souls must have been able to see each other through the eyes. It is said they are the window to the soul. I think I believe that. Anyway, we not only discussed marriage, but the lack of desire to have children. We both felt the same way on both subjects and agreed not to do either.

I knew as a youngster I didn't want any children due to overdosing on them in an early career of babysitting during my teenage years. One summer when I was sixteen years old, I had three very energetic boys I babysat all day long every weekday, and they were rambunctious trouble makers. They made me earn my money for sure. That's my explanation for my lack of desire to have children. Without the desire, I wondered in my head if I would be a horrible mother lashing out on the children with resentment. However, just in case, we said we would not make it a concrete decision until I turned thirty-five years old. I was twenty-seven then.

One night in late February out of the blue, we went out to eat at a place called Jimmy's behind our apartment building. While we were there having deep conversation, Will casually proposed to me. He didn't have a ring, but I don't think he expected to ask me to marry him that night. It sort of went like this, Will asked, "So what do you think about us getting married?"

I was surprised, but not, if you know what I mean. I told him I thought it would be great if we got married. Just as simple as that the decision was made. It was a grand moment, no ring needed. Now that we were engaged Will wanted to take me to select a ring. I told him I just wanted a plain wedding band and that no engagement ring was necessary to profess my love for him.

Will worked in the construction trade and I remember a very wintry, windy day in February, and he was supposed to be roofing. I was concerned, and told him he should call his boss to see if work was still scheduled for the day. His boss told him yes it was and that he had to go to work or lose his job. Being burdened with rent and other bills Will of course decided to work. I went to work that day as well.

I suppose we should have listened to that gut instinct many of us ignore. Will called me at work just a few hours after I had left the apartment. He told me he was hurt on the job that morning. He was up on a ladder two stories high fastening roof shingles from it. The wind gusted and pushed the ladder from the house with Will intertwined within it and he fell.

The rest of the construction crew on site didn't know what to do for Will. He then got himself into his truck and proceeded to drive himself to the hospital. Yes, he was in pain, but the guys he worked with were obviously incompetent. Perhaps they were in shock, or perhaps Will hid the pain and told them he would be alright and could take himself.

The doctors treated the broken bones in his left arm and right leg and kneecap with full casts to immobilize them and allow them to mend. I was frantic with the news of events. Will knew he shouldn't be at work that day, but felt forced to go to in. He was in fear of losing his job. In all honesty I would have done the same.

The next few weeks were interesting. He was directed not to get the casts wet which complicated bathing. He tried to shower with his leg outside the shower curtain which required a gymnast's flexibility and would prove to be impossible. We put large, black trash bags over his casts so he could shower, but the water still got in. Then I had a brainstorm of an idea. I grabbed a plastic milk crate he had, where he kept odds and ends, and tools. We emptied it and put it in the bathtub upside down to use as a stool. He sat on it in the shower and leaned his leg on the edge of the bathtub out of the water stream. He could wash himself pretty well, but I had to help him wash his back because he couldn't reach and only had use of one hand. I didn't mind that job at all...

Will was home on a worker compensation claim. He couldn't drive anywhere. He was always so full of energy that he had to be moving. We were both that personality type. The poor guy was going insane being shut in watching *The Price Is Right* and other game shows to pass time. We talked daily on the phone. I called him from my office while he was home to check in on him, and see if he needed me to bring him anything after work.

Will ended up suing the construction company he worked for. He should have never been working that day. Eventually, his boss called him and offered him some hours at the office answering the phone. Will almost jumped at the opportunity since it would allow him to get out of the apartment. He could talk to human beings instead of cheering for contestants on game shows. I mentioned perhaps he should speak to his attorney first. The attorney advised him absolutely not go to work and that it could be damaging to the case. With that, Will declined his bosses offer.

Departure

In February 1989, Will's father went to the hospital again with pneumonia and was very weak. Will was determined to go visit his dad. He was tired of sitting in the house and waiting for me to drive him to the hospital after work. After all, there had to be a way to drive. He had a full size truck with an automatic transmission which meant it was big enough to accommodate the cast. He finagled a way to get into the bench seat of the truck and off he went to the hospital.

He called me later and he told me he drove himself to visit his father. I wondered how on earth he was able to get that leg in the truck and positioned just so to enable him to drive. He did it and that was all that mattered. He would no longer be prisoner to our apartment after that. He regained his independence and I was happy for him.

Will's dad was in the hospital for several days and he would go visit him. He had nothing better to do and wanted to spend as much time with him as possible. He used to go to Brigham's on the way and bring his dad a frappe. Will would take a break in the evening and drive home to get me and we'd both go to the hospital until visiting hours ended.

His dad was so sick at that point things were not looking good and he took a turn for the worse. I got a call at work telling me things were getting very bad and that his organs were beginning to shut down. I left work and went to the hospital to be with Will, his dad, and his family.

I wonder if Will's dad somehow knew his soul was reaching the time of departure from this dimension. I never said anything because I didn't want to upset anyone. It wasn't my father or my husband dying. I didn't know what anyone was experiencing watching their loved one die; I had not witnessed death yet. I did my best to comfort Will and his family.

From time to time I would go to a common room down the hall and pray. I wanted to give Will's family some privacy. I prayed to God to give his dad strength and courage to get well. In that same prayer I asked God to take him and stop his suffering if he was supposed to go.

That same night the doctors and nurses told the family the time was coming, judging his vitals. All his family members were strolling into the hospital room with the revelation. There was one sibling missing still, Will's older sister. She lived a distance away and had small children. She was doing her best to get there to be with him in his last moments here on earth. I was in the room with his family; his wife was sitting beside him, near his right shoulder touching him with her hand. The elevator door opened and it was Will's sister. Will's dad let go the moment she arrived. Will's mom knew when he passed; she felt it somehow and announced it to us.

The crying began. Will was so emotional about his father's passing and I felt so helpless. I had to leave the room to let them express their sorrows and cry it out. I silently cried and prayed for Will's dad. I began to have guilt. How could I pray for God to end the suffering and take him? It was inevitable though, the professionals had already told us his organs had shut down, but still somehow I felt responsible.

The funeral arrangements were made and there was a wake. I had never been to a wake before. I lived on the West Coast prior to moving to Massachusetts. I had only gone to funerals involving a church service or mass, and then the grave site prayers and burial. Previous to the wake Will's mother advised us not to wear full black attire because his dad requested us not to. Perhaps it was his way to have us celebrate his life not his death.

I was with Will while he tended to his mother's needs in her time of loss. He was always respectful and willing to make many sacrifices to help family or anyone. This was a time of crisis and he was ready to be the man of the house and do whatever was asked of him.

Will's family arrived to the funeral home first. There was an open casket with Will's father in it to be viewed by all his friends and family. It was all so foreign to me, I had no idea what to expect. The family followed their mother in a line to the casket, and each knelt on the prayer kneeler provided at the side of it to say goodbye. Then they would rise and they moved to the side of the room and formed a receiving line. The rest of the room was filled with folding chairs set up in rows for all the guests to come in and pay their respects, and perhaps linger for awhile in support of the family.

The next day there was a Catholic Mass service held and then we all drove to the cemetery. The family was taken by limousine and Will's mother insisted I rode with them. I did not know her reasons for that; perhaps it was the wish of her husband. We arrived to the cemetery grave site and witnessed a peaceful, final burial service and said our farewells. I remember everyone paying their respects at the casket and leaving flowers as they departed.

I still felt so badly for the family and what they must have been going through. Will and I were very close even then, and he cried so much about his dad. He couldn't believe he was gone. I tried to console him and listened to him the best I knew how. I didn't know what to say to ease his pain though. I guess just being there for him to have someone to talk to and cry with was the best support I could offer him at that time.

He fought with thoughts and guilt in his head about not being here with his dad while he was in the Air Force and stationed in England until the middle of 1987. He somehow thought if he was home he could have kept him from dying. I knew that was wrong, but I could think rationally, I hadn't lost my father. I just continued to listen and never gave advice. Our journeys are our own, and Will was on his journey with gut wrenching, chest tightening pain that comes with it, with or without my advice.

Easter Eggs And Wedding Bells

Easter was around the corner. Unbeknownst to me Will had a surprise up his sleeve. It was the first holiday to arrive since his father passed away and I was expecting things to be quiet. His mother planned a dinner and said it was imperative that life resumed and that everyone involved made an attempt to live it.

Behind the scenes I planned on giving Will a basket filled with little novelties and candy. Smurfs were trendy at the time, and I happened to find an adorable one portraying a carpenter with a saw in his hand. It was made out of molded plastic standing about two and a half inches high. Will was a collector of sorts and a sentimental guy as well; I knew he'd like it and it was perfect because he was a carpenter. (That Smurf sat on his truck dashboard for years.) I was so proud of myself for lovingly filling that Easter basket with what I thought were the perfect trinkets and choices of goodies.

Will put a basket together himself and we exchanged them on Easter morning. The one I received from Will was filled with the traditional green, cellophane grass. He placed candy and some of those plastic eggs that come apart in the middle of assorted colors in it. I was impressed. I didn't even get that creative and everyone fondly calls me Margie Stewart.

Well, I shook one of the eggs and there was something inside, but it didn't sound like candy. I had no idea what was up his sleeve. It could've been nails or something for all I knew. I opened it and found a shiny new penny, a Hershey Kiss candy and an ENGAGEMENT RING! My heart was beating double time in excitement triggered by the magnificent beauty of the ring.

The ring was a complete surprise because we agreed to only get bands. I think I may have shed a pleasurable tear or two, and Will told me his family insisted I should have a proper engagement ring. He did a fabulous job picking it out; it fit me perfectly and looked great on my hand.

I was mesmerized by the sparkle from the many diamonds and it simply took my breath away. I had never worn something so grand and exquisite. I probably would've noticed it in the jeweler's case, but passed over it thinking it was too expensive.

The main stone was a half carat marquis diamond with three vertical rows of diamonds on either side of it set in channel settings. The rows were separated by thin bars of gold and extended all the way to the sides of the band. It was gorgeous and I absolutely loved the ring.

I also loved the fact that Will picked something so spectacular out for me. I never felt deserving of such luxurious things during my life. I knew he bought it to express his immense love for me and I wore it everyday and everywhere with pride. I was a new bride to be with all kinds of exciting plans to make now.

We selected a date for our wedding. Initially we chose May 19, 1990, we liked the ring it had with all the nine's in it. We let everyone in our families know about the date. Shortly thereafter, we were informed there was another family wedding in Florida that same day. We were told an important relative of Will's would not attend ours because of it, so we changed the date to please "the family." We moved the date to the following Saturday, May 26. We realized it was Memorial Day weekend, but nobody spoke up about it so we stuck with our decision.

Will and I determined our budget for the wedding by figuring out how much we could contribute weekly, and opened a savings account specifically for wedding costs. We had fourteen months to save for all the details involved in a wedding. I was pretty good at making a dime stretch to a dollar. With that, we got creative and put quite an event together. I used my talents and put my heart into every detail to make the day special. It had to be; after all I was marrying my best friend and soul mate.

Will was a great "groom to be" through all the planning stages of our big day. He was involved in mostly every element. We had fairytale ideas on a budget in mind, but with some determination we knew we could pull it off. We looked into having the ceremony outdoors at a large gazebo at Lake Quannapowitt in Wakefield. We inquired at the town hall about how we could make it a possibility. We were told they did not allow weddings to take place there, not for me, nor Princess Diana. That shot down our idea, but we did contemplate sneaking and having our nuptials there regardless of the rules.

Our search led us to a lovely place near Walden Pond. It was a historical manor house called the Codman House. There was the main house, a carriage house, and an Italian sunken garden on the premises. It was so elegant and romantic and we fell in love with the ambiance it offered.

The wedding would be in the garden where there were roses, a long pool filled with lily pads, and marble statue ruins lining the perimeter of the garden, once of museum quality. The reception would be in the carriage house and we thought of having live chamber music for the entertainment. We also envisioned that I would arrive by horse and carriage to exchange vows of eternal love with my husband to be. We had our hearts set on the place and discussed money and dates with the proprietor.

We shared our excitement with family members, but we always got the same response from Will's side. Why would you two want to have that? You should wear casual clothes like Dockers pants and polo t-shirts for the guys, and something other than a wedding gown for the bride. I wondered why they continued to rain on our parade. Then, the carriage house was unacceptable because some family members smoked and the site didn't allow smoking indoors. They did not want to be inconvenienced by having to go outdoors for a cigarette. All our excitement fizzled each time we were with family and shared our ideas about "our" day... Okay, we decided an outdoor wedding would not be wise in case of inclement weather. That was a good possibility in New England that time of year.

The hunt continued for the perfect place. We saw a write up about The Hartwell House in Lexington. It compared the interior to the house in Gone with the Wind. That thought raised my eyebrows and we contacted the establishment. We went to review the packages it offered. To our surprise it was affordable and fulfilled all the romantic and elegant hopes we were looking for.

It had a large, screened in patio area attached to the restaurant with a roof over it available for the wedding ceremony. It was connected to the restaurant with French doors. It overlooked a small pond with a fountain in the middle, with trees, rhododendrons, and flowers surrounding it. We'd exchange our vows at the edge of the patio abutting the pond with our guests seated behind us in rows of chairs. After the ceremony the reception would follow immediately in the restaurant. It was perfect for us.

We had both been married before in a church. The Catholic Church wouldn't marry us unless we attained an annulment, which is quite complicated. We weren't too concerned about that issue, married is married we thought. We scanned the yellow pages and successfully found a Justice of the Peace willing to marry us on our selected date. So it was settled.

We made the mistake of yet again letting too many details about the wedding plans leak out to the family. We were told a particular aunt and uncle would not attend the wedding if we had that particular Justice of the Peace. There was some sort of grievance between them. We cringed and made yet another change. We finally learned our lesson and decided not to offer anymore information about the wedding plans to family from then on. If asked how the wedding plans were coming; we decided to simply answer, "Just fine."

We had been pushed too far and became rebels with a cause. We were the only contributors financially, and felt no one had any right to ask us to make sacrifices regarding our day. That's right, "our" day. We scanned the yellow pages again, and in spite selected a woman Justice of the Peace. We contacted and met with the JP, she was lovely, and we reserved her for our date. We were happy to have a non-traditional surprise by having a woman officiate the ceremony. We had been pushed too far and were taking control now. From then on the plans had to have spark to them.

We had a list of creative ideas and necessities for the wedding. We kept track of them on a list and checked them off one at a time over the next year. Some ideas were eliminated due to being too expensive or impractical. Others, we were determined to have, and found a way to make them possible so we could give our guests a day of surprises they'd remember. We were having a lot of fun being sneaky and creative to give our wedding our signature trade mark.

We decided instead of the traditional DJ or band we would be unique and hire a pianist to play background music. There was a grand piano at the Hartwell House and the manager recommended some pianists for hire. We listened to someone play and we loved him so we hired him. He would play for the entire day, both for the wedding and the reception for what we thought was a relatively small fee. With that, we knew our day was going to be a classy event with yet another grand surprise for our guests. We had the bigger tasks for the wedding completed now. We decided not to rush with the rest and take a break from planning and scheduling.

Time To Play And Explore

―――――― ⌘ ――――――

We enjoyed each other and all the little, fun nights out and weekend excursions to a lake or the ocean, Red Sox games, nightlife in Boston, and fried calamari rings while people watching at Faneuil Hall, and our romantic interludes.

We used to play a game while we were at Faneuil Hall in Boston. We'd be strolling along and then take a seat on a bench and sip our beverages and talk. Will asked me once to point out men I'd ask out if I wasn't with him. I told him I felt awkward doing that. Then he told me he'd show me women he might be interested in, and convinced me to play the game. Of course we'd point someone out and then we'd always find some kind of flaw in the stranger walking by that each other selected, and wonder how they could even choose someone like that.

Will noticed I was drawn to the men who were well dressed. He'd point to a man less polished and ask me why I wouldn't pick him. I told him I just found a man sexier if he was dressed in fine clothing such as a suit, and immaculately groomed. Today they call that look Metro sexual.

I noticed the women he picked out were dressed as if they were on their way to work the street corner. I asked him why he was attracted to that look and he really didn't have an answer. I didn't possess that look at all.

Perhaps that's what fantasy is and also the purpose of the game we were playing. You select something you don't have and don't necessarily want either.

I didn't dress provocatively, I preferred a classier look. I liked tailored clothing and my figure carried it off well. I was slender at about one hundred fifteen pounds and five feet six inches in height. Will later revealed he liked that I didn't dress like a floozy, and that he bragged to friends and family about that fact and how he loved it. It actually comforted me to hear him tell me that, especially after our game at Faneuil Hall. I was happy regardless because he chose me and kept me.

We also took a trip to Cape Cod to go camping that summer. We enjoyed a great day on a lake canoeing. I had a fear of water, but with Will at the helm I felt comfortable and safe. The sky was blue and cloudless, and the lake was still and without many other canoes. We were lost in our world oblivious to our surroundings in our little, rented canoe. It was a remarkable feeling and we were in that state of mind quite often.

We enjoyed a few hours on the lake as Will maneuvered the canoe. I watched him take charge of the paddles in his tank top and muscular body flexing with each stroke. I loved his body; he was so strong and handsome. That day on the lake offered us the opportunity to fall deeper in love and enjoy each other simply.

We returned the canoe and then went to the truck and discovered it had been broken into. The thieves took all our camera equipment I was hoping to use to photograph some sunrises on the beaches. Needless to say we were quite distraught. We filed a police report, but knew the likelihood of them retrieving anything would be nearly impossible.

We went to our camp site with our tails dragging. We told the manager of the facility that we would be leaving due to our poor luck and inquired on a refund. The refund was available, but it would be returned by mail.

We spent the night at the camp site that night in the bed of our truck. It had a fiberglass cap with windows over it. It kept us from being eaten alive by the mosquitoes looking for a free all you can eat buffet. The camper adjacent to us had a dog tied outside his trailer door and it barked incessantly all night long.

I needed a bathroom in the middle of the night and had to walk a good distance for one. The neon sign on my back announced the free chow for the bugs and I was attacked by mosquitoes. Will also had to make the trek to the bathroom and he was eaten alive as well. That was one more thrill of camping we'd never sign up for again.

In the morning we packed up and headed for home. We decided since we were half way down the Cape we should take a detour and drive to the point. We went all the way to Provincetown. While the tide was out we walked along the beach collecting sea treasures left ashore. It was quiet and we enjoyed each other, and the tranquility the sea air and sounds offer to the soul. Later, we had some fried seafood for lunch in a small diner and then headed for home.

Still on the Cape we stopped at a rest area and witnessed a small pod of whales off the coast. It was majestic to see them out there in their natural habitat performing for the people on the beach. That chance encounter actually gave us an incredible high point of the trip and we didn't feel it was a complete disaster after all.

We never sat around to miss a day of opportunity in a world where it seemed we had it by the tail. As I mentioned, we just enjoyed getting out of the house and walking around Boston. We enjoyed extravagant excursions as well as simple strolls in the park with hot candied nuts or a sausage with fried peppers and onions.

Will was still dealing with losing his father and it seemed he was indulging in more beer on a daily basis. He was such a sensitive human being and I was so blessed to know and love him. We could confide in each other any of our troubles. He was deeply grieving and missed his dad so much and he'd talk to me about it. He would cry and I'd try to console him, and I'd hug him and just listen. I tried to convince him that his dad's spirit was here with him and watching over him.

I had never experienced such a loss and truly felt helpless at times. I could not imagine the depth of Will's pain. He must have felt alone on that journey, as I do now. He told me he'd be fine in time and the extra beer was only temporary until he felt better. It didn't govern his life in any way so I let it go at that.

Through example early in life, my mother taught me the ability of gingerly making a suggestion to someone, and letting them either heed to it or do it their own way. I'd have an idea about something and she gently offered her advice. Of course what do parents know when you are a teenager? She'd let me go ahead on my own and either succeed or crash. It was my journey and she trusted that God had the reins to keep me safe or let me learn a lesson.

I tried to give Will the same gift by just listening and being supportive, not a nag. He worked a full time job and was productive and he still treated me like a very rare, prized, crystal figurine. He put me up on a pedestal and treated me like a queen. I didn't feel I deserved being up there, but he put me there and enjoyed it. He adored me and with that I felt so loved and so close to him.

In the meantime, we enjoyed life as much as possible. Will was in the middle of a law suit against the construction company he worked for. In a short time they settled the case out of court. After the attorney got his compensation Will ended up with around $20,000.00. Needless to say, he didn't return to his job after suing them, but immediately found another one.

This newfound money was burning a hole in Will's pocket. He discussed with me some ways to spend his new fortune. We talked easily about decisions. I offered my two cents worth to him in a way not to push. It wasn't up to me to decide how he should spend his money, we weren't married. He was the one who suffered the broken leg and arm and all the turmoil that went with it. I think he just appreciated my opinion. I was glad he trusted me and could talk to me so openly that way about anything. We continued to share that luxury the rest of our lives.

He had a new Dodge pick up truck so he paid off the loan first thing. He was ecstatic. I was proud of him for wisely making that decision. He'd no longer be hostage to a car payment for four more years. Will still had some money left and we went places together and splurged on expensive dining. It satisfied that desire to have a glimpse of life on the other side of the tracks. We had more than money could ever give us. We had this strong connection between two souls and nothing was going to cut that bond. The next monetary decision he'd make was to pay off my engagement ring and wedding band. That was one less bill to be concerned about and we would go into our marriage debt free. What a great feeling that was.

After his father died, his mother needed some financial help so he helped her out a little as well. By then he didn't have a tremendous amount of money left, but did what he could in realistic terms. He also purchased a beautiful headstone for his father's grave site with love and pride. It was so important for Will to make certain his dad; his hero had a monumental stone.

Our New Home And A Secret

By autumn Will still had a little money in the bank left from his law suit and we decided to look for a house. Will had a dream of accomplishing a list of goals by a certain age and buying a home was a top priority. I was happy in our little apartment, but he had much larger dreams and wanted to pursue them now. He was a man on a mission. He found the woman he wanted to spend the rest of his life with, now all he needed was the American dream house with the picket fence. Will decided to use the last little bit of money he set aside for the down payment and closing costs of our new home.

We glanced at the real estate listings section in the newspaper each weekend to see what was on the market. We traveled to towns a little further away from the city of Boston. That allowed us to escape ties causing tension and find prices more in our range. We looked at several houses and were surprised how awful they were for the asking price. They were in disrepair or in horrible locations. We were on a hunt looking for a needle in a haystack, if you get my drift. Each time we searched we'd drive home feeling so discouraged.

After many disappointing trips to look at homes we found an ad for something called a condex. That's two homes connected with a joint main entrance in the front, and a hallway separating the two dwellings. Basically it was a duplex and you owned one side of it.

The price was within our reach so we drove to Haverhill to meet the realtor. He was smooth as silk as far as salespeople go, and we should have realized by the Mercedes sedan parked in the driveway. After his verbal presentation we were ready to sign on the dotted line even before we toured the house.

The realtor showed us the property, but the flooring was not installed. We had the choice of colors to pick from, and then they'd install carpet and linoleum. The home had a living room, eat-in kitchen, bath and a half and two bedrooms upstairs, an unfinished basement, as well as a full walk in attic. We had the option of having a staircase built to the attic instead of using a pull down access so we did. It meant plenty of storage and perhaps an addition someday. Off the basement was a sliding glass door and yard. We loved it and we swallowed the sales pitch, gave a deposit to the realtor, and signed the purchase and sales agreement right then and there. We were so excited to know that within a few weeks we'd be proud new home owners.

We had great news we wanted to share with the world. We told our families immediately about embarking on a new adventure. We scurried to locate and gather all the necessary information the bank required to process the loan. We both had all kinds of ideas running through our heads to turn that condex into our home. Will was thinking on a much larger scale with finishing rooms and building additions. I on the other hand was just concerned about curtains and furnishings. We had all those rooms to fill and not much furniture to put into them.

After a couple of weeks the bank contacted us and told us the original paperwork provided was misplaced. Of course we trusted the bank to be organized and keep track of it all. We didn't even think to make copies before handing things over to them. So once again we made calls and searched for all the documentation they requested and supplied it. They contacted us yet again, but for something different. Will had been in the US Air Force which qualified him for a VA loan. About a month into the filing process they told us they couldn't consider both incomes for the loan unless we were married. Neither of us made enough money annually to qualify for the loan alone. We were looking at closing on the house in January 1990, but our wedding was scheduled in May. We thought the house was perfect for us as well as being in a good location. We were heart broken. We scrambled yet again for a solution and an idea came to mind.

We already paid for all our wedding arrangements so we couldn't get our money back if we canceled. We wanted the house and the freedom it meant for us though. We were perplexed. We called the JP we booked for May and she was willing to marry us early, and then perform the formal wedding again on the original date reserved. So we just decided to elope secretly. No one would have to know and our well thought out wedding would still take place. It would be a divine event.

We went to the city hall and got our marriage license. Then we scheduled the mini wedding for VA loan purposes. We got two witnesses and drove to the JP's home in Waltham on the evening of January 12, 1990.

A coworker friend of mine gave us a wedding gift for that night. She recently won a hotel stay at a rather elegant place in Cambridge in a radio contest. She figured she'd never use it and surrendered the package stay to me and Will. It was for one night in a hotel suite and breakfast the next morning. We made the reservations prior to our elopement.

After our nuptials we took our friends and witnesses to the hotel restaurant for dinner and had an amazing night celebrating. After dinner we took the party to our hotel suite which was larger than our apartment. It had two bedrooms with king size beds in them, a living room, and a bar filled with alcoholic beverages and snacks. We pretty much devoured all that was in it and then called for a delivery that arrived via taxi cab.

It got quite late and our friends went home, then we had the most romantic evening in our hotel suite. Our life had just taken a huge turn and we were beginning a new journey together. We were bursting with love, joy and happiness, and our secret. We overcame our first hurdle.

When we returned to reality and our apartment, Will carried me over the threshold. He was such a romantic guy and I felt so lucky. I was still mesmerized by the fact that I had met and married Mr. Wonderful.

How could this have happened to me? I had been through so many struggles during my life. God finally granted me a gift you only get once in a lifetime.

Soon we closed on the house and were officially homeowner's as husband and wife. Will checked off another item on his list of goals and dreams that day. On moving day my uncle arrived with a borrowed moving van from the company where he worked, some guys for lifting, and it was snowing. With what seemed like very little effort we loaded the truck and were on our way to the new house. It was so cute; once we were there Will carried me over the threshold again, christening the new house. He treated me with such love and honor without having to think about it, it just came naturally. He treated me like I was a treasured gift and cherished me. It was a grand feeling to know that in my heart. I hope he felt the same warm feeling of over flowing love I had toward him as well.

Each time we would go to a family member's house we had to remove our wedding bands because they didn't know we were legally married. Our elopement would remain a secret just to avoid hearing more of why we didn't need to have a wedding. It was our day, our money, and what we wanted. We only eloped to please the bank so we could buy our first home together. Just because of a bank formality we weren't willing to give up our day of ritual and celebration.

Final Preparations

Even though we were already married we still had the big day to look forward to. We began to resume wrapping up the final details of the wedding plans. We selected our invitations, a cake, champagne toast glasses, the flowers, bridal party gifts and things of the like. We filed a bridal registry at the Jordan Marsh department store together and Will impressed me by picking out the china. There were some other small details to make our day over the top fabulous that I took care of along the way.

The creativity flowed and we came up with many ideas to make our day unique and give it flair. I came up with the idea of having bubbles blown at the wedding instead of throwing rice. I bought cases of bottled children's bubbles and removed the labels. I replaced them with hand written tags in calligraphy with our names and wedding date on them. I loved doing that sort of thing and by adding my special touch to our wedding day it was the icing on the cake. All the little details were falling into place as the day grew near.

I needed a wedding dress. I had been shopping in vintage antique stores throughout New England to find something circa 1940. Everything I found was extremely worn and in need of extensive repair due to age. I didn't want to be strapped with that chore and time was getting away. I gave up on that idea.

One day I stopped at a shop I just happened to find along my travels. They had an enormous selection of gowns to choose from. I had already tried on so many frumpy gowns and it just wasn't me. That day I took three gowns into the fitting room. I tried on all three just to give them each a fair trial. When I tried on the third one I knew it was perfect when I saw myself in the mirror. It spoke my language. It was form fitted all the way to my knees and then had a peplum at the base. It split off center in the front and gradually lengthened, cascading along the sides toward the back and formed a short train. The body of the gown was white satin covered with a rose patterned lace and iridescent sequins. It had long, lace sleeves and the peplum was satin. The entire gown sparkled when I walked in it as the sequins caught the light. I loved it and I ordered on the spot.

I browsed around the bridal salon looking at shoes and headpieces. I saw some adorable shoes, but cringed realizing that purchase would blow the budget, but I had a solution. My sewing and craft talents gave me an idea. I bought some satin shoes that could be dyed to match bridesmaid's gowns, but left them white. I visited a fabric store in Woburn that had a vast bridal department. I found sequins and pearls there to design my own unforgettable shoes. My gown didn't cover my shoes and I thought adding a little pizzazz would make the ensemble complete and unforgettable. I sewed sequins and pearls onto a piece of white fabric. Then with a glue gun I affixed the patch I created onto my shoes. Voila, it was perfect and only cost about a tenth of what the bridal salon wanted.

Now I needed my headpiece. I scanned the bridal magazine pages and found a pill box design I was attracted to. I felt it would compliment my stacked bob hair style and wouldn't overpower the gown. The fabric store I got my shoe supplies at also had everything for veils and hats so I went back and got everything I needed. I covered the pillbox form with satin and lace that closely matched my gown. Then I bought some netting and secured that to the hat and put some white silk, bridal flowers on the back to cover all the seams. It was perfect to the worst critic on the block, me.

We took care of all the little details for the wedding together after the gown. We selected the tuxedos in a dark shade of gray, with a barely visible black pinstripe. The ushers were in suit jackets with matching vests and bow ties. Will wore tails with a matching vest and ascot tie. He looked so sharp; I was probably drooling as he tried on the ensemble. You remember I mentioned my fantasy guy was finely dressed and groomed; Will was fitting that image there at the tuxedo store.

We were well within budget so we decided to rent a limousine to take us home after the wedding reception, just in case we enjoyed too much champagne. We made arrangements to have our guests join us there for more celebrating. We weren't leaving for our honeymoon until the following weekend. We were doing everything as first class as we could on our budget for the wedding. We thought the limousine would add just a little more flair.

We located a white 1962 Rolls Royce to accommodate our wishes. It was perfect. Our fairytale wedding on a budget had materialized. All that was left to do was mail the invitations, give the restaurant our menu choice and final head count; everything was all set to go.

Stirring Up The Hens

There was yet another uprising before the wedding on Easter Sunday, just two months prior to the wedding. From the other room, I could hear some family members cackling like hens in the kitchen about attire to be worn to our wedding. I didn't understand what the issue was; you wear what you want to wear. We were trying to keep it affordable for everyone, so we didn't ask anyone other than the ushers and best man to wear a tux.

It was a noon wedding so I didn't think formal attire for our guests was necessary. I was at my wits end with all the wedding plan bashing we had endured over the past ten months or so. I actually had an aunt mention that she may not be able to attend our wedding. She told me she didn't own any dressy clothing and could not afford to buy anything. I told her to wear what she had even if it was jeans and just to be there. Will and I wanted everyone to be there and we didn't care what they wore.

I walked into the kitchen that day armed and dangerous with anger and my hands on my hips. I interrupted the conversation between the women at the table. They were of the next generation older than me and did not speak their minds openly, but I did. I point blank told them, it just didn't matter what they wore to the wedding and explained about my relative. I told them to wear whatever they so desired and to just be there. I left the room as quickly as I entered thinking I handled it quite well, considering I was about to explode. I'm sure I shocked everyone, but someone had to finally take control and say it though. Finally, the dust could settle, or then again, maybe not.

That night our phone rang off the hook. Will's ears must have been burning from all the talking going on behind his back about me. One of the callers; a relative, asked him how he was ever going to control me. I remember he responded by telling them he didn't want to control me and that was part of the reason why he loved me. My cheerleader was speaking up for himself for a change and I was thrilled.

Later, we were told that one of the relatives would not attend the wedding because of what I said. Will asked me to call and apologize to her, but I refused. I told him an apology was not called for in this instance. I had spoken the truth and from my heart. He'd ask me to be "the bigger man" for the first time that night and apologize. I compromised and wrote a note instead. In that note I didn't particularly apologize, I just mentioned we didn't ask anyone other than the bridal party to wear tuxedos. We didn't want anyone going broke over rental fees, and due to that gowns weren't necessary for our guests. Then, I closed the note by telling her, the only person she would upset by not attending the wedding was Will.

The Big Day

It was wedding day countdown time. I confirmed all the plans two weeks prior to the big event just to be certain everyone's schedule matched mine. Now it was a waiting game for the day to arrive. Friends of Will's from the Air Force arrived from out of town a couple of days before the wedding and we took them to tour Boston. It was fun getting to know each other and hearing old stories shared between the guys. They were in the same unit on a base in England. It also gave us a big break from waiting for the wedding day to arrive.

Will and I always loved everything the city of Boston had to offer. We enjoyed the anonymity there as well. No matter where we went together I enjoyed a spectacular phenomenon. I felt as if the world around us stopped, and stepped aside for us to enjoy the magic between us. We were somehow able to phase out all distraction when we were in public and share a profound love between us. I enjoyed that for my entire marriage to him.

The wedding day arrived. It was sunny with scattered clouds and quite tolerable temperatures for May in New England. The previous day we had cold, damp and raw weather. I was concerned that our guests might need coats for the ceremony, but it all worked out perfectly. I met with my mother and sisters at the Hartwell House. We got dressed there; sipped mimosa's to cut the edge off our nerves, and met with the photographer for some pre-ceremony photos.

I think I was more nervous that day than the actual day we got married at the JP's house in January. In truth, it was probably due to the excitement of revealing our secret wedding plans to our guests. There was an element of surprise behind them. I wanted everything to be perfect.

The clock was ticking and everything was in place. All the guests were seated and the groom and ushers were in position with the JP. The bridesmaids and I were waiting for our queue to walk down the aisle. The pianist was playing *Ave Maria* and the soloist we hired was singing the lyrics. He also agreed to emcee the day's events. The song had so many verses and was continuing well after everyone was seated. I couldn't get their attention to cut the song short.

I could see our anxious guests looking back at me and my bridesmaids on standby, wondering why we weren't coming through the French doors and down the aisle. Finally, they completed the song and began performing *The Wedding Song* by Paul Stookey and we were signaled to begin the processional.

Staying with tradition, the bridesmaids went down the aisle first. Then I followed, making my debut as a bride and joined my best friend, the groom to exchange our vows. My uncle, who was also my godfather, escorted me down the aisle.

I could see Will's expression as I entered through the open French doors to greet him for our vows, with all our family and friends there to witness. He gave a grand gesture of a nod and let out a whew of a breath. That signaled me he was pleased by my appearance, and was eagerly waiting to take my hand, exchange vows publicly, and marry his princess.

When we reached the front row, my godfather kissed me and turned my hand over to Will. At that moment I was ready to give the performance of a lifetime. We were already married, but most family members didn't know. Somehow the formal wedding made me feel like I wasn't already married. We took great pride in our plans to create a special day, not only for our enjoyment, but to give our guests a day they'd also remember fondly. I think at that point everyone had noticed our subtle surprises unfolding and were anxious to see what was coming next.

The JP did a wonderful job delivering a message before we exchanged our vows. During the ceremony a family member did a reading by Robert M. Millay called; *The Key to Love*. I found it in a magazine during my vast research. It says so much to a couple embarking into marriage. If you pay close attention it gives you abundant wisdom on how to nurture a marriage through thick and thin. It describes what you should and shouldn't expect from each other. The message will in turn allow you to have a marriage that lasts forever if you remember it and apply it routinely.

We exchanged our vows and rings and we were pronounced husband and wife, then it was time for the kiss! It's interesting when it comes time for the kiss. You wonder what kind of kiss you would have in public. You're very excited and relieved the buildup to the event is over. We didn't rehearse that step. We embraced and tilted our heads and connected. We had a brief, loving, soft kiss on the lips, then Will lifted me to my toes while tightly hugging me and we kissed again. Will was able to completely envelop me when he hugged me. It gave me the most amazing feeling of safeness. We were lost in the moment for that instant and oblivious to our surroundings. The pianist began to play Mendelssohn's *Wedding March* for the recessional. We snapped back into reality after the kiss, turned around and faced the congregation of friends and family, and then Will threw up his arm and let out a small cheer and got everyone excited. We strolled down the aisle hand in hand toward the elegant party waiting behind the French doors.

Before the reception began we had our formal photos taken. The patio where the wedding was held was quickly rearranged and set up for a cocktail hour. There was a buffet table covered with trays of cheeses, crackers, and fruits for our guests to enjoy. It was to keep everyone entertained while we were detained by the photographer. There was a cash bar inside the restaurant to get beverages if they wanted any.

We took the formal photos indoors and then ventured outside where my uncle was waiting with his motorcycle. We planned ahead of time for him to bring his royal blue Harley Davidson touring motorcycle for our photos. I think he was honored I asked and proud to do it. Will and I were not bikers, but were intrigued by the lifestyle. Most of all, we wanted to have that little detail added to show our guests we liked

91

the element of surprise and perhaps shock. Our day was filled with those kinds of surprises still allowing it to be romantic and elegant.

The polished motorcycle was glistening in the sunlight while Will and I sat on it and its radio was turned on. The photographer and the video photographer were exposing film to capture the fantasy day of ours. The bridal party had some of the bottled bubbles and they were floating through the vantage point of the cameras. At one point Will kissed me and spoke to the spectators and photographers like they were paparazzi, telling them we would ride the motorcycle to Aruba. He explained there was a bridge they had now so we could do that. He was always the funny one with the clever remarks. We were enjoying our magical day in the spotlight. We had fun seeing our friends displaying smiles on their faces. It was proof they were enjoying the show, which was our intention. We had guests waiting so we moved the party back indoors.

It was time for the emcee to gather the crowd and direct them to the reception area. We elected not to have a seating arrangement since we were doomed no matter who we had seated with whom. This would be yet another surprise for our guests. It was our intent to keep tradition out of "our" glorious day while maintaining elegance.

The emcee introduced the bridal party and we made our grand entrance through the beautiful French doors and were seated at a table. Once again, to defy tradition, we didn't have a long table positioned in front of all our guests. Instead, we had a round table and we were all seated there. It was positioned in the front corner of the restaurant near a short, but wide staircase. It still offered good vantage to everyone, but with a twist.

Everyone was seated except for Will and me, and the emcee immediately asked the best man to make his toast. The best man was Will's only brother and he gave us the most exquisite and honorary toast imagined. He said, "Will and Margaret; when you travel along the sometimes bumpy road of life, may you look back and remember this day and the happiness you're having and that will smooth those bumps out. Cheers." We didn't know it, but there would be many times Will and I would do exactly that. Those wise words would come to mind and always made us smile. It couldn't have been a more perfect toast.

We selected an hors d 'oeuvre menu for our meal to please the pallet of many, including ours. We had been to so many weddings and received a plate of food never even eating it and thought it was wasteful. Our choice was different, which is what we were after anyway. The buffet included oysters on the half shell (one of Will's favorites), stuffed mushrooms, and Swedish meatballs, scallops wrapped in bacon, tea sandwiches, melon wrapped in proscuitto, spinach and feta cheese in filo, teriyaki chicken brochettes, Italian sausages with onion and sweet peppers, and salads.

The bridal party was invited to go to the buffet tables and get their meals first then our guests followed suit. Will and I enjoyed our assortment of foods immensely. I was indulging in champagne too so everything tasted wonderfully. Everyone ate and drank and seemed to be really enjoying themselves which was our goal. Most of all I felt like Cinderella when she got her happy ending when the glass slipper fit her foot.

We had the piano for background music and it was perfect for our special day. We didn't arrange for a dance floor because we wanted the day to be more like a cocktail party, rather than everyone getting completely drunk and falling all over each other while dancing. We had older guests too and I think they appreciated the light music genre.

Will and I did have a first dance in a cleared area near the cake table while the emcee sang; *Wind Beneath my Wings*, performed by Bette Midler then. I picked that song because it speaks of a hero being the wind beneath her wings. Will was that hero for me. We danced and I sang the chorus lyrics into his ears and Will began to cry.

He was a sensitive spirit and I think the day coming together was overwhelming for him. He told me he didn't feel worthy of marrying someone like me, that he didn't deserve someone so wonderful and dedicated to him. I reiterated that I loved him so much and we danced slowly and talked lovingly through our three minute song.

He told me while we danced that he wished his dad could have been there with us. I just softly told him, I know, and that I believed his dad was there witnessing our wonderful day and our grand love for each other. That dance was one of my most cherished memories of our wedding day.

It was time to cut the cake. The emcee directed the pianist and the guests to sing a song about cutting the cake. It was sung to the tune of *The Farmer in the Dell*. The lyrics are, "The bride cuts the cake, the bride cuts the cake, hi-ho-the derry-o, the bride cuts the cake," and I cut the cake. Then, the same jingle was sung, but they sang "the groom cuts the cake…" instead.

Will and I each had a plate with a slice of cake on it and were instructed to feed each other. I was on the receiving end first pleading with Will not to smear cake all over my face. I placed a dinner napkin over my dress like a bib in preparation for disaster. He fed me and I could feel him wanting to smear cake so I trapped his finger in my teeth to prevent it. He ranted and raved on about that.

It was my turn to feed him cake and I pretended I was going to get him good with it. I wasn't, because he was good enough to oblige by my wish for him not to make a mess with it while feeding me. The emcee and the crowd were cheering me on trying to get me to get him good.

His brother came up behind him and held his arms down for his turn. I was feeding Will the cake and his brother grabbed my hand and pushed it onto Will's face. Will couldn't believe he was betrayed that way and I swore I didn't do it intentionally. We wouldn't be certain of what exactly happened until we watched our wedding video a couple of weeks later. Yes, his brother was the force that made the cake smear on his face.

After the cake ritual we all began to mingle. Will and I moseyed around to all our guest's tables and said hello. We invited just over sixty people so it was quite intimate. We were able to pay attention to everyone that came to join us in celebrating our day. Even certain family members that said they would not attend initially did come. Later, we were told it was the best wedding they had ever been to. That was our intention!

Before the day was completely over we had to wait outside for the limousine which was running late. It was Memorial Day weekend and parades and detoured traffic caused the driver to be delayed. With that, an unanticipated surprise unfolded while we waited for the car to arrive. Suddenly, Will and a friend of his were carrying Gramps out from the foyer of the restaurant in an antique, wingback chair like an Egyptian prince. They strategically placed him in the shade under the entrance awning. He sat there and witnessed the activities while we waited for the limo.

The magic began to unfold as everyone began calling Gramps the Godfather. He thoroughly enjoyed the honor and proudly remained on his throne smiling ear to ear.

Will and I sat on the sides of the chair with Gramps smothering him with love and kisses. Will had gotten up from the chair and I gave Gramps a kiss on the lips. A few people witnessing the charming expression let out an ooooooh!

Will responded to that kiss by saying, "Hey, hey, hey, hey." The crowd roared with laughter.

I said, "Hey" back to him in an elongated pronunciation, as if what I did was perfectly acceptable.

He then said, "That's okay, he's my Gramps."

In the video you can hear the cameraman say, "This is magical." He did not know the meaning of his words in that moment. Our life was magical. The crowd became intoxicated by the loving display with Gramps smack dab in the middle of it all. Gramps said something about keeping the driver from coming for another hour and everyone laughed. I asked someone to bring me some champagne because I was sitting with my best man, Gramps.

Gratefully, the grand moment was captured by the photographer and on video. The car finally arrived and we were seated inside it, everyone left, and the grounds became silent as we drove off.

Will was an inquisitive soul and he asked the driver what it was like to drive a 1962 Rolls Royce. The driver offered to let him drive it once we got it onto the highway. Will accepted the offer and then drove us along the highway for several miles. The car would only go about fifty miles per hour and the steering wheel was on the right hand side. How many grooms can say they drove the limo with their bride in the back seat? It was fantastic that he did that.

He drove the car to a rest area and we stopped because I had mentioned I needed a bathroom facility. That particular rest area had no facilities, but I couldn't hold it for another half hour or longer. I wandered up into the woods still wearing my wedding gown. I located a spot out of view, hiked my wedding dress up, threw it over my shoulder, and relieved my screaming bladder. Will did the same, but of course it was much easier for him. He was shocked I did what I did, but I just couldn't wait. It was just another detail to put in the memory banks. The entire day and all of the events in it were extraordinary and I have remembered every detail for almost two decades.

We arrived to our home and Will carried me over the threshold again. He loved me so profoundly and I returned that love in equal or greater quantities to him. We truly had the most endearing partnership. We got into the house and many of our guests had arrived well before us due to our detours.

Everyone made themselves at home in our absence. Music was playing on the stereo. Burgers and hotdogs were cooking on a gas grill down in our basement. What?! Well, it was the only solution they could come up with since it was raining outside. I think many beers clouded their thinking on that decision.

The smoke alarms began to go off in the house, but they were hardwired so we couldn't remove the batteries to silence them. Finally, we located the breaker and dismantled them temporarily. We had a great time carrying on the celebration at our house. It was quite an eventful day and is etched permanently in my mind.

Will and I talked about our day a million times over the years. We also had our video and watched it several times in our first year of marriage. Then it became our annual ritual to watch it on our anniversary and have some strawberries and champagne. He truly was a romantic guy and that allowed me to think of him as my Prince Charming. I had a romantic heart as well so the two of us blended effortlessly. I married my soul mate. He was my true love forever.

Bon Voyage

―――――――― ⟨⟨⟩ ――――――――

The next Saturday we went on our honeymoon, a seven day Caribbean cruise. Neither of us had been on a cruise before and it seemed we were in for a week of enchantment. The ships itinerary included Aruba, Curacao, St. Thomas, Tortolla, and Virgin Gorda. We boarded the ship and the crew members made us feel like royalty. It wasn't like the old television series *The Love Boat* at all, it was much more elegant.

The first day we kind of got our toes wet while exploring the ship. We were issued something called "cruise highlights" in our cabin each day. It listed all the excursions and pastimes offered on the ship. It included all the entertainment to be found in each lounge, movies for the week, and fitness classes that were being offered. It even had talent shows, card games, and art and craft classes, wine tasting, Bingo, shuffleboard tournaments, among loads of other entertaining things to do while you were on board if you wanted to be busy. It also suggested dress for each evening for dinner. Some nights were formal and others were casual or costume.

The first night we explored the ship and all it had to offer with our directory in hand. On top of all the organized things scheduled you could go to the casino or shops. There were times we'd be at sea all day long so the on board excursions could be a fun take.

The first night I suffered an upset stomach from either sea sickness or the rich food. I had taken some complimentary Dramamine, but it didn't help. Will, my hero, came to the rescue and had a brainstorm that might help my stomach. He explained there could possibly be a remedy in a bar.

He asked the bartender for something I had never had before, called Bitters. The bartender prepared the tonic then I drank it and it soothed my stomach. That idea saved me; Will was brilliant in my eyes. I don't think he could have done anything wrong since I was so head over heels in love with him. He was perfect in every way.

We were at sea all day Sunday and found a comfortable spot on the deck with a pool, lounge chairs, and a bar with a calypso band playing the steel drums. We were enjoying a magnificent, blue sky matching the vibrant, blue sea in color. There was a cool, ocean breeze, making us unaware that the hot equator sun had the ability to rapidly burn our skin. As we sat on our lounge chairs the waiters brought us any drink we wanted.

The seating was arranged around a pool built into the ship deck. In that pool there was a tiled sitting area even with the waters level, probably about twenty feet wide and fifteen feet long. There was a type of curb around the edge high enough to rest your back against while sitting in there. The rocking of the ship created waves that went up onto the sitting area inside the pool and splashed over your legs.

The rhythmic rocking of the ship was hypnotic and was relaxing me in the perfect weather elements almost into a nap. Will was sitting in the area of the pool I just described and wasn't concerned about getting sunburned. I burn easily and tanned at a salon before our trip to ward off unexpected burning, but Will hadn't. He told me he was in Egypt, Morocco, and Turkey while in the military and never got burned. I argued and told him we were on the equator and it might be different this time. Especially since his legs were being splashed by water.

He didn't take heed to my warning. He was sunburned to his surprise, and his legs swelled from the severity of the burn. I never said, "I told you so." I did however, tell him he needed to elevate his legs and perhaps soak them in cool water or ice them down. He was a man, and his levels of testosterone would need nothing of the sort. He was really swollen and he looked like he had elephant legs. I couldn't help him further than I had already tried, he wouldn't hear it. He'd suffer those symptoms all night long and into the next day.

We arrived to Aruba Monday morning around eight o'clock. We spent time in a casino losing only twenty bucks and then wandered through town and enjoyed an authentic island lunch. While we were downtown a young boy passing by us on a bicycle called out to him, calling him "tattoo man" because of all his tattoos.

Later, we ventured to an outdoor mall filled with small boutiques connected under a roof. The corridor floors were covered in sand. We saw large parrots and toucans outside of the store fronts in cages or on perches. I was fascinated by their brilliant colors and the fact that they didn't fly away. We noticed a drug store in the mall and inquired within to see if they had Aloe Vera gel. We were in luck, they did have some so we bought a bottle of it and Will applied it to his legs immediately.

While we were wandering around that mall a gust of wind blew through the corridor and a piece of sand went into Will's eye. He was too uncomfortable with the sand in his eye to walk around anymore so we went back to the ship and tried to rinse it out, unsuccessfully.

We finally went to see the ship doctor, but he was off duty. They paged him and he came pretty quickly and then checked Will's eye. He actually found three grains of sand in it. The doctor flushed the eye, but the sand particles wouldn't budge. He had to place a topical anesthetic solution into the eye. Then he scooped the sand particles out with an instrument that sort of looked like a miniature, double ended spoon.

After the procedure the doctor dressed the eye with a patch. Just lovely, poor Will was on his honeymoon and was directed to wear an eye patch like a pirate. We went to our cabin to rest and clean up for dinner. Needless to say the patch didn't stay on for very long. Will wasn't about to parade around like that. I doubt I would have either.

Each night at dinner our taste buds experienced a sort of excursion themselves. Meals included island cuisine and extravagant meats like rack of lamb, duck, or stuffed lobster tails and other delicacies. The chef created magnificent desserts each evening for our indulgence as well. We were waited on by an expansive staff with smiles on their faces, always eager to please. I was in awe over the menu items and the complete first class experience every night. I was lost in the week of luxury with all the pampering provided on the cruise ship.

Tuesday we docked at Curacao. We noticed from the ship the Dutch influence by the brightly colored houses along the waters edge, in blues, yellows, and pinks. There were boats tied to piers in front of the buildings and I thought of Venice. The ship excursions were sold out, but a crewmember at the desk offered us a bit of advice. He told us to hire a cab and the driver would be more than willing to give us a private tour of the island.

We immediately found a cab driver willing to chauffer us around the city of Willemstad. He took us to the Curacao liquor factory in the Chobolobo Mansion which was typically on the ship excursion schedule. They made orange flavored liquors there. Will and I enjoyed learning about the cultures of the world. We loved listening to the cab driver that day while he told us of stories and adventures of his island. I think he enjoyed that we treated him like a friend, and not like we were spoiled Americans there to take advantage with our greenbacks. He even let me take his photo with Will at the liquor factory.

One of the days we were at sea all day long. We had heard about some sort of ship Olympics and that they needed teams for it. Will and I went to investigate to see what it was all about. We had attended a honeymooner's party earlier that week. Microphones were passed around the room that night. Everyone introduced themselves and said a little something about how they met, etc. Some people recognized us from that engagement and asked us if we wanted to be part of a team. I'm not usually one to jump into something like that, I wasn't confident in sports. Will was my guide and I seemed to follow his lead just before any adventure. The ship Olympics would be no exception. We got a team of six together and we called ourselves The Honeymooner's.

The Olympics consisted of multiple relay games each team would have to perform, and the first team to complete the task won. First, we had to all stand together as closely as possible so we could have our combined waistline measured. The team with the smallest one won. That meant we had to squeeze in together and suck in our stomachs.

We were all in good shape and young still, we thought for certain we'd win that segment of the games. To our disappointment we lost that leg of the race.

The next task was to dribble volleyballs down a basketball court on the upper deck and then back to the starting point, hand it off to the next person in line, and repeat it until all six on the team completed it. Next, we had to carry a volleyball between our knees as we walked down the court, and then lay it down on a lawn chair at the end of the court, and then jump rope back to the starting line. If you dropped the ball you had to start all over again. That proved to be quite a challenge. We all had suntan lotions on causing the ball to get slippery.

Everyone had competitive spirit during the event and our team thought we were doing so well. We didn't win those Olympic Games, but we did have a tremendous amount of fun. The referees gave us all Olympic Games certificates for being good sports.

There was a professional photographer snapping candid photos of the passengers throughout the trip, as well as portrait sessions on formal dining nights. The photos were posted daily on a row of vertical boards available for purchase in what was called the photo gallery. Each night we browsed for pictures taken of us. We ended up buying our formal portraits and a few candid photos, which included some from the Olympic Games.

We spent a day on the island of St. Thomas. We were previously informed that the duty free shopping was great there. We decided to shop for our souvenirs and gifts in the morning, and then go snorkeling in the afternoon. (I had practiced snorkeling beforehand in my sister's swimming pool.)

The stores on Main Street carried fancy items like jewelry, imported leather goods like hand bags, watches, and crystal. We weren't interested in any of that; we could get that at home any day at a mall.

We went shopping in the outdoor markets mostly. Will immediately found a T-shirt to add to his collection. As we moseyed along we discovered some lovely Dutch linen. We bought three sets of white pillowcases with embroidered cuffs. One set for each of our mothers and one for us. I thought they would be pretty displayed on a bed to dress it up a bit. We accomplished what we went there to do, and then recruited a cab driver to take us to a beach. We went to Coki Beach because we heard it was such an amazing place to snorkel.

Each morning on the ship we ate at the breakfast buffet. It was also served in the main dining room, but it was so early we elected not to go there. Besides, the buffet allowed us to sit outdoors and enjoy the sights and sounds of the sea, ambience in our eyes.

One morning a passenger told us to take a cake donut and bring it to the beach where we planned to snorkel. He told us it would dissolve in the water like fish food and the tropical fish would come right to you and eat it.

We remembered our donut that day for Coki Beach. I had it in my tote bag with our snorkeling equipment and towels. We got to the beach, shed our shorts to expose our swim wear and off we went to test the inviting Caribbean waters. We had our snorkels and sunscreen, and were ready to actually try them out for the first time since the swimming pool.

The sea water was about eighty degrees and you could barely tell it was any cooler than the air. Each island seemed to average a temperature of about eighty to eighty-two degrees Fahrenheit with a calm sea breeze.

We had the donut and let a piece crumble apart while literally in ankle deep water. These beautiful blue and yellow fish came right up and began to nibble the crumbs from around our feet. It was exhilarating. We had only seen fish like that in commercial aquariums. Will and I actually did go out deeper and snorkel for real after that experience.

My boss, a scuba diver, loaned us an underwater camera. We took photos of fish and of each other snorkeling so I could write home and tell about it. There were doubts I'd ever go snorkeling so photos were my only proof. It turned out to be the highlight of our trip, so we decided absolutely no more shopping. Instead, we were heading straight for the beach each day from then on to go snorkeling.

After spending some time in the ocean, Will suddenly noticed the swelling of his severely sunburned legs had gone completely down. The salt water was a miracle cure. He was thrilled to say the least and no longer looked such a fright.

The next day we arrived to an island called Tortolla with the option of taking a smaller boat to Virgin Gorda. We knew the trick about getting a cab to take us to a place of interest so we could snorkel, so that's what we did. Our cab driver asked us which beach we wanted to go to, but we didn't know. We told him to take us to the best one he knew of. That led us into a thirty minute cab ride over steep, winding roads, up one side of the island and down to the other side. He then dropped us off and asked what time he should come and get us. We quickly came up with a time and mentioned it to him.

There we were in the middle of nowhere. We trusted a man we didn't know to come back and get us after that long journey across the island. Well, we couldn't do much about it so we just went with it. We walked down a path to a beach and noticed a tall, wooden post in the ground with a white flotation device hanging on it. There were bold, black letters stenciled on it that read; "Brewer's Bay." At least we knew where we were.

We set up our towels and our snorkeling equipment and noticed we were the only people on the beach. It was perfect, it was secluded and we were on our honeymoon. The sand was white, the sky was blue, and the water was almost as blue as the sky. What more could we have asked for?

We snorkeled and I ended up sitting on the beach for awhile after taking in some sea water. I was ready for a break since water wasn't my comfort zone anyway. Will ventured further off shore to explore and take photos of the sea life invisible from the surface. I took photos of the scenery from the beach.

I got a little creative and sentimental, and carved our names in the sand with a stick I found. Then I carved a big heart around them. It looked like one of those love signs with initials in a big oak tree. (I took a photo of my handiwork and later framed it, which still sits on a shelf in our home now.) Will came back and saw it and felt so honored, acting like it was a cherished gift that I surprised him with. We were both very sentimental fools and I suppose it was like an instant, custom greeting card.

We were sitting on the beach, and after awhile we had a bit of a panic filled thought. We wondered if the taxi would indeed come back for us. We were seven miles from the ship and the walk was up hill fifty percent of the way. We decided we couldn't worry, because if we had been stranded, there would be a solution to our problem. Low and behold the taxi returned on time just as he said he would.

We boarded the ship and then took the complimentary boat ride to Virgin Gorda. We were game for squeezing in as much as we could on our trip. We were pleased with every other island so far. We ended up being so glad we elected to go see it too. It had white beaches and these massive, black, rock formations jutting up out of the sand with tall, lanky palm trees growing between them. They didn't look like they belonged there. It was like another world out of a sci-fi movie.

There was great snorkeling there as well. Will suited up to go see the sting rays and had the time of his life. In the meantime, I was intrigued on the beach by the amazing, foreign, rock formations, and the exotic beauty of the island. I was perfectly content to delve into my hobby and photograph the unusual landscape.

Virgin Gorda was our last Caribbean destination. That night we set sail for Puerto Rico, which meant we'd leave our fantasy life and return to reality the next morning. We had a debarkation briefing before departing the ship, and then we were off to the Puerto Rico airport and customs.

It was about ten o'clock in the morning and our flight home was not scheduled until late in the afternoon. It was hot and very humid there. We were burdened with luggage so we tried to see if we could get our flight bumped up. At first, the booking agent was not interested in accommodating us. I suppose he thought we were some wealthy, snobby Americans and he was going to make us wait since he was in control. We didn't give up our quest. We got into another line and spoke to a different agent and voila, we were on a flight out within a couple of hours. It got us out of the heat and home much sooner, and we were thrilled.

There's No Place Like Home

We returned home and we felt both sad and happy. We were sad we had to give up that lifestyle of what it must feel like to have a bank roll and be retired. We were however, glad to be back. Like Dorothy in the Wizard of Oz said, "There's no place like home." Things settled down for us and we pretty much had all we needed in each other to be happy.

When we got home there was a message on our answering machine telling us our wedding video was ready. We were confused since we were supposed to let him edit it, and then select three songs to be incorporated into it. When I called, he told me he couldn't wait to finish the video. He was excited to say it was one of his best efforts. He went on to tell me if we didn't like the songs he selected he would change them.

We were so excited we went to pick it up the next day and watched it that night. It truly was a magnificent production. It could have almost been nominated for an Oscar in the motion picture shorts category. The songs he chose ended up having sentimental meaning for us so no changes were necessary. One song in particular was especially important, although I doubt we would have picked it, but we were so glad it was included. It was the song called; *That's What Friends Are For*, performed by Dionne Warwick, Elton John and Stevie

Wonder. I danced with Will's dad to that song at his brothers wedding the previous year. It was perfect.

We both had jobs we went to daily just like many other Americans. We hurried off in the morning to work to earn an income so we could pay our mortgage and eat. If there was any extra after we paid the bills, we played. Each evening we met each other at home and had dinner together. I enjoyed cooking and we stayed in to eat most nights. Will enjoyed going out too so we did plenty of that as well. We explored our new town and found some good places to dine as well as some night clubs. Will was a great navigator and had a natural ability to find places to go to. I loved it and always left the driving to him. We rotated things around so we never got bored with doing the same thing all the time.

There was this one club on the river that had live music. We enjoyed going there from time to time and usually got a pitcher of beer and shared it. They had tall, cocktail tables with chairs like a barstool, but with a back. It was nice because you could watch the river and activity outside through picture windows. There was another bar that had a big screen TV and karaoke. We'd go there and watch people make complete fools out of themselves. I wasn't a good singer and I knew it, so I never attempted karaoke. Will however, was a good singer, but he never attempted it then either.

We discovered a fine restaurant that offered unusual cuisine and desserts, and dined there a couple of times for special occasions. The presentation was incredible, and the food was very pleasing to the palette. All the little details added by the chef created an illusion to the experience and made it worth the price tag. The food was so rich that we usually couldn't indulge in dessert, and I love dessert. Finally, I had the brilliant idea to go there, not for dinner, but for dessert and drinks instead. It was very romantic. I can remember going to so many places with Will and just gazing into his eyes. I continued to do that even after the honeymoon.

We lived together before we married, so we had our routine down pretty well already by our first year. If we didn't have plans for the evening we would have dinner at home. No matter what I prepared, Will always thanked me and told me how great it was. Even if I only made a tuna sandwich for lunch he always told me how grateful he was. In his words, he would say, "Thank you for dinner my honey, it was yummy." His gratitude made me feel like I was presenting a gift not just a meal. That sweet, little gesture of his made me feel so appreciated.

After meals and cleanup we would relax in the living room. We had a sofa and a loveseat, but the loveseat was hardly ever used unless we had company. Will and I always sat or we'd lie together on the sofa. I shake my head in awe over it still.

He loved the TV show Cheers, based in his city, Boston. He had this sense of humor that absorbed all the punch lines from that show, as well as others and commercials. He was brilliant that way. He stored the smallest of lines in his head and then he'd recite them later in a conversation where they were applicable. I always laughed even if it was a bad joke. I was in love, and loved that he was funny and tried to entertain me.

We had something so special, it is difficult to describe in words. I feel the emotion of intense joy in my heart to speak about the affection and love we shared. We enjoyed each moment with each other and never became bored with us. It seems it was a remarkable relationship rarely shared between people.

Since my husband died, I have had several people validate my feelings. They shared stories of how they could see our love, it was so obvious. They told me they've never known that kind of love even after thirty years of marriage.

Our auto mechanic told me one day he was sorry about my friend. I was confused and asked him who he was speaking of. He told me he meant the guy I always came to the shop with. I asked if he meant Will. He said yes. I thanked him and then told him Will was my husband. He was surprised and asked how long we were married. I told him almost nineteen years. He said I looked too young to be married that long. Then he told me it seemed like we were best friends and that we looked too happy to be married. I was grateful for the expression of sympathy and savored the compliment.

In our first year of marriage we explored the surrounding area of the town we called home and took day trips. We still enjoyed going to some of our old haunts in Boston too. I think it held abundant charm for us because we went there so often when we were dating. It held so many fond memories and milestones. Those moments locked in our minds eye were like the coals in a fireplace, and as long as the coals were still present the fire would ignite without much effort. Our magical life together was almost effortless.

We discovered places of interest on the northern shore of Boston, closer to home. We could get there rather easily and had the greatest time just being with each other. We went to Salisbury Beach in the summer time. I wasn't the greatest fan of the beach crowds of summer though. It seems beachgoers feel compelled to have food with them, calling the seagulls to fly overhead. I was concerned about the likelihood of being splattered with a gift from those birds in flight above me.

Will had fantastic childhood memories of the beach and loved the boardwalk, all the rides, and foods available like an amusement park. We always had to get square slices at Tripoli's Pizza. Then to satisfy a sweet tooth we got fried dough sprinkled with a cinnamon-sugar topping. There's nothing like going back to being a child in your mind. He took me around town and shared his wonderful stories with me. It didn't take me back, but it was great for him and I wasn't about to rain on his parade. Besides, like I keep on saying, I was with him, nothing else mattered, and we had fun together no matter what we did.

We found another beach closer to home both quiet and pristine at Plum Island. In the winter we walked along that beach while the tide was out. We found complete solace without another soul around. We wore our down jackets, stuffed cotton in our ears, and walked the beach and gathered little sea treasures like shells and rocks we'd come upon. We had a crystal bowl at home we displayed our trinkets in after beach excursions. I loved the solitude while lost in our own world out there walking, talking, and holding hands with my husband, my best friend. We'd be half frozen from the cold, winter, sea air, but it didn't matter, we were together and alone. Those days at the sea nourished our souls; two souls meant to do that together as if it was our planned journey, it seemed so comfortable. It was just phenomenal.

We didn't take a summer trip that year since we had already gone on the honeymoon cruise in June and had the time of our lives. Day trips around the area were the perfect getaway in my eyes anyway. We incorporated some visits to see our families as well. On many Friday nights we drove to my mother's house, ordered takeout fried seafood platters, rented videos, and hung out there with her and my siblings. It was always very casual and we had a great time. We lived far enough away to have our own lives, yet close enough to attend weekend gatherings and things of the like.

A friend from Washington State visited us in Haverhill that October. She arrived at the peak of the fall foliage season. Will was a history buff. He was in his glory showing her all the historical sites in and around Boston during her visit. He got great satisfaction being the teacher and tour guide; he was like a walking encyclopedia. We saw many sites in Boston along the famous Freedom Trail as well as the USS Constitution, the Kennedy Library, and Faneuil Hall, and as she put it, the Atlantic Ocean. She lives near the Pacific Ocean.

Will's grandfather worked at the Sheraton Hotel in downtown Boston then. He offered us some complimentary trolley tour tickets so we stopped in to see him. He was the head bellman and looked so fabulous in his official uniform and white gloves.

After a short visit, we got aboard the next trolley and saw even more important historical locations. We learned so much and had loads of fun at the same time.

We all had a wonderful visit. It was the first time she met Will too. She was glad to have the connection now, and know who I was talking about when we shared stories on the phone or in letters. Will and I enjoyed being hosts and getting an excuse to go see the sites of Boston and the surrounding area. It seems one never gets around to sight seeing in the town they live in until they have someone to show it all to.

On the way to the airport we took her to a fish market in Boston to buy live lobster. They offered to pack them securely for airplane travel so she made her purchase. She took four lobsters home with her as a surprise dinner for her family. It was actually an exciting adventure to carry live lobster aboard a plane. I had flown to the West Coast myself on several occasions carrying such a package. You can sense the other passengers looking at you when they realize what's in the box. They seem envious.

The brilliant, fiery foliage colors of autumn come quickly and depart even quicker in New England. We took every opportunity to get out and absorb nature's magnificent canvas each fall season. We enjoyed simple day trips relatively close to home mostly. We usually just got into Will's truck and followed the black ribbon of highway to wherever it would take us.

There is something magical about being alone with someone you love and adore, and witness the transformation happening all around you. It was always fun stopping for an occasional walk, an ice cream, or cup of coffee and dessert too. But truth be told, it was more about the companionship than anything money could buy, we were so deeply connected and thoroughly enjoyed every moment together.

Christmas Jitters

The holiday season was upon us and we would be torn on what to do. Whose house would we go to for dinner or dessert? We tried to squeeze it all in and please everyone, unsuccessfully. We always tried to have a good day and ended up aggravated and miserable by the end of it. The holidays are meant to be joyful, but somehow joy was always buried under our anxiety. Thanksgiving was our first holiday to divide between two families somehow, and it was emotionally exhausting.

Next, Christmas would come along and we were not even savoring the thought of how to handle that holiday. We somehow wished we could run away. It wasn't that we didn't like being with family. There was so much tension in the house that we both had stomach aches. We could feel the negative energy strangling us. Due to controlling personalities constantly making us feel inadequate, we felt like we were walking on eggshells during those visits.

We knew holidays meant tradition so we once again tried to please everyone. Christmas Eve was a big event with Will's family. My family kept it kind of small so it was fine to go to my in-laws for the festivities. We would once again enjoy interesting, yet fun Italian cuisine, as well as laughter sharing stories of years gone by.

We still had our private Christmas Eve waiting at home for us, which made performing our duty for the holiday almost bearable. After we got home and got comfortable we had our own quiet ritual that we started the prior year. We'd have a beer, a glass of wine, or some champagne and open our gifts to each other. We still opened a gift one by one, alternating turns to seize the moment. We really did well at selecting gifts for each other. I never received anything I hated or had to return.

I had a keen ear for listening to details. Sometimes I would get Will a gift and he wondered how I knew he wanted the item. He mentioned things in passing and I stored that in my memory banks like he stored joke punch lines in his.

Christmas Day arrived and it meant we had to divide the two families up. Someone in his extended family recently bought a home, and it was decided she would have Christmas dinner at her house that year. We would eat the main meal there, and then hurry off to spend the latter part of the day with my mom and my siblings.

Christmas Day was another day of a variety of foods surprising my eyes and my palette. I was introduced to something I still had not had the pleasure of tasting that day. Actually, I had never even seen it before. We were invited to get our plates and serve ourselves buffet style in the kitchen. I got my plate of spaghetti, then I proceeded to get some sauce, and suddenly there was this strange thing lying across my spaghetti! It was about ten inches long and an inch wide with tentacles all along one side of it.

My eyes must have bulged out of their sockets like a cartoon character. I asked Will what it was, and he told me it was octopus. Now that was a first for me. I had eaten calamari and tripe, how bad could this be I thought? Okay, I kept my cool and took my seat at the table to Will's right, since he was left handed. We would bump arms while we ate so this seating arrangement made dining more peaceful.

I was eating my spaghetti and getting my courage to at least try the octopus. I had to watch everyone at the table and learn the technique so I knew how to eat it. Well, it appeared everyone was just cutting it with a knife and fork, as if they were eating steak, and popping it right into their mouths and chewed.

Okay, I followed their example. I was chewing and chewing and chewing, but it was not breaking down enough for me to swallow it. It was like eating a rubber band an inch thick. My eyes must have had a

112

look of fright in them and Will noticed just in time. He rescued me; he told me it was okay not to eat it. I'm sure he was just so pleased that I at least tried it without a huge fuss. So, he casually took the leg with the tentacles on it, put it onto his plate, and continued to eat. He was the Italian and grew up eating that way. I was perfectly content with my plate of plain spaghetti.

There was a little bit of heavy air from tension in the house, but everyone behaved themselves and there was very little bickering. The day went rather well after the excitement of getting to eat octopus for the first time. Next, we had to drive to my mother's house for the plans we made with her and my family.

We were late and missed all the festivities; we hadn't quite hurried off soon enough. My siblings had already gone home and my heart sank into my toes. I felt like I was a disappointment again. It wasn't fair; my mother was put on the back burner. She didn't get us for Christmas Eve either and I felt like I cheated her. We spent some time with her, but after she worked so hard to prepare a meal and everything else involved with Christmas, she was exhausted, so Will and I went home. I felt horrible that I did that to her and my siblings. It was all because we had tried to please too many people. We would be tugged that way for all the holidays to come in the future as well.

We came up with a solution to our holiday heartache. We would flip flop the holidays and then rotate them every other year. We thought the plan was genius, but it didn't work. The strong, one sided tug was pulling us to our death on the desire to celebrate the holidays at all. We felt like we had only one choice, to spend the holidays with our family separately. We tried that and were told that was unacceptable, that we should be together for the holidays since we were husband and wife. Yes, indeed it was, but we just didn't know what else to do.

Double Anniversary

After the holidays and all the stress that was attached to them we escaped back into our own world, and had one secret celebration of our own. It was our first wedding anniversary of our elopement. We planned a special evening and went out to dinner at an authentic Italian restaurant we had been to before. It offered elegant ambience and a scrumptious menu. Will liked to order all the courses, so we got appetizers, an antipasto salad, and our entrees. That particular night we were bold and ordered snails for our appetizer. That was yet another food I had not tried in the first quarter century of my life. Will told me childhood stories of how his grandfather got snails in Boston and brought them home to eat. I was willing to try them; after all I had already sampled some pretty exotic foods, I thought.

The snails arrived to our table, and I found it interesting that they came inside rather large shells, almost as big as my fist. They provided us with little forks and tongs to retrieve the meat with and I laughed to myself. I imagined flipping the shell over to the next table like Daryl Hannah did in the movie *Splash*. I cautiously attempted the task, very lady like, and I managed it with finesse. I tasted the snail and it was delicious! They were sautéed in garlic and butter, and then placed inside the shells just for presentation purposes. They tasted similar to sautéed mushrooms.

It was a successful evening with a little added adventure. We held hands and gazed into each others eyes as we often did over a meal. We had a glorious first anniversary celebration. After our romantic dinner we went home to continue indulging ourselves in ritual and love.

We had planned a special night at home which included watching our wedding video, sipping champagne, and having strawberries and whipped cream. We were two hopelessly, happy romantics in love. It was an evening filled with small simple details that would define our lives later.

We watched our video, reliving that enchanted day. We laughed and had such joy together at home. We especially loved the toast our best man gave that day in Lexington. That tradition became an annual event for many years to come. The fun thing about it was the elopement was still a secret. We had something precious of our own that nobody could destroy with hurtful words.

Our May wedding anniversary arrived and we celebrated it in the same dazzling manner. We had dinner at the restaurant where we had our reception. A dear friend surprised us with a gift certificate to eat there. It was a perfect idea to go to the place we got married and celebrate our first anniversary.

We enjoyed a romantic dinner and the reminiscing of events on our wedding day. Afterward, we watched our wedding video again with delightful dessert at home. Only this time we included a gift to each other. Even though January was our legal marriage date on paper, our hearts were caught up in the May anniversary. After all, it was the actual selected date before we had the dilemma with buying the house leading us to elope.

For our first anniversary, Will being the humorous man he was, gave me the traditional gift of paper. Yes, he gave me stationery. I opened my gift in surprise, and of course he explained and then handed me a second gift.

He liked to give me things I would never buy for myself. He bought me a fine piece of Lalique Crystal. It was a frosted crystal, nude figurine of Pan and his Fair Maiden sitting on a rock embracing each other. I absolutely fell in love with its exquisite beauty. It somehow reminded me of our passionate love for each other. Will began a collection of the Lalique series for me after that.

Puppy Love

One evening in June that year, we found ourselves in the mall wandering the corridors, enjoying snacks from the food court, and window shopping. It passed time on the colder and rainy days when you preferred to be indoors, but needed some outside stimulus for your mind. While we were there we poked our heads into a pet store. Our bodies soon followed our heads, and we saw a black and white Siberian husky puppy with magnificent, blue eyes. We thought it was perfect timing to start our family of the four legged variety. Besides, the dog with the piercing, blue eyes had already stolen our hearts.

We asked the clerk to let us see the puppy. He took him out of the glass enclosure so we could play with him. He was absolutely adorable, but a bit shy. It seemed like he desperately needed a home. We took him home that night, along with half the inventory in the pet store. We got bowls, a brush, collar, leash, a book on the breed, and some toys; we were ready to be parents.

Our new baby had beautiful, bold markings and a mask around his eyes typical of the breed. We wanted to give him a regal name to match his looks. We thought of King, but I wasn't sure it was right for him, after all he was Siberian. Again, you have to realize Will and I liked being unique, so we came up with the perfect name still along the lines of King, we named him Czar.

We were labeled "DINKS" by our peers. That is; double income no kids. We planned on keeping it that way, but now we did have a dog. We fit the current trend of the yuppie mould. Having a new dog changed the way we would pass time. We enjoyed nature every chance we got. Some found it peculiar that we catered to our dog and ventured to the woods now instead of the city.

Will and I didn't care about labels; we knew who we were and what we were. We were comfortable with ourselves and let the winds of the Universe lead us where they may. We were no longer concerned about what was being said at the water bubbler. I think we liked making the sparks fly to a degree, just to make people aware that we were in control of our life now.

That first year with Czar was fantastic, well, except for the house training period. We bought a book written by a British woman who had Great Danes so we could learn about training our puppy. Her theory was that there were no bad dogs, only bad owners. So we followed the guidelines in her book and things went well for the most part. We had soft hearts, so Czar did turn out to be quite spoiled, but he was well behaved. He learned many tricks early on, and he was always rewarded for his honorable performance with a dog cookie.

We took Czar walking each day after work. We had a cemetery close by and we walked him there. At the same time we enjoyed reading the old head stones. There is a lot of history in those old cemeteries.

Finally, we put up a picket fence around our yard. It enabled us to play ball at home with him if we couldn't always squeeze in a walk. The fence turned out to be money very well spent. It became the *white picket fence* of the American dream.

We spent a lot of weekends hiking with our dog at nearby forests and lakes. We took Czar to the ocean during the off season and walked the vacant beaches. We went to Boston and we'd wander around the Public Gardens, Boston Common, and Faneuil Hall. We loved it. Czar used to chase squirrels in the park; he almost tried to climb a tree once to catch one. That dog went everywhere with us except to work. Eventually, that changed as well. Will was in the construction business and Czar went with him and waited in his truck while he worked.

Fireworks, Foliage And Dark Clouds

We experienced that feeling of oblivion, as if we were the only two people in the world almost everywhere we went. It is an amazing talent to have, and be so in tune with each other when you are together. It was such a gift. The bond between us became woven so tightly that the sharpest scissor, knife, or sword could never cut it.

We experienced yet another romantic interlude that summer over Fourth of July. Another couple friend of ours called, and asked if we were interested in going on a cruise in Boston Harbor to celebrate the holiday. The invitation sounded fabulous. We had not done anything quite like that yet, so we accepted.

Will wore Dockers and a dress shirt tucked in with his tan Sperry Topsiders, he looked great in anything in my eyes. I wore a dark pink, tank style dress made of cotton jersey knit with a coordinating jacket in bright, summery colors. It clung to my body exposing my thin physique and womanly curves. Will was over the moon when I dressed like that.

The cruise included a buffet dinner and live band, reminiscent of a wedding reception. During the meal there was jazzy background music playing. After that a band played Top Forty hits to dance to. Will and I danced on the parquet floor for awhile and enjoyed it thoroughly.

Watching him dance and on occasion dance silly made me smile until I glowed.

It was warm down below where the party was even with air conditioning, so we went up to the top deck to get some fresh air. It was a breathtaking sight. The night sky was crystal clear and the Boston skyline was vibrantly lit up. There were many smaller sea vessels in the harbor as well. We pretended we were on a private yacht for a moment.

Our friends joined us on deck shortly thereafter, and the fireworks display was about to start. When you're on the water the fireworks are doubly beautiful. You not only get to see them light up the sky, but you see the colorful lights reflect off the waters surface as well. It was incredible.

There was a band playing patriotic music during the pyrotechnics performance. I was amazed by the beauty surrounding me, but most of all I was in awe of the love I felt for Will and his for me. I had goose bumps on tens of thousands of occasions being with the love of my life. What we had was absolutely extraordinary.

Summer was always a very busy time for us. Each weekend was earmarked for escaping from the long work week, and having fun in all the hours possible. We always found something to do, and a way to enjoy life and each other from simple to grand style. Time always went so fast for us because we were always doing so much together.

Once again autumn in New England was upon us. We were fortunate to have weekends off together. If we didn't have a project or errand on the "honey do" list for the weekend we'd usually get in the truck and take a ride. We always had a cooler with snacks packed as well as a leash and water for Czar.

We never had a set itinerary, we just let the roadways guide us and end up wherever they took us. Will was very good at driving to nowhere and ending up somewhere. We almost always found a great park or trail system to walk with our dog. Then we usually found a diner or an ice cream stand too, and stopped for lunch or a sundae. When we got ice cream we usually also got a small cup of vanilla for Czar. He absolutely loved it and we got great joy sharing it with him. We enjoyed hundreds of those weekends in our lifetime.

The holidays were approaching again, and I felt a big, dark cloud of doom was lurking about. They weighed heavily on us. We couldn't please anyone with the visit schedule, least of all ourselves. It just didn't seem fair somehow. I love that we can be with family at that time of the year. I just don't think you should feel like you need a stiff drink or a couple of valium tablets to survive it. The pressure was unbearable.

We ended up shutting out our harmonious world for the winter holidays again for the sake of others. We always tried to keep the peace because conflict was so heart wrenching. It just seemed easier and responsible to do what we were asked and submit. I don't know about Will, but I could feel my stomach tie into knots, waiting for a conflict to occur during a holiday dinner, it seemed inevitable. In previous years it always happened sooner or later. I just wished we could run away from it all. Will told me he wished we could do our own thing as well, but he was concerned about hurting people in the family. We did the *right* thing for the family and attended the annual get together, but felt unfulfilled because the holidays left us feeling sad and empty.

The positive point in it all was that we knew we would eventually go home. We would get to indulge in our own wonderful tradition, already four years in the making. We were creating deeper meaning to our tradition each year. Those moments alone in our enchanted world allowed courage to blossom and strengthen in our hearts, without us realizing it.

Eventually, we would find freedom from the stress and anxiety of the holidays each season. They would become joyous for us in the end. Will and I debated on the subject and arrived to the only logical solution. We had been pushed too far once again, just like the wedding plans. It would give *us* freedom, but wouldn't be popular with the family. We'd spend the holidays alone in our own special way, a new tradition would be born, and we found a cure to the holiday panic.

Tasting The Good Life

Upon entering the year 1992 we celebrated our second anniversary on January twelfth. I had seen an advertisement in our local newspaper for an all inclusive night in Boston. The package included limousine travel into the city and dinner at Schroeder's Restaurant in the financial district. At an irresistible one hundred fifty dollars, I booked it.

My concern now was how to get Will to dress up and get into a stretch limo without telling him why. I revealed what I had up my sleeve for our private celebration and he was ecstatic. The surprise was blown, but we still had a fabulous night to look forward to.

On the big day we were all dressed up and waiting for the car to arrive. I already had a dress in my closet that I bought for my office Christmas party so I wore that. It was black, wool knit, and was form fitting with a deep cut V in the back to just below my shoulder blades. The entire neckline, front and back was embellished with large faux gems in red, gold, and violet, surrounded by shimmering black and gold beads and sequins. Will was showering me with compliments when he saw me dressed so elegantly. I bashfully basked in the adornment I could only accept from him. He also looked marvelous in his suit I might add, and he was my dream date for the Red Carpet.

We enjoyed champagne and each others company during the forty minute ride into the city. We liked to tangle in high society lifestyle on occasion and this excursion would be no different. We reached our destination and the driver opened the door for us. He then ushered us out of the car and into the restaurant. I felt like a celebrity with such service.

The maitre d' seated us and gave us a menu that included fine cuisine and items we hadn't tasted before. We were both full of adventure and ordered appetizers, soup, and entrées unknown, but incredibly pleasing to our senses. We enjoyed a five course meal that lasted for over two hours. After dinner the driver took us around the city to see what remained of Christmas lights. We had a spectacular evening and were soon on the highway heading home.

Will and I lived a life of hard work, but enjoyed time playing too. That year our tax return presented us with a bonus of cash we hadn't expected. It was sort of like getting a winning lottery ticket. We elected to spend it frivolously and splurged on another cruise. We looked forward to the elaborate vacation. We had experience with cruises by now, and decided to dress up a bit more on the two nights designated to formal attire.

We invested some time and money in a few pieces to add to our wardrobes for the trip. Will was so fun to shop for. He had a great body to dress and I loved the men's department. He and I went to the mall together and picked out several items for him to try on. He tried some suits on, complete with shirts and ties, and came out to model each one for me. I thoroughly enjoyed that, he had a sexy physique and he was built like a model. I had a warm feeling inside my heart that he felt so comfortable dressing for me and trusted my opinion. He looked so fantastic in each suit that it was a difficult choice to make. We finally decided, and purchased a suit with two shirts and two ties to go with it. We returned home smitten with our choices. We made such a great team.

I shopped for something to wear on the cruise myself. By chance, I found a little boutique called Michael's. The clothing on the mannequins in the window display attracted my eye immediately. They had a captivating, glamorous line that was out pricing my wallet though. I always had champagne taste, but a beer pocketbook.

I was approached by a salesman as I browsed through the racks, and he asked me what I was shopping for. I told him I needed something for formal night on a cruise. However, I had almost made up my mind that I was in the wrong store for my budget.

He convinced me to go to a dressing room and that he would get some dresses and bring them to me. I found that request odd and wondered how he would know what I'd like to try on. I did as he directed and soon he came to me with about a half dozen dresses.

All were quite elegant, but I didn't think I would like them once I had them on. I wasn't confident my body type was of one to display in such exquisite and revealing dresses. He asked me not to judge the dress on the hanger and to trust him. I decided to go with the adventure.

With the dresses he also brought me nylons and shoes, and instructed me to put everything on, and then exit the dressing room to view the ensemble in a full mirror to see the entire look. I was dressed and did as he asked, then he put earrings on me to match the outfit. He was absolutely right; I looked incredible, even in the dresses I condemned only moments ago.

I felt like I was shopping on Rodeo Drive in California, it was a divine experience. I had settled on a gorgeous fuchsia outfit that was very form fitting and shimmered in the light. It had a short skirt and matching jacket style top. The V neckline was embellished with a large, three dimensional ruffle made of the same fabric, in lieu of a collar, mimicking a feather boa. It had Austrian crystal buttons that looked like jewelry to fasten the jacket closed. The earrings matched the buttons very closely made out of the same type crystal. I was ready for the cat walk.

It was something I wouldn't normally buy for myself because of my lack of self-confidence. I knew Will would practically faint when he saw how stunning I looked in the dress, so I went ahead and took the leap. It was almost the same exhilarating feeling of what my wedding dress did for me.

The salesman was aware of the two formal nights on the ship, and asked me about another dress. There was another one that I almost went for instead of the fuchsia one. I went through the same wonderment trying it on. I looked great in both, but wasn't sure I could afford the two of them. I was of frugal mind coming from the childhood I had. I had difficulty spending money frivolously on myself. In the end, I was convinced rather easily that I'd be pleased if I purchased both dresses, so I took the plunge. Besides, I would be the belle of the ball in my husband's eyes wearing them, and that made it so worth it.

I was an insecure sort when it came to my appearance. I did not like to attract the envious eyes of others, so I usually dressed conservatively. Will on the other hand was proud to display me in public as if I was the best prize any man could win. We used to joke about my being his trophy wife. It certainly wasn't the case, but he wanted to show the world his wife because he felt I was so beautiful and I was all his. I was the blue ribbon he acquired at the 4-H fair.

I had striking looks, but I was in denial due to childhood trauma during my school years. Anyway, I modeled the dresses, and my endearing husband could not wait for me to get the opportunity to wear them and be on his arm. In all honesty, neither could I. He had a way of making me feel precious to him even without words, his eyes spoke to me. With those displays of affection and pride he helped my self-esteem blossom.

In May we went on the second cruise, the maiden voyage of Royal Caribbean's Majesty of the Seas. The timing was in sync with our second wedding anniversary, we celebrated in style. Once again, we left our simple life behind and lived like royalty for a week at sea. The ship was even grander in both size and beauty than the first one we sailed on. We enjoyed another exciting week of beautiful islands, tranquil, sandy beaches, nightlife on the ship, walking arm in arm on the upper deck, gazing at the stars over the horizon, and more love between two people that ever seemed possible. As someone once put it, "We can see the love ooze out of the two of you." We were oblivious to the world around us, and let our love and the Universe that put us together guide us through a remarkable week.

By now my confidence had grown stronger since the time Will and I first met. He gave that to me. He had his moments of parading his trophy wife in her new, sexy, formal attire in the public eye all week long and he was in heaven. I must say he looked phenomenally fabulous as well. He was my six foot two, dreamy, tall, dark and handsome prince. I was on his arm and was not about to share with anyone. Will used to tell me that times like that were the best boost to his ego ever, and I must admit it was an ego trip for me as well.

As with the first cruise we stopped at many wonderful islands. This time we were in the Western Caribbean. I would have to say our favorite place visited that week was Jamaica, where we experienced Dunn's River Falls. It was one of the most incredible excursions I have ever been on. We got off the ship and rode a bus to the falls and were given a brief description of what to expect. Then everyone on board followed our guide to a small gated area. We were then instructed to form a line and follow him. We arrived to a clearing and we were standing on a sandy beach where we could see the ocean ahead, and to our left was a magnificent water fall. Interestingly enough, we were going to climb up it. At that point our guide asked to hold onto our cameras, reassuring us it was only to keep them from getting wet.

The guide asked us all to form a human chain by holding hands. There were about fifty of us and he didn't want anyone to slip. He also warned us of what to do and what to expect during the climb. I was leery about making my way up the falls, but once I got in motion I was fine. Will was able to convince me to try things and calmed my anxiousness about it when I wasn't so sure of myself. My sense of adventure had a safety net, but he was able to help me let go of it and enjoy the challenge.

We walked to the side of the falls, getting sprayed and splashed with water along the route. It was a beautiful sunny day, the sky was clear blue and the ocean matched in color. The stones and boulders used for our path seemed porous and weren't slippery at all. That discovery gave me confidence that I was indeed going to make it to the top of the falls.

There were a couple of fabulous vantage points to stop for a photo, and the guide carrying all of our cameras around his neck offered his services to do so. At one point we were in a pool of water in front of the falls and Will and I had our picture taken there. There were a couple of other points we stopped at and a ship photographer was with our group taking photos of everyone too. They would be for sale at the ship gallery later.

We climbed to the top of the waterfall and I was filled with such excitement I wanted to do it again. It was quite a sense of accomplishment for me to do something like that. I was so glad we took the chance and went on the excursion, and that it turned out to be so fantastic. Every time I heard someone was going to Jamaica for years to come, I always recommended that tour.

We returned to the ship soaring with an energy filling us from that journey up the falls. Then, we still had a wonderful evening to look forward to just like every evening aboard. We had an incredible meal and Las Vegas, cabaret style entertainment each night.

The most wonderful thing about the cruise for me was the continuous time I had with Will, my husband, my best friend. We had each other to love and adore twenty four hours a day for seven days.

A special thing about a cruise or perhaps any trip away, is you can get lost in each other. We were solo in an environment that allowed us to try so many things, experience cultures, try foods you can't get at home, and we lived in a magical dream state. We had no phones so no one could call us and we couldn't call anyone. It was truly an escape to paradise.

The dream came to an end and the adjustment was difficult for the first day or so. We always melded back into our actual life and were happy to do so. Life on the other side of the fence was great for a taste, but life at home in our comfort zone was more truly ours and we were glad.

Canine Capers

One day that summer we were at the vet with Czar and noticed a newspaper with pet adoption listings in it. We saw a Siberian in need of a home and thought it would be great for Czar to have a companion. We contacted the organization immediately and discussed the requirements.

The protocol for adoption required home interviews and a trip to see the dog before we could adopt. Someone came to our house for the interview, and evaluated the setting to determine if a dog would be comfortable and happy living there. They were extremely pleased to see we had a fenced yard, because the dog we were interested in had been traumatized being tied out and abandoned.

We received the nod of approval for the next stage of the process. We drove about two and a half hours to meet the dog, Ivan the Red. We had to bring Czar with us so he could also meet Ivan and see if they were compatible. The meeting and interview went well and we were approved, but there was one glitch, we couldn't proceed for twenty-four hours. They required that we sleep on the decision to be certain we actually wanted to go through with it. We drove all the way home and then back the next day.

On the return trip we were guided through all the steps of bringing another dog into our home. We were advised to keep their toys separate and to keep their sleeping quarters separate as well. We signed all the paperwork with the promise to return Ivan if things didn't work out as planned. We took both dogs home and they were best friends instantly. The ride home couldn't have been any easier and was peaceful the entire way.

We got home and brought the two dogs into the house and let Ivan sort of sniff his way around. Czar seemed very passive about it and wasn't concerned about Ivan taking anything that wasn't his. We let them go out into the fenced back yard to see how that would go. All went superbly. All the warnings we got seemed to be obsolete in our case. We fed Ivan and Czar and that went amazingly well too.

It was time for bed and we let Czar go to his normal sleeping area on our bed upstairs. We made a sleeping area for Ivan in the kitchen. We had been warned that there could be severe problems if we let the dogs sleep together.

We went to bed after the dogs were settled. I felt badly leaving Ivan blocked in the kitchen alone in his bed with some toys. I was only following instruction. Ivan began to howl immediately after I got into bed. I went to see if he was alright, he seemed fine. I tucked him in and went back to bed myself and he began to howl again.

We elected to ignore it and thought he would quiet down in a few minutes, but he cried for over an hour. We couldn't quiet him down unless we were with him. We went against the advice we received from the rescue organization, and let him out of the kitchen to make a bed of his own. He ran upstairs before we could even turn the lights out. Czar was already up there sleeping on our bed. Ivan assessed his surroundings for a moment and then jumped up onto the bed as well. Will and I looked at each other waiting for a fight to begin. Ivan walked in a circle a time or two and then lied down on the bed, curled up, and went right to sleep as if he were meant to be there. Czar never made a motion to let us know he disapproved, and we all got a good night sleep after defying the rules.

Having a second dog worked out marvelously for us. Czar had company and they were not under foot when I got home from work. The two dogs went outside and played in the yard while I prepared dinner. Before we got Ivan, Czar required more attention. I had to try to cook dinner and play fetch in the house with a tennis ball at the same time. Having two dogs was the best of both worlds both for Will and me, and for Czar and Ivan.

We continued our weekend treks hiking throughout Massachusetts and up to New Hampshire. We were fortunate to have a lake near our house with a well maintained trail surrounding it. We went there frequently and it didn't seem to have much foot traffic. The dogs loved walking there and they would absorb copious amounts of information along the trail through their noses. They'd also leave information behind for the next canine to travel the path.

In the summer we took hikes near water so the dogs could take a dip and keep cool. In the autumn we enjoyed hikes in the White Mountains of New Hampshire with many leaf peepers from across the country. We enjoyed breathtaking, panoramic views of trees of many species lit up like fire there. Even if you've witnessed the transformation the trees go through several times, you realize it's still somehow different and unique each year it occurs. Having the dogs helped us find nature and our deep yearning to be in it.

With research we found little two room cabins to stay in, so we could lengthen our day trips hiking for weekends or longer. They allowed pets to lodge with us so it was perfect. We took at least two trips during the summer and then another one in the autumn and stayed at the simple, little, efficiency cabins in the mountains. They were inexpensive and quaint and thought to be built in the 1950's. We enjoyed stepping back in time while we were there. We found our home away from home. We enjoyed the simplicity of the rustic cabins that sat right along the Pemigewasset River in northern New Hampshire.

At night after we hiked all day long, and then enjoyed a dinner prepared in the cubicle sized kitchen, we'd lie in bed and listen to the water rush over the boulders in the river right behind the cabin. It sounded much like a water fall. There was a screened in porch on the back of it so we'd leave the door open during the night. We listened to natures concert filled with sounds from the rushing water and wind blowing through the trees. It was majestic, pure and simple. We vacationed there for years.

Throughout our stays we inquired at the ranger stations to seek out trails suitable for hiking with dogs. The authorities willingly gave us maps and advice on where to go, as well as where the best scenery was. We had our back packs, water bottles, dog snacks, and lunches with us, and we were ready to become one with nature.

As I mentioned before, Will was so smart, brilliant in fact, that he was able to navigate his way around the woods that would impress an Eagle Scout for sure. I don't know why I was surprised; he was capable of doing whatever he put his mind to. Even if he didn't know what the heck he was doing and was faking his way through it, he did a superb job and impressed me. I had complete faith in him, he could whisk me away to any place and I willingly followed him.

We ventured along many trails off the Kancamagus Highway near Lincoln, New Hampshire, and usually hiked some of our favorites over and over again. It was funny, sometimes we would pull into designated parking areas and the dogs would get so excited in the back of the truck. They barked and howled uncontrollably and tried to push the cap door open with their paws, anxiously trying to get out and hit the trails. They had dog business to tend to and wanted to do it now. I think they truly believed we only hiked for their benefit. Well, it did bring us abundant joy to watch them enjoying the hikes so much.

It was so peaceful to get away from suburbia and enjoy nature, our dogs, and feel so close. I can't express it enough, we just loved every moment we had together. Even with time passing our love never seemed to fade.

With the adoption of Ivan we discovered an organized sled dog club in our area. We attended a meeting and found it interesting. The club opened our eyes to a new adventure, the world of mushing.

It led us to volunteering at one particular dog sledding race in February. We were entranced by the pandemonium of jumping and barking dogs hooked up to their ganglines, attached to wooden sleds, with their masters known as musher's ready to tackle a sixty mile trail. It was exhilarating.

The mushing bug bit us and we soon began testing the trails on our own. We acquired the necessary equipment piece by piece and trained our two dogs to pull sled. Since we didn't have a team large enough to compete in races we strictly practiced the sport in a leisurely manner. Either way it was exciting to partake in a new adventure. That was the thing with Will; with each adventure he would apply himself one hundred percent. It was amazing to see such zest for all he did.

After many fantastic journeys over the summer and autumn seasons that year, we began to feel the darkness of doom falling over our heads, the holidays were approaching. Don't get me wrong, we loved the opportunity to give, and to have our own Christmas alone, as well as holiday parties that came with it. We loved the season and what it was capable of doing for our hearts. The problem was the magnetic pull we felt dragging us down into a deep, black hole.

We felt like skipping the holidays and the anticipated horror altogether. That year we had a brainstorm idea. We enjoyed such peace in the mountains, and realized it was the answer to our problem soon to arrive. We had to tell everyone we would be out of town for Christmas. It was our answer to sanity and freedom we longed for, finally.

Christmas In The Woods

After doing so much exploring, and discovering incredible places during our hiking expeditions, we decided it was time to take action on our genius idea of avoiding the holiday ulcers. We called and made reservations for a lovely cabin near Weirs Beach, New Hampshire. From there, we planned a menu and we'd have our first Christmas away. It would be a safe haven as well as our first romantic Christmas alone, just us and our dogs. We felt selfish, but that feeling wore off quickly once we enjoyed a peaceful holiday.

We told the family ahead of time we wouldn't be attending the festivities that year. We didn't make peace with the announcement. However, it was done and we knew we had to chart the new course we were on, or regret it later. It was a new adventure and we poured ourselves into the strategic planning of it all. In a short time what felt like bleeding ulcers induced by stress of the upcoming holidays healed miraculously. It was the smartest, most courageous decision we made at that point in our life together.

Before we'd go away to our secret place in the woods we attended our office Christmas parties together. My boss's wife held a party at her home. Everyone dressed up festively, and enjoyed gourmet finger foods and mingling throughout the evening. Will's office party was held at a lavish restaurant in a Boston hotel.

We had been on the cruise and already had formal attire for the parties, and I wore the fuchsia pink outfit from it. Will was so proud to show me off anywhere I would join him at his side. (It would take me many years to get used to being escorted by such a proud man.) He thought I was so beautiful and told me that I was his supermodel all the time. I did not feel I was as beautiful as he portrayed. I was stuck on wanting to be average after my self-confidence was shattered during my teens, and a previous marriage.

We delighted in yet another enchanted evening and enjoyed a lovely meal, and then danced the night away in a club on the premises. I felt like Cinderella again waiting for the stroke of midnight to end the magic and take me back to reality.

The glimpses we had of that elegant lifestyle were enough to make it fun. However, I was perfectly content not to trade my humble life for it. I assumed it would become mundane if I lived that life full time.

In the process of making plans for our trip to the cabin for Christmas, I worked on the menu. I planned on making a ham, a duck, and all the side dishes that went with a holiday dinner. We came up with the duck idea because of its size. It was compact enough to take along and would cook faster than a turkey. We packed our food, bags, dogs and their essentials, and our Christmas gifts, and left town for a couple of days.

We felt like the only people on earth for good reason during our cabin stay, we were the only ones at the site for the holiday. We arrived at the cabin, unpacked, and got our bearings in the small, but quite charming temporary home. It was a bit more upscale than others we stayed in and had an efficiency kitchen. We had to use our imagination a little to find room for our things and groceries, but that was part of the magic.

There was a fireplace and firewood was provided, so Will built a fire. Then we relaxed and put up our feet, and breathed in the peaceful silence of the woods. We didn't have any anxiety over our decision to avoid the hustle and bustle, or tensions of Christmas at home. We really loved it, and it became our newest, deeply satisfying tradition.

The next day was Christmas Eve. We took a tour of the area and discovered a great place to go on a nature walk with the dogs. It was cold, but refreshing; the air was so clean in the woods. The silence there was almost eerie, but it was comforting to our souls. As we walked I could hear my footsteps crunching in the snow as well as the wind blowing through the trees. As the evergreens swayed I heard them squeak and I heard the sound of water running across rocks in the brook. The brisk air made our noses and cheeks turn red, but I didn't feel the cold. I only felt an inner peace that nature offers free of charge. With that, we knew in our hearts we absolutely made the right decision about going away for Christmas.

Later, we had our Christmas Eve meal. It wasn't the traditional production with lobster and spaghetti, we improvised. Instead, we ate cheese and crackers, shrimp cocktail and then spaghetti with a red sauce. It was perfect for just the two of us, the only two people that existed in our world that day.

That evening Will became director again and we shared abundant, childlike joy and laughter while opening our gifts. Many came wrapped beautifully, but disguised with some sort of item in the package that jingled to conceal the contents inside.

We even had gifts for the dogs. It seemed they took pleasure tearing the paper off themselves to discover a squeak toy inside. They chewed on their new prize until it no longer squeaked, which usually didn't take more than ten minutes in their case. We loved spoiling Czar and Ivan, they were our children.

Christmas Day was as lovely as the prior day. I prepared a feast in the tiny kitchen somehow, and we enjoyed the good food and companionship. That Christmas was therapy for our souls. We were somehow under a spell cast by unknown entities that gave us such a deep love toward one another. That bond was stronger than ever and strengthened as time went on. We could not go back to Christmas past after our experience nestled away in a small cabin in the woods, no matter the price.

We returned home feeling refreshed and refueled, ready to face our recourse. We heard much nagging and pleading not to leave town and abandon the family the next year. We experienced a holiday that felt like a dream and allowed us to know euphoria. It was a tall order to fill by asking us to sacrifice that gift to ourselves next year. Besides, we only went away for Christmas; we still had Thanksgiving and Easter with family.

Keeping The Flame Lit

In 1993 life was going perfectly for us. We had a home in the suburbs, our two dogs, and most importantly we had us. Will left the trades and made the transition to a new job as a hotel maintenance supervisor. It was closer to home and he performed mostly indoor work, which was a plus after doing carpentry outdoors in all seasons.

He liked the change of pace and the variety of work at the hotel. The only down side to it was that he was on call twenty-four hours a day for emergency situations, and had to carry a pager. He was called in to work constantly and it became aggravating to me. It was a good job and he liked it so I tried to be tolerant.

Will's boss came up with a solution for our being apart so much. He offered to let us use a vacant room so I could go visit him when he worked the night shift and things were slow. We could have meals together at the restaurant on the premises as well. It seemed like a great plan, we just had to be together, the separation was killing our spirits. We were even authorized to bring our dogs with us.

We accepted his offer and I went to the hotel. It was great to get some quality time together. I preferred we spent more time in our own home, but we didn't have that luxury at the moment, so we improvised and made the best of what we had. I could have spent the night in the hotel with him, but elected not to. He was on call, and in and out of the room, and I was more comfortable at home in my own bed.

Besides, I had to go to work in the mornings as well as take care of the dogs.

Will was employed there for only about seven months. The hotel changed hands and they cleaned house and let many employees go. Will was not under the axe, but he didn't want to work under the new management. It all worked out for the best actually. I won the best prize of all; I had my honey home with me.

He had his contacts since he still did some side work, keeping his own company, Red Horse Construction going. He worked on getting that rolling full swing again, but the construction market took a hit from the economic recession in the early 1990's. I still had my job in dentistry and made a very decent wage, which allowed us to pay the bills even during slow times. I enjoyed what I did and loved Will so much, it really was effortless to work extra hard to keep our home and achieve our goals.

Will struggled with not being able to provide me with a princess life with a never ending bank account. I didn't come from the mould of the rich and famous, or that lifestyle. I was quite content and never asked that of him. I knew the love we had was worth much more than any amount of money could ever buy. You can't buy the perfect life; you have to make it happen.

I loved every detail of our simplicity. I think that is how we were able to enjoy a day out, just the two of us. Being in nature or in the city with a cup of coffee in hand gave us an outing to stimulate our brain, and we had each other. What more could we have needed?

While doing some construction jobs he won bids for, he hired subcontractors for plumbing and electrical installation on his work sites. With those contacts he ended up finding a full time job doing interior work for another construction company. We discussed the idea of doing remodels for a supermarket giant in Massachusetts. It was good money and steady work; however, it meant working third shift.

It was a difficult decision to make. We once again were taken from each other for the sake of employment. Will's ego had taken a depressing blow being out of work, and he had to accept the job offer to feel like he was contributing, if for nothing else. We agreed taking it would be good for the money. We left a window of departure open in case the toll on our marriage was too much to endure.

Due to the same economic recession I ended up working odd hours at my dental office. Our patients were in a dilemma as well, and they felt like they could not take time off from work to attend to their dental needs. The cry for evening hour availability was getting loud.

After studying the sparsely scheduled appointment book and a staff meeting, my boss decided we had to change our hours. We had to either agree to that or have internal layoffs. The doctor I worked for was a good man and did not want to let people go if he could avoid it. I certainly needed my job so I was in agreement to the change.

The new schedule was grueling and didn't leave much time for any extracurricular activities. We worked later into the evenings and it disrupted my normal sleep routine. I found myself getting home around ten o'clock at night and watching television until three o'clock in the morning. Everyone was in the same boat, and I just rowed my oars and tried to be grateful I had a good job.

Will left our house at nine o'clock at night to get to work and I got home an hour after he left. Then, I left in the morning about an hour before he returned from work. We were two ships passing in the night. We kept missing each other and communicated by leaving each other notes everyday, it was horrible. We were at the mercy of the economy so we held on tight and did what we had to do.

We did have weekends off together, but he wouldn't get home until around eleven o'clock in the morning on Saturday, and then needed some sleep. I would creep around the house downstairs doing chores not to disturb his rest. Sometimes I went to the grocery store and got that errand done on my own, even though I was used to going with Will. We did everything together, even that. I was strong and knew I could hold on for better days. We at least had Sunday together and worked hard to make the best of that day.

If crunch time came to finish a remodel at the supermarket, he had to work weekends too. Sadly, that did happen quite frequently. I dreaded all the hours he had to put in. We were spending more time apart, but we needed the income. I was getting lonely, but we had no choice.

He took his lunch each day in an igloo cooler. I usually prepared it and left little love notes on his napkins. He thought that was the most fantastic idea and gift of love from me. He told me he hated to use them because they were so sentimental with the greetings I added. My intention was to make him feel close to me.

We both had mushy, romantic personalities, and felt the love seeping out of each other and into our hearts by just looking at each other. It is an indescribable feeling to put into words really. There was just a transcendent vibration coming from our bodies, communicating to each other unbeknownst to us consciously, that made us feel so in love. I am certain we were soul mates.

I came up with a solution for the weekends apart. I knew what store he was working at and I had weekends off so I went see him at the job site. Friday nights I got out of work at five o'clock. I drove home and fed the dogs, let them out to relieve their bladders, and then loaded them into my car.

I felt like I was preparing to go out on a date, timing everything exactly to see Will on his dinner break. I packed a dessert or some sort of treat for us to share. If I didn't have anything at the house I stopped to pick something up at the store. Sometimes I got something as simple as a candy bar and soda for us to share together.

We were so grateful for all the little thoughts toward each other, we felt cherished. We didn't require extravagant gifts; we just loved to know we were thought of. Our idea to see each other worked out marvelously. I got my dose of my husband and then went home. I had sweet dreams because I got to see him and physically be with him for longer than two minutes.

Love notes are great, but no physical contact for weeks at a time was like being held in a dungeon with no release in sight for me. We enjoyed our little picnics at dinner time in the parking lot of the supermarkets. Like I said, it never mattered where we were as long as we were with each other.

A Bump In The Road

Eventually, the remodels were finished and the job ended. Will was out of work. He looked for a job, but the economy hadn't quite bounced back yet, and he wasn't having much success. He decided to get back into the trades under his own general contractor's license and revive Red Horse Construction Company. It was a slow process, but we had high hopes of things taking off for him, and I supported his decision. I felt it was better than not working at all. We had been through a lot with the odd hours we were keeping for a little over a year with our jobs, and now money was tighter which was raising our stress levels. We could feel the tension, but we did our best to overlook it all and fall into each other as we always had.

We decided we needed a break. We managed to find time and a little bit of money to get away to a place where nature resides best, the White Mountains of New Hampshire. We were able to stay five days for just over a hundred dollars. We had a bed, a shower and a small kitchen, and that was all we needed after a full day of hiking and sight seeing. Traveling with frugality allowed us to make the trip possible. We brought all our food for meals and snacks as well as for the dogs whenever we traveled.

We splurged and ate out one night during the week. It wasn't always easy to find a good restaurant tucked away in the mountains though. We discovered many greasy spoon diners and it was barely worth eating out. I prefer a good home cooked meal over that type of food any day. We did stay at one place that had a nicer restaurant and we didn't mind the treat out then. They served steaks, poultry, and seafood, and even Maine Lobster. Will loved a good steak and I didn't make it at home often, they just seemed to taste better in a restaurant. So when we went out, Will got steak and I usually got seafood.

Our favorite place to stay was in Lincoln, right along the Pemigewasset River. After a full day of hiking we returned to the log cabin to unwind. After we fed the dogs we went down to the river behind the cabins for more tranquility. We had long ropes we used instead of leashes for the dogs when we were there. That enabled them to wander further in the river. They could not be trusted off leash, which is said to be typical of the breed. We had seen posters in the woods with photos of lost dogs on them. We weren't about to take that risk with our dogs.

After our lovely trip to the woods, we had to face the day when all the splendor of the mountains had to be left behind. We seemed to have much less energy and passion when it came to packing for the trip back home. We were so drawn to the woods, but we had commitments like a home, and jobs, and had to return.

Even though Will and I were enjoying life and our time away and alone, darkness began to hover over us. With the recession and lack of work in the trades we had fallen behind on our bills. The mortgage was especially strangling us. We were caught in the scenario many other home owners were in since property values plummeted that year. Our house was now worth $30,000.00 less than we paid for it. I worried more than Will, but of course, he always helped me see the bright side of things. We were both working and he convinced me that matters would stabilize soon.

Will hid his stress rather well from me. He protected me by taking me away from our daily surroundings to forget our troubles. We shared a lot of laughter and tired to hide from our hardships whenever we could. We lived in a fairytale world when we were together, and I was able to deny that things were as bad as they were then. Of course, when the phone calls started coming in from the mortgage company we were snapped back into reality.

Will had begun drinking a little more beer than usual after his father died. He was able to function and maintain a job, so I figured he had a high tolerance to alcohol and was actually fine, even though I was concerned early on. It had been almost four years since his father passed away and the beer consumption hadn't decreased.

It seemed now that I was in denial myself. I wanted to hold onto my happy life with Will and couldn't imagine being without him. I think I let the drinking ride, since whenever I brought it to his attention we would begin to argue. Will always won, because he was able to justify that since he only drank beer he couldn't possibly be an alcoholic. I understood his argument and hated to make waves, so I let the issue rest. I couldn't handle being at war with my husband, so I just avoided conflict whenever possible by biting my tongue, just hoping things would finally fix themselves.

We tried to cut back on all spending and worked overtime to catch up financially, but we continued to fall behind. I felt like I was treading water in a lake with cement shoes on, waiting to lose the battle and drown. We tried to work with the bank and we paid our mortgage each month when we could. But, after several months of paying it late it spiraled out of control. Suddenly, we were three months overdue. We continued the struggle to catch up so we wouldn't lose our home. We thought of selling it, but the value dropped so low we would have taken a huge loss and couldn't afford that either. I looked over our budget each month and couldn't find anywhere else to cut back.

Will and I were under enormous pressure trying to fix this problem. I think we began to harbor resentment toward each other. Somehow it was easier to blame someone else. Communicating about the issue became a heavy burden. It was like listening to a broken record, so we held our disappointment and anger inside to avoid it altogether. In the meantime, we just kept trying to stay afloat, but it was wearing on us.

Will's business wasn't doing great, but okay, and out of necessity he contracted most of his jobs much closer to Boston where the money was. He had difficulty finding a crew he could depend on though. Every time he had to leave the job site they took long breaks and got nothing accomplished.

At the end of the week when payday rolled around he noticed he was getting more and more behind schedule. He ended up letting some employees go and did the work himself, to catch up. He couldn't afford to pay people not to work.

Working with a smaller crew meant he had to put in more hours and he did so willingly. I must say Will was a very hard worker. When he needed energy I think he reached into his pocket and found more. Somehow, we both had strong work ethics, whether born with them or taught, but it was good that we were similar that way. We understood what it meant to do what you had to do to get the job done.

Will had a particular carpenter that began to creep into his personal time. He was like an invasive weed growing around his legs pulling him downward. He felt like the man he hired needed his time more than I did for the moment, so he kept him on staff. I struggled with that because I got a sense I couldn't trust him.

I warned Will of the vibe I was getting from him. Our dogs didn't trust him either. They never barked at anyone, let alone treat them as if they were suspicious of them, but it was different this time. I gave my warning and had to let Will determine the path he would take at that point.

He spent a lot of time with the man. On occasion, he spent the night in the city with him so he could get to the job site early and avoid an hour commute. I was amenable to that, but my gut instinct was sending me warning signs. I didn't want to badger Will and be the nagging wife though.

I noticed that he was drinking more than usual and I expressed my concern about that too. It worsened and was taking over his life.

I felt him pushing me away as if my love for him was no longer precious or needed. We had a remarkable relationship prior to this hurdle for years. I couldn't understand why he was suddenly abandoning me. He denied any of my accusations about drinking or abandonment. I then spent many days and nights alone wondering what I did.

I felt our marriage crumbling. Perhaps the overwhelming inability to catch up on our mortgage was taking its toll on him now and this was his escape. Drinking with someone that didn't mind him doing so, was more tolerable than facing a wife that didn't understand.

Will was no longer able to contribute to the household budget. (Another clue I ignored.) He said he was losing money on his jobs. I'm not so sure he was even working at this point. He was still trying to convince me that things would be alright in the end, and asked me to have faith in him.

I was working and scrambling to put enough money aside for our bills, but it seemed hopeless. We just continued to fall behind. Now, the number one reason why marriages collapse was taking its toll on ours, money problems. Our boat had sprung a leak and we couldn't bale the water out fast enough.

As time passed I was getting more upset and knew I couldn't do it all on my own. We always communicated pretty well prior to this hurdle, but now Will was taking the defensive and our discussions turned into arguments. I kept trying to get him to see I desperately needed his help if it was all going to be just fine, like he kept telling me it would.

All the bickering created a wedge between us. I tried another tactic and avoided quarreling altogether. It always made me feel like I was the only one who understood what it was going to take to pull out of the mess we were in. Will's wheels were turning in his head I'm sure. I tried to ignore what was happening, but my personality wasn't capable of doing that. I began to feel neglected, and anger was boiling up inside of me because things were so out of control. My control.

My husband found refuge with his friends and began to stay out late, and sometimes just not even come home. I struggled with that because we were always together. We were great partners and could accomplish anything we put our minds to, or so I thought. We got off our charted course now and were becoming distant. I was taken out of my comfort zone because I never had to share Will before. I was his best friend and he was mine.

I was in denial and a classic enabler, but hadn't realized it yet of course. I was still trying to hold on and keep our heads above water. I was confused about how everything soured so badly right under my nose and I just didn't see it. I was a perfectionist and I didn't want to see it. I had a fairytale life and wasn't ready to give it all up and walk through the gates of hell.

Will had become emotionally detached. He couldn't bear the pressure of dealing with our current situation, or a wife that was so upset with him because she felt as if he let her down. He continued to stay out late and when he came home we fought. He told me one night that he came home late because he knew there'd be an altercation and he wanted to make it worth getting yelled at. That statement made me feel like crap and wondered why I was putting up with it all.

What I still didn't see though, was that he had run to alcohol to self medicate his problems away. He hid alcohol so well. He didn't display obnoxious behavior and I never knew if he had even had anything to drink. I didn't want to look too deeply at that either because I couldn't fix it.

After a few months of this erratic behavior and still not catching up on our bills, I finally reached a point of asking for help, or walking away from the marriage. I wanted to make things work and in order to do so I asked Will for three things. I told him I wanted to see a counselor first and foremost, and that I also wanted us to attend church again. We got out of the routine when the work schedules no longer left room for it. I then asked that we court. I wanted to see if by dating again we could get the dwindling flame of our love to reignite to full capacity. It was hard for me to ask for all of that. I was usually the one to stay quiet and wait for the turbulence to pass if there ever was any. We never encountered seas so rough before though. It was time for intervention or the ship was about to sink.

Will agreed to appease me by granting my three wishes. We did everything, but it was a struggle. We saw a counselor and she asked each of us a list of identical questions. There were some regarding drinking and he felt she was accusing him of being an alcoholic. I think it made him realize he was, and the guilt came roaring up at him then. That was the first and last visit to her office together. We discussed our session in the car afterward, and he told me straight out she was taking my side. That was ridiculous, but then again he needed an excuse to feed his denial.

It seemed as if Will was not ready to go the rounds necessary to find the happiness we once shared. I still didn't want to believe I had lost the battle to save us. At times I went to my corner and sat on my pity pot and wished my problems would all go away. From time to time I would put on the boxing gloves and come out to try to find a solution to our issues. I still so badly wanted to believe all was fine, and that Prince Charming would ride up on his horse, and rescue me from the evil queen's tower. The draining arguing was getting us nowhere. If anything it was driving the wedge deeper.

I am a type A personality and not only do I hate conflict, I don't like losing or throwing in the towel. I have a lot of determination and am always dependable and responsible, and those traits played a role in all of this.

I had exhausted all avenues in the battle field of the current state of my marriage, but I had a new plan. I had read something once about having a bird and loving it so much that one should set it free. If it shared the same love toward you it would fly back. So I tried reverse psychology and let Will have all the freedom he wanted. I figured if he really believed in fighting for us he would indeed go away, but come back to me. My plan backfired.

The man who befriended my husband was still beckoning him for social meetings and drink. Will was being pulled in two directions. The choice seemed obvious to me. I thought he would easily choose the love of his life over a man he owed nothing to. It finally dawned on me the drinking was the underlying issue. Doing the work to reignite the flame of our love proved to be too difficult for Will. The call of the beer would extinguish all hopes of recovery for us. With this revelation my heart was broken.

In the meantime, I read some Al-anon literature. I had already left some Alcoholics Anonymous pamphlets for Will, but he denied there was an issue and refused to read them. I discovered my actions and holding on were enabling him to continue to drink. He desperately needed to get help, but I alone could not convince him to do so. It was easier to hang out with his friend that accepted him and his addiction.

I came to the point of having to make a very difficult decision. I was going to turn the tables and abandon my husband, and the thought of it gave me gut wrenching pain. I did not know where else to turn because my words were being spoken to deaf ears. I moved out.

When I first left, hoping to make my husband realize I meant business, I took just a suitcase worth of clothes and our dogs. We had three now, since we adopted a mixed breed while visiting a shelter earlier that year, hoping to volunteer. I hadn't really anticipated being gone for long. When he returned home and found me gone he called me at my sister's house. I had left him a note with information regarding my whereabouts. He wanted me to come home.

I was deeply hurting because of his actions of leaving me in the dust while he spent time with his drunken friends. Somehow, I had to pick myself up and try to live with the situation at hand, or walk away. I had had enough. It took a lot of courage and strength for me to leave, and I knew I had to stick to my decision.

Will was mad, but still couldn't see the answer was so simple. I was willing to do the work, but I couldn't share him with the beer and his neglectful ways toward me.

He called me a couple of times trying to finagle a deal to get me back home. I already knew what my conditions were. In the meantime, we agreed to be separated for a few days and try to do some soul searching.

He also asked that I bring the dogs back to him. I told him I couldn't because they were in danger living with him. He was broke, never home, and still drinking, and they required care he couldn't afford. I made a deal with him and gave him the dog we had recently adopted. I never quite bonded with him and he actually frightened me, so I let my husband have him. Will loved his dogs and I am sure he felt like the one dog he had with him was his only friend.

We tried the courting part of the three wishes we initially agreed to. I settled for a percentage of them thinking I could pull him out of the darkness and get him back into my loving arms. I still had hope; I knew we were soul mates.

He was captured by a grip of demons in a beer can, and he couldn't see how he was hurting me through his submersion in alcohol. He needed help, but didn't want to accept mine, or anyone else's yet. He was still in denial of being an alcoholic. I cried enough tears to flood the basement of my house through that stage of my life.

Our courting basically consisted of going to the grocery store to fill his refrigerator, money was tight. I was still enabling him. I loved him and saw he was headed down the road to disaster; the least I could do was make sure he had food to eat. It was so hard to detach myself completely. Enabling was like an addiction to break as well. It was too hard for me to do.

The final demand I made, was that Will stop spending time with the supposed friend that shared time with him only in a bar. I was under the presumption that he was going to let the leach of a man go. I'd hoped he had finally come to realize our life together was far more important than what he was choosing instead.

We had times scheduled to talk on the phone in the evenings to stay in touch and try to work things out. I called as planned to find Will wasn't home. I left messages on the answering machine, but didn't get a return call.

I paced and endured stomach aches induced by anxiety feeling like volcanic eruptions, I was certain he wasn't going to choose me. I was hurting so badly and did not want to believe the once wonderful love we shared and expressed constantly was over.

After a couple of weeks, I finally made the most difficult decision I had to make in my life. I called my husband and set up a time for me to meet him at our house. I was ready to end my pain and let life as I knew it go and say goodbye to Will forever. I couldn't go on the way I was, it was too stressful and taking its toll on me emotionally and physically.

I went to see him with my wedding rings in hand. We talked, and I just felt I wasn't reaching that lovely soul inside of him that I knew and loved so much. Something very dark had a tight grasp on him and I realized I couldn't break the grip alone. I told him it was killing me to do what I was about to do, but he seemed to be staring into space as if not to hear a word I said. I think he was spiraling down some deep, dark hole and wasn't going to come out of it until he hit his personal bottom.

With tears in my eyes and my hands shaking I gave him my wedding rings, reaching for symbolism, and told him our marriage was over. I hoped my handing the rings to him would really tell him I needed him to begin to take me seriously. We were on top of the world once and I didn't know how it all crumbled right beneath our noses. He seemed upset about the statement I just made, but didn't express any anger. I knew he was too far gone for me to reach him.

I am not a quitter and felt I gave it the honest college try to pull him out of the trenches of hell. The spell he was under was more powerful than any burst of love I could show him. He was drowning in a sea of despair and I continually threw him a life preserver, but he never reached for it. I was too late.

I left him sitting at the kitchen table and I cried in disbelief. He had the chance to come running after me to beg for another chance, but didn't. As much as it was killing me inside I knew I had to do it. I knew I couldn't help him out of his drowning pool. From all the literature I read about alcoholism, it would take a major wake up call to reach for the cup of sobriety. I thought my message that night would be just that, but apparently it wasn't quite powerful enough.

I was living out of a suit case trying to find myself with half of my heart missing. I felt as if a part of me died. He was my best friend, and the love of my life. He was what made me smile when I was blue. We had no contact after the day I gave him my rings. I closed the door unless he made the move to reconcile. He knew my wishes so I had to leave it up to him.

I thought about him constantly and I wasn't sure I made the right decision to leave him. The heart wants something so badly that the mind gets confused, and plays out scenarios to try to construe a way to make things work out. I was constantly engineering a way in my head to have a new start with Will. The ball was in his court though and I had no control. The monster holding him hostage was bigger than I was.

He was still not giving me the attention I required and craved, and everyone and everything else always seemed to come first. I was out of ultimatums and tired of what seemed like a one way struggle. I determined there was nothing left to salvage. It was over as far as I could tell and I went to my house only to pack all my things. He was home when I got there. He was upset that I was giving up the fight.

With that, he took off so he didn't have to witness me taking everything I had brought into the marriage.

Once again my husband begged me to come back home and that he was ready to work on our relationship seriously. I had been trapped into believing him before. I had given him so many chances. I stood my ground and the game had to be played by my rules now. Will was very hurt, but so was I. He couldn't understand why I left. I explained until I was blue in the face. He was drinking more than ever now and thought my demands were ridiculous, and decided it was fine that I left and he was tired of the fight too.

A Dark Place With A Flickering Light

—⁓—

I decided to accept that I lost the battle I fought so hard to win. I was trying to accept my life's new direction alone. Several weeks went by and I received a phone call at work. Will had been arrested and was in the county jail in Cambridge. The caller gave me a brief explanation of what transpired and landed him in jail. She told me he wanted to talk to me and wondered if I would be willing to listen. I was in shock with the news and of course agreed to listen to what he had to say. We arranged a time when I would be available to talk on the phone via a collect call from the jail. I saw it as my ray of sunshine breaking through ominous clouds.

Will called just a day or two later. I was eagerly anticipating the call; I needed to know what exactly happened. I could not imagine him ever doing something so bad he would end up in jail. I answered the phone and agreed to the operators request to accept collect charges from Will. There he was, finally I got to speak to him. The first words he said to me were, "Hello my honey, I love you." I almost cried at that very moment. Then he said, "I'm so sorry." Those words sent a warm rush through my body. I heard the man that I loved so deeply tell me he loved me and apologize. I immediately told him I loved him too, and in that moment I suddenly felt hope tapping me on my shoulder.

He put into his own words the evening's events that would have him arrested and put into jail. The leach of a man strangling Will with his invasive, weed like vines wrapping around him, had led him to disaster. They worked together that day and went drinking afterward. They ended up at that mans apartment in the city and continued to drink all evening. Will had one of his dogs with him that day. They were in the apartment completely polluted by alcohol, and probably never even ate any food that day. The man began kicking Will's dog because he was growling at him. I understood why the dog growled at him, he had given us the same clue months beforehand. It was our initial warning, but it went ignored.

Will proceeded to tell me he continued to kick the dog while wearing a pair of work boots. He told me he demanded the man stop kicking the helpless animal, but he refused. I was shocked the dog didn't attack out of self defense, but perhaps he was hurt. Eventually, Will was driven by alcohol and anger and a fight began. I never saw Will angry in my entire life. He was provoked by an instinct to protect his innocent dog. The fight went from bad to worse, and then Will armed himself with a utility knife he carried for cutting sheetrock, and went after the mans face, but cut his throat instead. Will was in shock by what he did and was instantly sobered by his actions and adrenaline pumping through his veins. He dialed 911 and waited for emergency crews to come rescue the man lying there unconscious and bleeding. He was arrested for his crime when they arrived.

I was crying in disbelief listening to my husband's confession. I could not imagine him ever being that angry. We rarely even yelled at each other in all the years I knew him. It happened and it was history now. Poor Will was sorrier for hurting me than he was concerned about what he was facing with a possible prison term.

After hearing his apology and I love you, I told him that was all I needed to hear and would be willing to take him back. I still loved him so deeply and I knew he did not hurt me intentionally, his addiction was controlling him. I had done my research on alcoholism and knew that to be the case. Will asked if I would visit him at the jail. I agreed to and wanted to see him at the soonest opportunity. I was about to embark on a new journey with the man I love.

Visits at that particular jail were Tuesday and Thursday evenings, and also on Saturday afternoons. I went immediately to see Will. His family forfeited their visit that day so I could go see my husband privately. I went after work and drove about forty minutes to get to the city. It was unfamiliar territory to me. Will knew the area and told me what exit to take from the highway, and how to get to the jail from there. I had my notes in hand, and drove with butterflies in my stomach from fear of the unknown and excitement to actually see him.

I had never been to a jail before and never dreamed I would ever go to one either. I arrived and searched for a place to park. It was downtown and the only parking available was metered along the streets, or in a garage a few blocks away. I circled the jail until I found a parking space only about a block away. I was nervous being in the city walking at night all alone. I tried to set all my senses on keen alert to avoid being attacked.

I made it to the courthouse and entered through the doors. The jail was on the top floor. Immediately, I had to remove any metal items from my person and walk through the metal detectors. It buzzed in warning of my body harboring metal somewhere. It was my belt buckle, so I removed it and walked through the test again. My heart was beating out of my chest; I was scared just being there. I felt like a criminal trying to hide something even though I wasn't. There is something about that environment. I felt like I was being watched through suspicious eyes just waiting to catch me doing something wrong. I was honest as the day is long and I had nothing to hide, but still felt I did somehow.

After clearing the security entrance, I was among a line of other women waiting to visit inmates in the jail upstairs. My heart sank seeing everyone ahead of me because there was a limited amount of visitors each session. It was first come first serve, but I didn't know that ahead of time. I drove straight from work and still faced a rather large crowd in front of me. I almost gave up hope that I would get the chance to see Will that night. I remained seated, and tried to mind my own business among all the other visitors speaking languages foreign to me.

All of us waited there until the announcement that the waiting area in the jail on the seventeenth floor was open. Everyone made a mad dash to the elevator which was armed with a guard. There was only one elevator that went to the jail. I suppose for security reasons it had to be that way.

I arrived to the upstairs waiting area and still had no idea what the protocol was for a visit. I carefully watched what was going on around me as I stood in line behind the other women. It led to a small window similar to that of a bank teller. There we registered to see the inmate of interest and supplied them with a driver's license. I wasn't the first in line so I learned the next steps by observing the seasoned visitors ahead me.

My turn came, and I handed the security officer behind the window my driver's license with my cold, but sweaty, shaking hands. He asked me who I was there to visit; I responded, and he told me to get in another line. The women all got lockers and put their personal belongings into them. No personal items of any type were allowed into the visiting area, so I followed suit. Some visitors were turned away due to lack of space. I was fortunate, and was in line eagerly waiting for the next step in the process to eventually see Will.

The large clock on the wall reminiscent of the ones in school slowly ticked away, minute by minute. It seemed like it echoed throughout the room over voices speaking in foreign languages as I anxiously waited. It took another thirty minutes for all the processing to take place. After everyone checked in, a guard had to notify all the inmates that had visitors waiting.

Finally, another security officer opened a large, gray, steel door at the head of the line I was standing in. We entered one at a time and went through yet another metal detector. It was so sensitive that even under-wire bras were setting it off. My insides were shaking and I had no idea if I would get clearance, but was certainly hoping so. I had invested about two hours of waiting time along with nerves laced with nausea to get to that point. It was my turn and I cleared through the final security stage of the visit.

Just on the other side of another steel door was a narrow hallway that was U shaped. It surrounded a square room enclosed in shiny, gray painted concrete, cinder block, steel, and glass. The windows appeared to be about an inch thick. In the glass were small circles framed with aluminum and a perforated screen inside of it. At each circle there were two stools. Each inmate could have a maximum of two visitors. I was alone.

I noticed there was no particular order to follow and the women sat on any stool they chose. I sat on one myself and we all waited there. Within a few minutes men dressed in orange jumpsuits and state issued white canvas, slip on sneakers began to enter the square room on the other side of the glass. They each recognized their visitor and sat inside the window opposite them. Will arrived within a few minutes too.

I was elated to see him at last; I was so sad that it was in that manner though. He was not that kind of a man; he was a good person and did not belong there. He was caught up in that expression we all say so casually, "in the wrong place at the wrong time." We couldn't hug or kiss, only talk through the little hole in the glass window. We each held back tears that pooled in our eyes, trying to keep our composure in front of a tough crowd, to protect him while he was behind those walls.

Through his eyes, I somehow felt he was completely genuine about getting our life back in order. I was so happy Will requested a visit from me. He expressed his gratitude for the gift I was offering him, to stay by his side through the tunnel of the unknown he entered. We were in it together now. I loved him and I wanted to be there to help him in any way I could. We swallowed our pride and did what we had to do to follow the new game rules of our life.

By then bail had been set for my husband at $100,000.00 cash. I was among the working middle class sector and was lucky if I had $100.00 in the bank. Even if the entire family pooled funds together we could not gather that amount of cash.

I contacted an attorney to see if they would handle Will's case. They were interested in doing so, but they required a $50,000 binder. Okay, where was I going to get that kind of money? I didn't know where the nearest money tree was. Our family wasn't in the position to put that kind of money together either. Our only hope now was that Will got a decent court appointed attorney.

Will was hopeful to get guidance from an uncle of his that worked at the county courthouse downstairs. He tried to help us by telling us who we would hope to get as judge and prosecuting attorney, but that was all the help he was able to offer. We were in the middle of this dark, scary maze alone. At least we had each other. Will had me cheering in his corner. Will was also very bright and learned some of the ropes of survival to avoid conflict while he awaited court hearings.

I continued to visit my husband three times a week there at that jail for eight months. I never got completely used to going to that place, but I knew it was my only option to stay connected. Will made me some promises at the very first visit and I felt hopes warmth helping me walk my new path. He once told me before we were even engaged that he never made a promise he couldn't keep.

He began AA meetings, was sober, and could see the world differently now. He was once again the Will I met, knew, and loved. I knew he was worth whatever it took to get him home and resume our wonderful life.

I was in the middle of taking adult confirmation classes at my Catholic church to become a godmother to my niece. One evening our instructor brought guest speakers into our class to teach us about something called "laying of hands."

We were in pods of six, and after some instruction and inspiration we did such praying over each other. I went first in our group. I sat in a desk chair and the other five stood and placed their hands on my shoulders, and began to pray randomly while I sat with my eyes closed. My body began to feel hot and I opened my eyes and I couldn't see anything but bright, white light as if I was looking at the sun. I couldn't see anything or anyone in the room, not even the room itself. But, I could hear the prayers, except that they had become jumbled and sounded as if they were praying in tongue. I felt as if I was going to faint.

I did not share this with my instructor or anyone in the class. I thought I was just going to faint and accepted that as my explanation. I didn't want to embarrass myself. A few days later I did end up telling my mother the story about my experience. She told me I received a healing by the Holy Spirit. After that healing, I felt more relaxed and able to let go of things out of my control, and allow God to take it over.

Later, I told Will about what happened at my class. He confided in me that he went through something similar. He was speaking to a visiting priest and shared about his shame in what led him to being arrested. He also talked to him about his sadness over losing his father, and the healing episode almost identical to mine occurred then. I thought it was ironic we both experienced such an event. With that, I decided we were going to be alright because our higher power was going to make it so.

As time went by Will had to make several court appearances. His attorney kept him abreast of the schedule, and through phone conversations Will let me know what was happening in that regard. He needed some suitable clothing for court and I managed to deliver them to the jail where they would be stored until he needed them. Before it was over he'd go to court several times just to determine whether or not he would have a trial. There seems to be a lot of negotiating that takes place in the world of criminal law. I took time off work to be there for all of them, but most of all to support Will.

Before any court appearance took place Will suffered an injury. I discovered it when I went to visit him and noticed his face was quite swollen on one side. I asked him what happened. As he spoke through the side of his mouth he told me, nothing. I had a career in dentistry and told him there was definitely something wrong. He tried to tell me he fell and hit his head while cleaning the toilet in his cell. I wasn't certain I could believe that and pressed him further.

He couldn't contain his lie and he told me he was attacked from behind in the weight room and suffered a blow to his face. He called it a sucker punch. It happened that day and he had a witness. I told him he must report it and that I was going to call at the end of the visit and report it myself. He promised me he would go to the infirmary and have it looked at. We continued our thirty minute visit as my heart beat out of my chest in anger and worry for Will. He was in a scary place and wasn't safe.

At the end of our visit I reminded him to see the doctor about his face. I also called the office from the payphone down stairs before I left to go home. He called me the next day and told me he had been taken to Massachusetts General Hospital to be treated for his broken jaw.

He was treated like a serial killer while he was there. He told me he was escorted to the hospital in his orange county jail jumpsuit, handcuffed and shackled, and then handcuffed to the hospital bed to be treated. I sensed his humiliation. He wasn't the man they were all afraid of, but they didn't know him. They set his jaw and wired his teeth together so it would heal and he was returned to the jail.

The next day was a visiting day so I went to see my poor husband. Of course, with the latest turn of events I was worried sick about his welfare. His teeth had wires and orthodontic bands on them to make his jaw immobile for six weeks. He couldn't eat solid food so they provided him with a canned drink called Ensure. It had the required dietary supplement to keep Will fed, but it didn't seem to have enough calories to carry him through to the next meal.

He maneuvered a way to put soft foods into his cheeks, getting them behind his molars and into his mouth to dissolve between his tongue and pallet, and then swallowed. Mashed potatoes were the ideal food for that technique. He was quite proud of himself, being able to devise a way to get more food into his stomach and stay healthy. He was in good spirits considering what he had been through.

There was a lot of bantering back and forth between him and his appointed attorney. He insisted a trial would not serve him well in his case due to the severity of his charges and circumstances. Neither one of us understood that rationale though. He kept telling us that considering the crime Will committed he would serve nine years in prison. I gasped at the thought.

The victim contacted me and told me he did not want to press charges. I told him to contact the attorney, but he never did. He had a paper trail a mile long among other things and did not want to set foot in a courthouse, or jail.

I thought for sure a jury would have sympathy hearing Will describe his attempts to save a dog being beaten to death. Then they would understand why he hurt that man. I considered it defending a poor helpless animal. I think I could be pushed to hurt someone to rescue my dog as well. I really believed Will could convince a jury and they would give him probation or community service at the most. The attorney told him there just aren't that many animal lovers. We thought we had to trust him, we felt like we had no choice. We didn't have money to pay someone that probably would have listened to us and agreed to go to trial.

I was asked to appear at another court appearance in March 1995. I was told nothing was going to happen that day, just more of going through the motions. The attorney told us the date would most likely get rescheduled again, as it had been done several times before. The court system is good at doing that to you, in attempt to hear the many cases waiting to be heard. You follow the protocol and rules, etc., and they pull the trap door from beneath your feet at any given moment without thinking about what they do to you. You are just a docket number on the books and each time the date is cancelled you go back to square one. Time kept ticking away with my husband in jail not knowing what to expect next.

I went to court that day alone, expecting it would be a waste of time and energy to be there. I was sitting waiting for Will and his attorney to enter unless it is was once again postponed. My stomach was in knots, feeling guilty of some crime just because I was at the courthouse dealing with jail matters.

Will's docket number was called and his attorney motioned he was present. I was caught off guard, I didn't expect this to happen, and I was not mentally prepared. Will was ushered into the court room from a holding cell handcuffed and shackled. His feet were not able to move more than about six inches at a time. He more or less shuffled them like a person with advanced Parkinson's disease rather than walk. He was then seated at the side of the courtroom where a jury would be if there was a trial.

It was breaking my heart to see him treated that way. I knew he did what he did to save his dog. He was not that kind of man, nor did he ever have a prior record of any kind. The ruling had to be favorable, it just had to.

The judge and attorney exchanged legal jargon while my heart was beating out of my chest. My hands were sweating and my stomach was nauseous, almost to the point that I thought I might faint. I could only imagine how my husband felt waiting to hear what the courts saw fit for his destiny. We were told the guideline was nine years, and I just prayed that would not be the outcome today.

The sentence was finally given and Will was not set free that day. He didn't receive the maximum sentence; however, he did receive a prison term of three to five years. That court appearance was only supposed to be a day of going through the motions. I was alone there to compute the message the judge just presented.

I began to cry silently, and my tears strolled down my face after yet another dagger penetrated my heart. I lost the battle trying to help Will be set free and given back to me to love, to hold, and to cherish for all time. The authorities began to take Will away and as I watched, my mind slowed things as if it were a dream.

The attorney that I felt failed us somehow managed to stop them, and motioned to me to come say goodbye to Will. It seemed impossible to endure what was about to happen. He was cuffed and shackled still. I dried my tears of disappointment away and looked into his eyes and told him I loved him, and then I hugged him and gave him a kiss. It was only seconds and then it was all business, and they took the love of my life away. I was surprised, but happy to get that opportunity. It was the first physical contact I had with him and would be the last for awhile.

The attorney explained to me what the sentence meant out in the corridor. Will had to serve three years in the state prison system, less the eight months he already spent in jail. That was a relief. After the three years if the parole board saw fit, he would be released to a one year simultaneous parole and probation period, and then one more year of probation once parole was completed. There would be no appeal. We had to take our medicine and do the best we could with what was dished up onto our plates by the justice system. We were somehow grateful the sentence was not for nine years.

Doing Time

Will was moved from the county jail almost immediately. They would not tell me where he was going, I imagine for security reasons. I had to wait until he arrived to a new facility, be registered, and issued an inmate number before he could call me to tell me where he was. It was almost two weeks before I heard from him. He finally called me collect from the state prison in Concord and gave me all his new information, including his inmate number. That number would be the only way to identify him for the next twenty-eight months. In order to receive mail or visits we had to use it, and I memorized it quickly. Will and I were so connected and determined not to let this "bumpy road in life" wear us down.

Finally, I got to see Will, it was a Saturday. The weekday visits were Tuesday and Thursday like the first place he was incarcerated. However, the visiting hours were at noon time. Unfortunately, I was working those days and the commute was too long to squeeze visits in over my one hour lunch break. We were at the mercy of the prison system, and they weren't there to make life easy for anyone. I can understand that, since they are probably faced with many inmates and visitors that do all they can to beat the system.

The prison was surrounded by a concrete wall and barbed wire taller than anyone could see over. I saw watch towers behind the wall overlooking the entire property from the parking lot. I entered through the front doors of the prison to register for a visit. It was a very old building and the appearance reflected it. The interior walls were painted a gloomy, gray color and the fluorescent lighting was poor. It reminded me of an insane asylum from the movies.

People waiting for visits spoke many different languages that echoed off the cement walls. It created a chaotic setting for my nerves. It was strange and new to me. Like the first place, there were many people before me that paved the way. I was able to observe and learn the ropes just like before.

The protocol was the same mostly, except I discovered you could bring quarters into the visiting room. There were vending machines in there and you could buy sandwiches, sodas and coffee, and candy. It was permitted to buy items and share them with the inmate. I wasn't aware of the quarter policy so I didn't have any with me that day.

I had to store all my personal belongings in a locker. Once visiting hours were announced I passed through the security section, including a metal detector. Next, I entered a large room filled with chairs lined up side by side in several long rows. I sat in a seat and waited for Will to enter the room, which took anywhere from five minutes to half an hour.

I was eagerly waiting there to see my husband. I had not seen him since he received his sentence a couple of weeks prior to that day. We spoke on the phone, but somehow it just wasn't enough. I needed to see him physically, to be assured he was unharmed. So many crazy thoughts and images went through my mind from watching too many movies, or television programs depicting prison life.

Will finally arrived, and I stood up and watched him walk toward me, and we embraced. There were guards in the room watching every move. Will and I never broke the law before and we were on our best behavior that day. We enjoyed being able to sit across from each other, hold hands, and gaze into each others eyes. The visits were bittersweet. We conversed and expressed our extraordinary love to each other through small mannerisms no one else could translate. I felt like I was on the right path even though it would prove to be trying. I saw a light at the end of the tunnel and knew Will would eventually come home to me again; we had the date on paper.

That visit and all the ones that followed fueled our spirits, and gave us the energy required to endure the remaining years of his sentence, and leave it behind us forever. In the meantime, we wrote a letter to each other every night. We began that ritual after my very first visit to see him in Cambridge. It was basically our chance to ask each other "how was your day" since we weren't able to in person. Since we were cut off to one visit per week the letters helped to keep us connected. I was living outside those walls of darkness and gloom. Will carried the heaviest weight of the journey and I was willing to support him any way I could. I felt the heat from the torch of hope, and it was reigniting that flame that was extinguished all those months ago. That school girl feeling of giddiness returned each time I checked the mail box, or went to see the love of my life.

Will ended up serving his sentence in five prisons across the state of Massachusetts. Some of the facilities involved a drive of up to two hours, but I went regardless. I shared the visits with family and friends, since they allowed two visitors per session.

I became a warrior in the battle of bureaucratic, red tape woven throughout the state prison system, and observed some changes with the aid of the board of health. Not only were the public restrooms filthy, they were without soap, toilet paper and paper towels, and the inmates were living among roaches and rodents. Will inquired once and was told they could not hire an exterminator due to security reasons. I discovered that was not so, and filed a complaint, which did indeed result in the hiring of a professional to rid the compound of pests. I understood the concept of prison, but it didn't mean disease should have the opportunity to run rampant in it.

Each week the routine was to drive to whichever facility he was in and spend two hours with him. There wasn't much to share between us, since we were writing letters to each other every day, but we enjoyed being together physically. We talked casually, held hands, and even laughed a little. I was so glad to give him the gift of getting out of the cell block for a brief visit and break up the monotony for him. Will confided that each time I came to see him he was put through a strip search. I offered to reduce our visits, but he told me he wouldn't give them up for the world. With each one we realized his release date was that much closer. We didn't begin a serious countdown until the final months though; it was still too far off for that.

Each day when our sessions ended it was difficult to hold my tears back and leave him there in the awful place he was held in. I had to appear strong for him since I was the one with the easy end of things. I experienced a more normal life outside the concrete walls and barbed wire, while he was inside barely getting an opportunity to get fresh air, and having to abide by petty rules and mind games. I didn't like the fact that he was in prison, but we didn't have a choice in the matter.

He used to joke to me about how he was the only one in prison that was guilty of any crime. He said, all the other men there had "deniabetes." That was Will's humor coming out even in a dark place. He made the word up for all the other inmates living in denial. He combined the word denial with the word diabetes and came up with deniabetes. Get it? Many of them claimed to have been sent to prison because an informant told, or some other excuse, and never admitted to any kind of crime.

Will's amazing sense of humor was his gift to me and his family, so we wouldn't worry so much about him while he was in that terrible place. We accepted the fact that if he could give us a laugh or two, perhaps the authorities hadn't suffocated his spirit, and he was actually doing okay.

He once told me that due to the charges and nature of his crime that he admitted to, he was considered dangerous and that was his saving grace and other inmates avoided him. If he could almost kill a man, then he wasn't someone to be reckoned with. It eased my mind a bit, but I still wasn't sure if he was just telling me that to keep me from worrying. We were both trying to protect each other the best we knew how.

I praised him in each letter for hanging in there so well, in hopes that he would hold onto the dreams that would come true one day. He wrote to me about his visions of us being reunited and the goals we could strive toward once he was home. We had a date on paper that meant freedom for him, and we could reclaim our life together.

At one point near the end of Will's prison term, someone in his family called me at work and verbally attacked me. She seemed to enjoy throwing a wrench into situations. Will and I had been through an incredibly difficult journey and it somehow strengthened our relationship. The woman on the other end of the phone told me she would see the day that Will and I divorced. She caught me in the wrong mood that day, because I had courage in my pocket, and I calmly responded to her. I told her, if she was so sure of what she just said, that she could go down to the Cambridge courthouse and file the paperwork to get the procedure started, and then I hung up on her. I stood up for myself even though she upset me. In the rest of my years with Will I never once heard an apology form her for that assault, or any others. I never told Will of that encounter, I didn't want him to dwell on more negative family issues. Besides, I knew she couldn't hurt us.

Will took jobs while he was in prison to help pass time, earn time off his sentence, and earn two dollars a day for his canteen account. He could also receive money for his account through private deposits, either by mail, or at check in time of a visit. Canteen was the prison commissary where he could purchase toiletries, stamps, stationery and some non-perishable grocery items.

To save on his account balance, whenever I wrote him a letter, I placed an extra sheet or two of writing paper and an envelope in it, so he could reply. He could receive books of stamps in his letters as well, but a prison clerk checked all incoming mail, confiscated them temporarily, and reissued them after they were searched for drugs. I always mentioned any enclosure, so he could check the inventory and his canteen account to be sure he was getting all the items mailed to him.

I had books mailed in directly from a bookstore for Will's thirst for knowledge and entertainment. He discovered college correspondence courses on animal husbandry and small farming issues he was interested in, and with prison approval I ordered those for him as well. Basically, as long as the items came directly from a college or book store they allowed it into the facility. With all the books, courses, and jobs in the prison he was keeping his genius IQ and inquisitive brain active and engaged. All the studying he did ended up helping to pave the way for our future.

I had Zig Ziglar's book; *Courtship after Marriage* mailed in to Will. He's a motivational speaker and his book on marriage was brilliant. I was reading abundant self help books at the time, and found that one a lot of fun. Will read it and enjoyed it so much that he passed it around to other inmates who expressed interest. It was a great tool for us even though we weren't living together.

Will had leadership talents so he got involved with military veterans in prison and became the chairman, running weekly meetings to help them prepare for their release into the free world again. They were entitled to certain aid and programs, but without being informed, the veteran inmates were released into society without any guidance other than to see their parole and probation officers.

Will had a passion for veterans and wanted them to succeed outside the prison walls. Many of them had families that gave up on them, and had no network, or any idea where to go for help to find jobs, or a place to live. Will knew if he could end up in prison anyone could, and he wanted to offer equal opportunity to all.

Once you are freed you are on your own. You walk out of the gate and fend for yourself with a felony strike against you. Look on any job application and you will see the question that asks; "have you ever been convicted of a felony?" When you check that box you may as well kiss the opportunity goodbye. It happened to Will, he knew all too well.

Prison isn't typically considered a very pleasant place to be. Somehow, Will was able to extract anything minutely positive of the experience, store it, and apply it to life skills in his future. During his incarceration we both changed, and we learned what was precious to us. Will took all he learned and transformed himself into a magnificent human being. He was always an extraordinary person, but now he was at his best.

As if chairman of the veterans group, college courses, a job, and visits wasn't enough, he also became very involved in church again, and helped with AA meetings. Prison and exactly how he landed there that fateful night, opened his eyes. He filled his days with all the positive influence he could find, to survive and leave that place a winner. With all his efforts he earned two months off his sentence and was released in April instead of June 1997, after serving thirty-four months behind bars.

Overwhelming Challenges

My life sidestepped and took on a new normal… Shortly after Will was arrested the mortgage company notified me our house was heading into foreclosure. I lost the fight even with all the worry and watching my marriage go down the drain. It was impossible for me to pay all the bills on my own, so I let it go. I was disappointed, but I didn't really care anymore. It was only material things and they could be replaced.

At the moment my two dogs and I were living with my sister and her husband. I was grateful and tried to help out in every way I could since they were not charging me any rent. She graciously recommended I pay off my bills, so I would eventually be on my feet again and able to live solo on my salary.

I was not accustomed to accepting such gifts. However, with that I became debt free, but with bad credit due to the delinquent loan on my house. Space was tight there and I didn't want to be in the way so eventually I looked for a place to live on my own.

I met up with a lot of closed doors. I was continually turned down because I had dogs. They were house trained and well behaved, but the landlords didn't want to risk it. I would have lived in my car rather than give them up though.

I ended up moving into my other sister's house. She had a room in her basement and I could stay there. She and her husband didn't want any rent either. In return for their support I helped out around the house and yard with whatever I could. My life was upside down and keeping busy helped me hide from my pain and fear of the unknown.

After a few months, I decided to begin to repay my debt to them by funding a remodeling project for the basement. I was going to be there until Will got out of prison. My brother in-law and I did the work together. Again, staying busy was the magic tonic that chased away my blues.

I am the type of personality to deal with whatever challenge comes my way. The years of dealing with my husband being in prison were just another building block. In the early months, before he was sentenced, I was a wreck. I was unable to eat and survived on diet cola and iced coffee. For my mental health I was keeping a journal and tried to remain calm. However, what I was dealing with now was so large, and I struggled with giving up control. I was afraid and it was consuming me. I ended up having a mini nervous breakdown.

One day at work I could not contain my tears and anxiety. I was doing too much, but didn't know it. I was dealing with legal matters and the possibility of Will serving nine years behind bars. I was overwhelmed and didn't know how to let go.

From my office, I called several psychiatrists to seek help. Nowadays, insurance companies dictate how medical professionals operate their practices. I was insured, but did not have a primary care physician to give me a referral. I had never been sick and was not aware of the protocol. I still lived in the days when you could go to any doctor if you needed one. I never knew to make any other arrangements. I called everyone listed in the Yellow Pages, but no one would take me as a patient.

Finally, I spoke to a receptionist at a private practice, and once again was told; sorry, but you need a referral. I couldn't believe I was turned down again. It was the last number to call in the phone book, my last hope. I lost it during that conversation and began to cry. I told her I would pay cash for a visit and keep insurance out of the scenario altogether. She told me she couldn't do it that way. I was shocked. We live in America, and no one takes cash anymore! I was almost suicidal at that point. I told that woman that it is no wonder people jump off bridges and kill themselves. There aren't any doctors willing to help them when they are in dire need. This particular receptionist seemed to get it, but it was office policy and she had no voice in the matter.

I broke down into tears again. My boss witnessed the breakdown and cancelled our dental patients. He put me into his car, and drove me to an emergency room. We waited for hours, but I did finally see a social worker. The policy was of course to slip into a hospital gown while I waited. When she came to examine me she commented on some red marks on my back. I could sense that she was wondering if I had been abused and was concealing information about it. I told her that I had sensitive skin and had been leaning against the ladder back chair for over an hour, to explain the marks. It was the truth. I had been defeated, but not beaten.

She asked me, what I suppose are considered routine questions, and then left me to wait for a doctor. It seemed like another hour went by and a psychiatrist entered the exam room. He barely spoke to me, or inquired about my state of mind, and quickly wrote some scribble onto his prescription pad and sent me on my way. He gave me the feeling it was quitting time for him, and in order to hurry off he made his assessment hastily.

After four or five hours I was free to go home. I was expected to take some five milligram, generic valium, and get over my problems. He did not set up a second appointment, nor did he give me any other recommendations, just to take the pills.

I guess he knew what he was doing. That night, those tiny pills sent me into a slumber of about twelve hours. I woke up feeling groggy, but felt rested at last. Each night for a week I took a tablet and fell into a comatose state until morning. With that, I was rejuvenated and relaxed enough to finally eat something solid. I had lost fifteen pounds and could pull my jeans down without unzipping them. My battery pack was recharged, and I was ready to take the tiger by the tail and fight to the finish.

I still had anxiety and sought therapy on my own. I also went to church and prayed harder than I had ever prayed before. Every time I knelt and saw Jesus on the crucifix, above the church altar, I cried. I explained that to my therapist and she told me it was quite normal. I was trying to let go of my need to control and let God help me.

My life seemed to have no direction. I woke up and did what had to be done to get through my day. I usually kept busy, and when I wasn't I found something to do. It created enough distraction that I could function to the point that no one knew I was suffering. I am not one to sit still anyway, and when I'm stressed I'm even worse.

I continued to work full time. I worked on the basement one room apartment, took care of my dogs, and lived sort of on auto pilot until Will was finally sentenced. I couldn't focus on much, since there were too many unknowns causing my brain to work in circuit overload mode, making me unable to cope with much other than a structured routine. I lived with my two nieces as well and had a lot of fun playing with them. When I was with them I could let my problems go and be a big kid.

After the sentencing I was able to grasp what had been doled out and made some sort of sense out of my life. I had already agreed to stand by my husband through this journey, and I hadn't changed my mind. Now we had a date of actual release and I formed my life flow around it all, and went through a transition into a type of survival mode. I was wonder woman. I could multi task and take care of matters as if my brain was like a computer. It seemed almost effortless to cram everything in and still walk tall and smile. I had my new routine and still had my youthful energy, and just did what had to be done.

Many people in my circle seemed to think I was taking on the impossible. I have been through many difficult times in my life and learned to be tough and deal with it. It was my genetic code to just take it all on. What was my option, walk away and feel like a quitter? I couldn't do that. I felt like I had hope. I still loved my husband very much.

With writing my daily letter to Will and a journal entry, a couple of collect phone calls during the week, my job, family, and my dogs, it all kept me grounded and gave me strength to walk the path set before me. It was one that I chose to take. I guess I always seem to compare my struggles with another person, which could be much worse and realize I can do it. I don't know where that strength comes from; it kind of just comes natural. Or, it could be a bit of bull-headedness.

I'd have to say my dogs gave me great joy and were also good listeners. I could cry and they would instinctively come to me and try to console me. Czar was sick and had grand mal seizures due to what was diagnosed as epilepsy, since he was age one. He died by the time he turned four, two years before Will came home.

It broke my heart to lose him, but I grieved silently. I had guilt over why I couldn't make him well. I did everything the vet asked and he still continued to get worse. I was busy with daily life, my job, as well as my new situation, and being there for Will that I sort of blocked the loss out somehow.

When he died I wrote a letter to Will in the first person as if Czar wrote it. In it he apologized for having to leave this world. He told Will to be proud of "the mama" because I did a great job taking care of him and will continue to do so for Ivan now.

I still had Ivan and he was a loving, regal dog. He became my true comrade and we did everything together. We took time for our peaceful walks at Carlisle Forest, rides in the car for an ice-cream, or just to do errands. He was my buddy. He filled the void of not having Will, or Czar by my side now.

I also became intrigued with self-help books. I read many that dealt with relationship issues, finding the child within, and spiritual journeys. I am also a music lover and found it helpful to listen to CD's through headphones. It was meditative for me. Music sings to my soul and it helps me relax and escape.

I was sober and never turned to drugs or alcohol during this phase of my life. I already saw how addiction almost completely snuffed out my marriage. I knew I didn't want to travel that road. Therapy, reading, music, and friends and family, helped me more than anything else.

There were a few people in my corner that supported me by listening when I needed to relieve the pressure valve. I went to the West Coast one time to see some dear friends and get away. Will insisted that I go. It was hard to leave him, but I knew his family would visit and it was only for a week. I sent him post cards from all the airport layover points, and Washington State, and British Columbia, Canada. I needed him to know I still loved him even though I wasn't there.

I had a lovely time on the trip, but my personality faults made me want to be home with Will. I had this craving to be with him all the time. He was the only person that made me feel good to be loved and in a way I never knew before. It was free and painless.

I felt all of this return when he called me after he was arrested and told me he loved me and how sorry he was. I just knew in my heart he was back from the darkness. I wanted to be with him to soak up the love he willingly gave me free of charge.

We mastered the art of communicating during the forced separation of prison. There was never a stone unturned between us. We shared everything about our feelings and even just the day's events. We had been through something tragic and had nothing left to hide from one another. We talked just as if we were at home having dinner, except now it was between barriers like concrete, barbed wire, and the bars of prison.

Will had a parole hearing three months before he was released. In order to be considered he had to have a pre-approved place to live. I had not secured an apartment yet, so we got clearance for him to live with me at my sister's house. Just afterward, I did locate an apartment, but we could not get another evaluation until after Will was released. We didn't want to take any chances so we left things as they were for now.

In the meantime, I cleaned and moved our things into our apartment. We stayed at my sister's house for a couple of weeks until we got the go ahead. We moved in right away and began our journey together again.

Will had some anxieties of living on the outside. He had been conditioned by the prison environment to always watch his back. He witnessed some horrific events and initially he told me he could never discuss them.

About ten years later my husband did tell me he saw a man killed in a facility he was in. He was thrown from the second tier, and landed on his back on the floor below with other inmates waiting there to attack him, and they killed him. I can't imagine my husband felt safe there, especially after the broken jaw episode. He tried to make me think he was doing well enough so I wouldn't worry.

For the rest of his life he was always telling me how sorry he was for putting me through that. He told me I didn't deserve that life. I had a choice in the matter and I elected to stay. With that we ended up with the gift of a rich, but simple life.

Early on after his release, he felt like he was being followed when we were in public. He scared me, but he was in therapy and I wasn't going to push him. He was attending AA meetings and doing everything right so I wasn't worried.

Eventually, he did however, slip rather nicely back into our life. He resumed position of head of household and got a job immediately. He was also in seventh heaven to be reunited with Ivan. He had not seen him for three years. Ivan welcomed Will home as if he had never been gone. He was such a special dog and loved us both so much.

Life for us was better than starting where we had left off. During the time apart we had time to heal and find ourselves and each other again. We had time to think about the past and forgive. Without that we may not have been able to make a go of things so easily. It wasn't only time that healed us, we both did a lot of work for it as well.

Free At Last

April arrived, and like spring I had butterflies in my stomach as I drove to MCI Shirley, the minimum security prison Will had spent the last few months at. I was thrilled he was being released, but I suppose at the same time, I worried that perhaps they'd discover they made a mistake and would not let him go.

After a journey such as prison life you'd be amazed at what your mind is capable of imagining. You become conditioned by so many road blocks, and red tape of prison, and government bureaucracy that you get trapped and tangled in along the way.

In the end, I had worried for no reason. Will checked out, was issued his personal belongings, and we walked out of that door without looking back. We went straight to my car, had a real kiss, and left the grounds immediately.

Will and I rejoiced as we drove away from that prison forever. It was hard to grasp the thought that the day had actually arrived. He was on parole. He had to report to the county courthouse in Cambridge and sign his paperwork for that new journey. They allowed twenty-four hours to accomplish that task, but Will was the type of man to get it done without putting it off. Any screw ups at that point meant his freedom could be revoked for the remaining two years, and we weren't willing to risk that.

We took care of the formalities to the last detail immediately, even with all the aggravation of doing state paperwork. He was assigned his parole and probation officers closer to where our apartment was, and we drove there to report directly after we left the courthouse. Of course, the parole and probation offices were not in the same location, there was a forty minute commute between them. We went to both places and took care of all the mandatory requirements so he could live outside prison walls. Will took it all very seriously because I think being free took on a new meaning for him.

Our new found freedom was awkward; it almost didn't seem real. We could touch and kiss, and gaze into each others eyes at any moment without a visitor permit, a pat or strip search, or fear of a guard telling us we were sitting too close together. We had just hiked the highest mountain and experienced many bumps and bruises along the way, but we finally reached the summit and found freedom, utopia, the air was so clean there and no one could take it away from us.

I was told by many people in the early stages of Will's incarceration to give up on him. They told me that I deserved more and could do better. However, I knew there was a reason I felt compelled to wait for him. I was certain he was my soul mate and it is something precious to know and love them. Those on the outside looking in didn't know that feeling, or they would have held off on their mindless advice. I knew I made the right choice to stay with Will and could endure the test before me.

I was glad I put the utmost effort into it and conquered the battle. The prize for me in the end was worth all the miserable moments. I finally had my honey home with me. Surviving those three years made our lives rich. We reached for the stars and achieved many goals we set for ourselves as a couple once he was released.

Living in the free world required some adjustment. Will suffered post traumatic stress disorder due to cruel behavior modification forced onto him by his environment. In celebration of his homecoming I took him out to eat at the Outback Steakhouse, but we had to leave before we finished our meal. He felt as if he had to constantly watch over his shoulder to be ready for an attack. It became unbearable when he went to the restroom and came out in a panic; he apologized and told me he had to leave.

It broke my heart to know he was living with such a burden, but I couldn't fully understand since I had not lived in prison. He told me once that there were some violent things that happened there he could never tell me about. I took care not to ask him to do anything that may be too difficult. With some counseling and practice, and developing a new routine, he began to feel more comfortable in his new surroundings in freedom.

We were a married couple that just survived yet another "bumpy road in life." We no longer had wedding rings since we had broken up and they were pawned off for cash. We bought new bands, and with them we hoped the symbolic token would profess publicly with pride, that our hearts were taken by another.

After a couple of months went by I threw Will a pre-approved welcome home party. He was concerned people would attend only to see the freak ex-convict, but I explained that would not be the case. I thought it would be the easiest way to get to see all his relatives, and let them all see for their own eyes he was doing well, and was indeed not a freak. We compiled the guest list of family and close friends, rented a small hall, and hired a DJ to play music and karaoke.

Our family members brought potluck dishes, and with that we enjoyed a buffet luncheon. Will enjoyed himself and seemed at ease with all his relatives, it was the perfect ice breaker. With karaoke he sang two songs on stage that day and charmed his way deeper into my heart if that was possible. The first one was a song Carole King sang called; *You've Got a Friend* and many of his relatives joined him in the sing along. Then in solo he sang a song performed by The Proclaimers called; *I Would Walk 500 Miles (I'm Gonna be…).* He dedicated it to me, and sang it as if he were serenading me while he walked toward me signaling me with charming hand gestures; the lyrics were from his heart. I was starry eyed with that sweet display of his love to me that day, as I had been many times years before.

Life Is Grand

Will was home for three months, and the hoopla was over. Life began to settle down for us. We both had jobs and were once again so in love we couldn't get enough of each other. After all we had been through; we wouldn't take each other or life for granted. There was some sort of spiritual growth experienced through that chapter of our lives. It brought us to a higher level.

We had the same requirements most Americans have as far as working so we could survive. Somehow though, we found simplicity would grant us magnificent peace in our hearts. It was as if that entire ordeal helped us find a deeper meaning to life. With that, we made new rules to live by; we were in charge, not anyone else.

We knew we wanted to be able to live a lifestyle that allowed us to continue to enjoy simplicity, and all the gifts it brought to us. We had the perfect plan. We both worked full time jobs, but lived on one income. We downsized by cutting out all unnecessary expenses and watched our savings account grow. At that point in time we were renting a small apartment in a two family home, and the landlord allowed us to have our dogs, which was crucial. We were determined to find the homestead of our dreams to fulfill our passions and goals in life. The downward spiral that led Will to prison and robbed us of three years in the free world, led us to peace and the desire to live our precious life together the way we so chose. In a way it could be considered a gift, a blessing in disguise.

We continued to enjoy each other and our dogs on weekends doing things to entertain ourselves for very little, or no money. It involved lots of packed lunches, free excursions to Boston, to trails, lakes and parks that allowed dogs for walks, hikes and dog sledding, movie night at home with borrowed videos from the public library, and homemade pizza. We had each other; we didn't need anything else, I cannot stress that factor enough. We could have been stranded on an uninhabited island together and still found true happiness with each other.

That year we also continued with our quiet Christmases away. We got permission from the parole and probation officers, and stayed in a small cabin nestled in the woods of the White Mountain region of New Hampshire. We got over yet another hurdle in life and realized exactly how important our time together was. We endured enough conflict with family politics and knew we weren't required to be a part of that anymore; we were different now, somehow.

We had an extraordinary love for each other and it was up to us to make our life together what we had hoped for. We chose to go away every opportunity we got to make up for lost time, which created more magical memories for us. We finally learned how to let the criticism and battles slide off our backs like the water rolls off the feathers of a duck. We were survivors and no one could take that away from us or hurt us anymore. Most of all, we knew we had to make our life what we wanted regardless of what others said.

Will purchased his first dog sled that year and became actively involved in the sport again. He received subscriptions to Mushing Magazine while he was incarcerated and it kept his passion for the dogs and sledding alive. Will was the sled driver and I was the dog handler for the most part. I enjoyed being on the snowy trails with him and our dogs though, no matter what my title was.

We were also involved in a rescue organization to offer care for and find homes for unwanted Siberians. It was the same organization we adopted Ivan from and we got first notice of available dogs, which led us to adopting another Siberian.

The dog we adopted had been abandoned and developed something similar to Jekyll and Hyde syndrome. One moment she was sweet and mellow, and then the next she became wolf like and attacked us. We did all we could with training and tender loving care, but eventually she bit Will's hand, drawing blood through a pair of leather work gloves. She had bitten me twice previously, but not as severely. At that point we decided to put her down. It broke our hearts to do it, but after working with her for seven months it wasn't getting any better. All the professionals agreed we did more than most would have. We also couldn't take the risk of a neighbor or one of our family members being bitten.

Just a few days after that incident we received a telephone call about another Siberian needing a home, Sasha. She was a two year old and was in custody of the animal control officer. She needed to be placed or would be euthanized immediately. We drove to the location to meet her. She was sweet, and Ivan loved her, and we adopted her that day. Within a couple of months of that we added a Siberian puppy to our family.

Will was hired to build an addition to a whelping barn for a friend of ours who raised Siberians for sale, the show ring, and dog sledding. He took me there one day while he worked. I sat and visited our friend's wife and also got the opportunity to be with Will for the ride there and back.

After a bit of time passed, I was asked if I was going to go out to the barn to see the puppies. I had no idea there were any puppies, but it didn't take much provocation to get me to go see them. Who can resist puppies?

They were an unplanned litter of four and only two were spoken for. I rolled in the hay in their pen in the barn and played with them. They were crawling all over me, licking my face and ears, and made me feel like a child again. Then our friend asked me which one I wanted.

It finally dawned on me what my husband's intention was by taking me along for the ride that day. I approached Will, and asked him if he brought me there in hopes I would fall in love with the adorable canines, and not be able to walk away from them. He denied all implications with a grin on his face, which was a dead giveaway to me that he did indeed have ulterior motives.

When he was finished adding to the structure we discussed the possibility of getting a puppy. I was against the idea since we lived in a small apartment and already had two dogs, but I did have a soft heart and came up with a plan. I told Will he could have one, if our friend was willing to make some kind of barter arrangement for his services of working on the barn. I really didn't think he would go for that, but to my surprise he did, and in that instant we became proud new parents to a white Siberian husky. She was too young to take home yet so we had to leave her in the barn with her mother and siblings for a few more weeks.

Once she was old enough we went to pick her up and brought her home with us. However, beforehand we had to get all the necessary gear for puppy-hood. It had been a while since we had a dog so young. We picked up our new baby and named her Isabella. Sasha absolutely loved her and cared for her as if she was her own. Ivan was interested, but pretended not to be if we noticed. It was a lot of work, but Isabella proved to be smart and the transformation to adolescence went relatively easily.

Will had two great dogs to go dog sledding with. Ivan knew his sledding commands and Sasha was willing to run and learned quickly. Isabella was still young, but we tried her out on the gangline anyway just to see how she would respond. We discovered she was a born sled dog for lead position. Will was so proud of his accomplishments regarding the sport. He took every opportunity to take our nieces and nephews for rides in the basket of the sled. It was an invigorating experience for Will and me, as well as a fantastic opportunity and gift for the kids. It was a great thrill and hobby for winter, which in New England is quite long. Our pets were like children to us and they ran the household for the most part. Being a small team, we only did short trips, as not to overexert them.

As our savings account for our future continued to grow we began to search out the perfect homestead for us and our dogs. We had contemplated moving to Montana in the early stages, but I thought we should stay in New England closer to family. I lived on the West Coast before I met Will and my family lived in Massachusetts. The distance made it difficult to see each other over a seven year period. Yes, it's easy to say you'll fly home to see everyone, but saying and actually doing it are two different things. I never seemed to financially arrange many visits. We compromised and came up with the idea of buying property with a maximum of a five hour drive from home. That way we could visit more frequently.

Will's grandfather was aging rapidly due to Parkinson's disease. We used to go visit him on Sundays. We brought him dessert I made and witnessed his face light up when we presented it upon our arrival. Those were special days for all of us and I knew Will would miss him if we relocated too far away.

I am grateful we elected to stay close by. Will's grandfather ended up passing away. Had we moved to Montana he may not have been able to attend the wake and funeral. Fortunately, Will was close enough to say goodbye and go through the rituals of loss and letting go.

The quest for our homestead took us to Maine, upstate New York and northern New Hampshire. We looked at a small house in Maine in an ocean community with seven acres, but it was ready for the demolition ball and over priced for its condition. Then we ventured to New York to view a home on forty acres with incredible views of rolling hills, but again the house needed to be condemned. It was also next door to a large dairy farm, and the smell migrated right to the parcel we looked at. I'm not sure I could have stood that in the summer months. We became discouraged and gave up our search for the time being.

We continued to save, and knew in the back of our minds we would eventually get back on track and find something perfect for our needs. You know, sort of like the expression; when you fall off the horse get up and get back on it again. About six months passed and I was in the bank on my lunch break and came across some Century 21 real estate brochures. Just for reading material I picked one up and went home to eat lunch and let the dogs out. I leisurely scanned through the pamphlet while eating, and found a posting that might be worth checking into. I didn't get overly excited about it since we had been disappointed previously.

That night I returned home from work and showed Will the home listing. The house was an old 1870's farm house sitting on twenty-seven acres along a river with mountain views. The price listed was so low it was scary and we could only imagine the condition of the house. We were going to be in the area for a few days to pick up a custom made dog sled Will ordered, so we contacted the listing agent.

Over the phone they gave me a brief description of the house and we scheduled a date to view the property. I asked the agent what was wrong with the house since it was priced so low, and he told me there was nothing wrong with it. The price was about a fourth of what homes were going for in our region, but of course, we lived in a completely different world in comparison.

Dreams Materialized

In October 1998 we met the realtor and followed him to the house to take a look around. Not to our surprise it was old and badly needed some updating. I had my trusty Nikon camera and a video camera with me, so I journalistically recorded our tour of the house and the surrounding property. We followed a trail going into the woods toward the Upper Amonoosuc River with full view of mountains surrounding us. We heard all the sounds of nature in the air as we walked, and fell in love with the land and the possibilities it offered. It sang to our souls and we pretty much forgot about the disrepair of the house.

We put down a small deposit that day and then drove three and a half hours home. Will and I talked about the land and its potentials, and became very excited about our discovery. We had recorded our tour so we could watch the tape when we got home.

We watched the video that night in excitement and then showed it to our families. They didn't share the same enthusiasm, but we were drawn to the land and instantly knew we belonged there. We knew the house required some work, but it didn't need to be torn down and we thought we could handle the renovations ourselves. Will was a highly skilled and licensed carpenter so we figured we were all set to go in that respect. We could envision the house with our imagination added in. Our hard work and sacrifices to save for our future homestead finally paid off. We then proceeded with all the banking involved in purchasing the property to make it ours.

In the meantime, Will accepted a job working at a dairy and cranberry bog in Carlisle, near the apartment we rented in Massachusetts. We used to walk the trails and sometimes rode our mountain bikes at the state park adjacent to that farm in summer and autumn, and went dog sledding there in winter. The sweetness of the job was, along with a salary they offered a place to live as a perk. The home was on the second floor of what was called the bog house. It was a large loft with an open concept design. We spruced the place up a bit, moved in, and soon felt right at home there.

We had a great view of the cranberry bog and forest surrounding it. We had access to trails to walk the dogs, ride our mountain bikes, and train the dogs on our wheeled rig in the autumn for winter dog sledding. In winter, the bog was intentionally flooded over and allowed to freeze, and we ice skated on weekends or evenings by porch light. There we enjoyed tranquility of the woods and witnessed many sunsets worthy of being depicted on an oil canvas.

Living there helped us make the transition to a life in the country that we were already working toward. We had jobs, but at the end of the day we had peace in our hearts, and our souls were being nourished by nature surrounding us. We were both deeply driven toward finding that tranquility we knew at that farm forever.

We had big dreams for the old farm house we bought, but would not move in right away. We decided we'd go up on weekends and do some remodeling first. We weren't actually certain if we'd ever move there or just use the house for weekend getaways and then retirement.

The house was in livable condition, but the standards were not quite ours. Renovations were complicated and required complete makeovers of each room. It proved to be a difficult task to accomplish on weekends alone. We spent seven hours commuting each weekend, arriving late Friday night and leaving Sunday by early afternoon, so there wasn't a lot of time to work on the house. We took some extended weekends and even a full week on occasion to tackle some of the larger tasks, but it was going so slowly.

The first months we owned the house we worked furiously on the bathroom. The previous owner had placed the old fashioned, cast iron bathtub outside of it, since the existing bathroom was too small to accommodate it. It was in the pantry, only separated from the kitchen and front entrance by a curtain, making bathing quite drafty. We knew we'd be at the house Christmas week for our annual holiday getaway, and planned the challenge of full demolition and reconstruction of the bathroom then.

Previous to the rebuild of the room, I managed to find an old bureau at a second hand store to use as a sink vanity. I also found an adorable cabinet circa 1950, about six feet tall with glass doors on the top half and wood doors on the bottom half, separated by two small drawers in between. I refinished both pieces and we placed them in the bathroom, making it a charming environment. Will cut a hole in the top of the bureau to house the sink, and then we treated it with marine polyurethane to protect it from water. Half the fun of the remodel was the hunt for the perfect items to give character and charm back to the old farmhouse.

We gutted the bathroom over the week between Christmas and New Year. As we tore down the walls we discovered many trinkets from yesteryear in them. There were old books, shoes, newspapers, old liquor bottles, and toys. We kept several items and put them out for display on a shelf. Will was so clever he managed to make the bathroom four feet longer, which allowed us to accommodate the furnishings and tub into it. We strategically rearranged the floor plan as well so we could ideally place the plumbing fixtures.

Will did all the new framing and I followed behind him hanging insulation. It was a nasty job, but I put on all my protective gear and placed it all with precision, as instructed by my teacher and husband. We installed lighting, sheetrock, the sink, tub, toilet, and flooring that week. The room was a masterpiece, and by seeing what we accomplished there I was able to envision the entire house after our hands touched it.

Will performed miracles in the world of construction, he had hands of gold. He had the intelligence and I followed his lead and therefore, we made a fantastic team. We even joked about how we could have a television show to teach do it yourselfers how to take on such tasks in their own homes. Later, we saw a TV show with our idea already on PBS. Will was certainly handsome enough to be a television celebrity, but he chose to live a simpler life with me.

The efforts of renovation continued each weekend and we were devoted to the work involved to achieve our goals. The entire house needed restoration, to include; new windows, insulation, kitchen cabinetry, and the entire works. We knew what we were capable of after the bathroom folly, but it was going to take some perseverance. Fortunately, we were able to tenderly push each other and stay motivated while we lived in two places, and tried to get our house to the point of where we could live in it full time.

We adopted our fourth Siberian husky that year, a nine month old named Duke. His owners were a young, college student couple that just plain bit off more than they could chew trying to go to school full time and train a puppy. We took Duke into our home and tried to keep the excitement of a fourth dog into the pack to a minimum. Managing Duke was a challenge, but in time we taught him the house rules and he became quite a charming addition to our family. He was a big, strong male and enjoyed working with the rest of the team in harness, dog sledding, and Will was in musher heaven. It sounds like a lot of aggravation, but in reality all the dogs had a routine and we all lived together harmoniously.

Some weekends we just didn't have enough steam to dig in and work on the house and opted to play instead. In the winter months we dabbled in dog sledding, and then in dry weather we hiked or took country drives exploring. In our travels we discovered a dairy farm close to our house that sold non pasteurized milk straight from their cows. Will liked milk and the fact that theirs was organic, so we purchased a gallon each weekend while we were in New Hampshire. After a few visits to buy milk, being as outgoing as he was, Will made an impression on the farmer who soon offered him a job. The salary was low and we knew we couldn't live on it, but became tempted.

After much analysis and discussion we decided to move and accept the job, while I continued to work in Massachusetts three and a half days a week. The hope was that I would eventually find a job in dentistry near our new home.

An Amazing Leap

In June 2001 we packed everything we owned, took an amazing leap, and moved to New Hampshire. Our peers thought we were insane for doing so. Our new town was very small; in fact so small they call it a village and only had a population of about five hundred. It was our new home and we rather liked that it was isolated.

We had twenty-seven acres of unspoiled nature, with protected land that could never be developed adjacent to ours surrounding us at all times. We savored the idea that we'd always have our humble, little place in the woods without the possibility of it being over developed in the future.

We were not only surrounded by God's green earth, but so many animals too. One weekend we were in the house and we actually saw a bobcat lurking about on the hunt for food. We could not believe our eyes when we noticed him outside the bedroom window at the edge of our pasture. We knew we also had snowshoe hares on our property because we had seen tracks and suspected he was searching for one. We also saw white tailed deer, moose, bear, fisher cat, fox, coyote, turkey, great blue heron, and many other bird species on our natural wonderland. We decided we would not allow hunting on our land, offering sanctuary to all the creatures that wandered it.

We noticed that nature was more accepting of newcomers than the people of the region we now called home. We were labeled "Flat-

Landers", a name given to anyone arriving from below the mountain ranges of New Hampshire. People assumed anyone moving in came with money, and ways and means to change the area and spoil it somehow. We had no intentions of doing anything to change the North Country. After some time passed we made some friends and it seemed many finally accepted us, realizing we were just regular folks looking for a peaceful life.

The house was still in need of major refurbishing. We had wisely purchased most of the expensive stock and stored it in the attic ahead of time. We knew we would replace all the windows and doors, so in preparation we bought supplies and stored them. Our goal was to do the remodeling without taking out any further loans so we could keep our mortgage low.

When we moved in, we decided to only unpack what we absolutely needed for the time being. There was a full size attic that measured about twenty-seven feet long by seventeen feet wide and served as perfect storage. Living there certainly made it easier to work on the house and we planned a project for each weekend, whittling many tasks off the list more quickly. On occasion we experienced a feeling of burnout and took a much needed break to rest, or go play and explore the world around us.

Will was enjoying his new job working with the cows. He had some dairy experience from Carlisle, so he was already a step ahead of the game. He was so intelligent and learned quickly that he was capable of doing any job put in front of him. I was glad Will was happy and was feeling productive and had a sense of accomplishment. At some point in ones life you have to realize you must do what you love and not worry about how much money you earn to have a happy heart. Moving to New Hampshire allowed Will to enjoy that gift.

I continued to work in Massachusetts at the dental office. I left our house on Tuesday mornings usually by five o'clock. I took a small cooler with snacks and my lunch in it, and an overnight bag for the three nights I'd be away. I stayed at my sister's house in the evenings. I wanted to repay her and her husband for giving me such a generous gift, and helped out as much as I could around the house while I was there.

In the meantime, Will and I were together for three day weekends, and continued our efforts to make the big dreams we had to transform our old farmhouse into a showcase home. Will was a very talented carpenter and I was an eager apprentice, and we did the entire project alone, together. Will was amazingly patient with me and I watched and learned as we went along. I tend to be good with my hands, however, the tools and techniques involved in carpentry were foreign to me.

We not only worked on the house both inside and out, but we had work on the land as well. One of the first things we did was installing fencing around the house so the dogs had a large area to run and play in. We couldn't trust them to run loose and return home due to traits bred into them. We live in the country with neighbors who have livestock, such as cows, goats and chickens. I can only imagine our dogs chasing animals around someone else's farm, and being shot on the spot for their mischievous behavior. We weren't willing to risk that, we love them too much.

We had big plans to make a trail system that would wind through, and also make a loop around our entire property. We no longer had to drive to the mountains for a getaway, we lived there. Groomed trails on our homestead would allow us to enjoy dog sledding at home.

Weather permitting, we took time off from remodeling work and took to the woods. The previous owner started a loop around the land, but never completed it. Will and I navigated our way past roadblocks, around a swamp and a hill, but with some good old fashioned ingenuity we accomplished our goal of making trails. Having them allowed us to walk with our dogs easily each morning before we began our day. We even put some lawn chairs in our woods up on a hill with a clear view of the mountains. It became our place to escape and be one with nature.

It was great to get outdoors, and get some fresh air and exercise instead of working all the time. The dogs were in their glory as well, and if they heard the leashes or dog sledding equipment jingle, they were up and ready before you could even announce you were taking them to walk or sled. We even decided to make signs like the ones in the state forests, and name our trails, brooks and ponds, just for fun.

It was one of those tasks on our very long "to do" list and we never seemed to get around to it.

We completely gutted one room at a time in the old farm house with Will doing most of the heavy work. I mostly retrieved tools and supplies until he could do something without my help. I became quite talented in certain aspects of the building trade though. I mastered the insulation work, placing tile and grout, and painting walls and trim. Will gave me the job of painting trim, since I had the patience and precision for it without getting excess paint where it wasn't supposed to be.

We strategically planned our projects requiring the two of us while I was home on weekends. When I wasn't home Will did other projects alone and I'd be mesmerized by the work he completed in just a few days. I felt so lucky that he could do what he did with his hands and that he was willing. I could see in his eyes and mannerisms that he had done all the work as a gift to me. He was thanking me for working so hard at my job and presenting me with something so impressive in return. All our dreams for the house were unfolding before my very eyes, although our efforts to remodel lasted several years in the end.

During this phase of my life I learned how to handle sheetrock, joint compound, paints, poly, caulk, and insulation, loads of power tools, a tape measure, and all the many details of building a house. I also learned how to read my husband better than ever before. We worked so closely together that I could sense his mood changes. I knew I experienced mood swings when my blood sugar began to fall from neglecting to eat. We always had a big breakfast and then we walked the dogs, and then immediately got to work in order to get as much done as possible. We had so much to do we just put our noses to the grind stone and worked so hard and forgot to eat lunch.

I noticed Will got a little cranky around two or three o'clock in the afternoon when we worked together. Actually, we'd both get a bit testy and begin to take the defensive and bark at each other. I finally realized it was the blood sugar, and I learned to take a deep breath, excuse myself from the work area, and make some coffee and lunch, or put some pastry together. We'd eat lunch which tamed the grouchiness away and we became our charming selves again.

Will and I were aware of each other so intensely, that I noticed him clenching his teeth at times, which usually meant he had something stirring around in his head. That was my queue that he needed to talk, so I gently approached him without too much provocation and offered him my gift to listen. I read the book; *Men Are from Mars, Women Are from Venus*, by John Gray and learned men and women think differently. I always knew when he needed to talk, so I'd put the offer to listen on the table and allow him to go to his "cave" first, unless he was ready to talk at that moment. That book helped me understand the male ego and relationship issues, and the authors suggested technique worked marvelously.

My husband had a deep, sensitive side to him that allowed him to communicate comfortably, which I loved and it kept us connected. He'd talk to me about something that was bothering him and with my God given, natural counseling ability I'd delicately offer him some advice. We'd engage in our typical philosophical discussion and then feel so good afterward. I loved all that Will did for me, and I was glad to be able to repay him by letting him vent while offering him a gentle ear.

In return, Will offered his natural gift to me. Not because I held things in, but because I struggled with bouts of depression. He automatically knew when I needed a lift out of the doldrums, always having the brilliant idea to just get in the car and take me some place. He was quite stealth like and always made it sound like he wanted to go out, but indeed it was to pull me away from my demons. He tenderly nudged me, because being in a depressed mood I wasn't willing to just get in the car and go. Somehow, he knew it was the best medicine for me and he'd have me back to my old, smiling self again, enjoying life and his presence. This frequent effort on my husband's part was performed without my sensing it. What a God send he was. He was my hero and always knew when he had to valiantly ride in on his white horse and rescue me. We were so good for each other; we were both very lucky to have known that kind or love.

In August 2003 I found work closer to home in New Hampshire and left my job in dentistry of fifteen years. It was a difficult day, but it meant I would be home full time and see my husband more often than just three day weekends.

Will had a construction business called Patriot Contracting which was still in its infancy. He did both interior and exterior work on residential and commercial levels. Business was slow, but as long as I was working we would be alright while the company grew and expanded.

I started my new job and felt out of place in the beginning, but eventually, I no longer felt like the new kid on the block. It was an adjustment since I had not changed jobs for such a long time. I was good at what I did, but I constantly felt eyes on me. As I entered a room the chatter immediately stopped and made me feel like the talk was about me.

Within about four months I felt more like a part of the team, but it wouldn't last for long. I don't know exactly what happened to be honest. I just felt like I was walking on eggshells due to being treated poorly by another employee. I'm not sure what I ever did to make her treat me the way she did. Perhaps it was due to her insecurity. We actually had two very heated confrontations at the office and I had never experienced that in my life before. I can usually sense something is about to blow and walk away and let the volcanic lava flow without burning anyone.

After some time went by I realized the chatter around the office wasn't about me, but instead about the woman I was uncomfortable around. I tried to avoid any further conflict, but found it too difficult, and she continued to verbally attack me without warning.

I tried to keep the peace, but it got to the point that I wished I could die. I wanted my car to mysteriously skid off an icy road over a bridge or down an embankment as I drove home from work. That's crazy! I had to get past that idea. God was probably wondering when I was going to smarten up and figure it all out. I finally talked to Will about it all and he intuitively knew the dark force at my office was killing my spirit. Before my body could absorb anymore poison from the toxic environment there, he just lovingly told me to leave the job. I am not a quitter, but Will gave me permission to leave and I felt immediate relief.

I called my old boss of fifteen years and explained how the job wasn't working out. With that he told me my old position was still available. He had hired several dental assistants in the seven months I was gone, but none of them seemed to have the endurance for the job. My sister was willing to let me stay at her house with the same arrangement as before, so I returned to my old job with my husbands blessing.

Quality Time

It was hard on us to be separated during the week. We depended on e-mail and phone calls to each other to stay connected. I kept telling myself, and Will, that I was not doing anything different than a business person who had a job that required traveling. We were secure with each other in our marriage so we didn't have to worry about either of us roaming and being led astray. We still hoped the work arrangement was temporary. Those days of separation made us appreciate our time together even more.

Every Friday I'd have that fluttery feeling of giddiness, even after all our years of marriage, knowing I was going home that day to be with Will. When I arrived, after the three and a half hour drive, he'd meet me in the driveway. We'd embrace and kiss and then he'd help me carry my bags into the house.

The bulk of our home remodeling was basically complete. We were just working on some minor details. We prioritized those tasks and continued to work on them in between excursions. Will worked on some of them while I was at work. By the time the weekend arrived we seemed to be more interested in taking a break from it all. We had developed a routine and spent our time together doing many of the same things depending on the season. We were just happy to be with each other no matter where we were.

Due to finances we learned to be frugal, but could still enjoy the simpler things in life abundantly. We usually took a ride to town to get a cup of coffee and pastry. Sometimes we would venture down the road less traveled and take a scenic drive to nowhere, but end up somewhere. Will was still very talented at navigating his way around and showing me a fabulous day. Along the way we always found places of interest and stopped to poke around to pass time. We both loved antique stores, flea markets and even a good yard sale. Our day trips were always an adventure and created the best quality time one could ask for.

We enjoyed being at home too and we'd find ways to relax without going anywhere. Sometimes we'd just hang out on our deck and wait for nature to present itself. Our dogs played below us in a large fenced in yard while we sat with a magazine or book, and some binoculars sharing small talk with each other.

We always took walks at home on our trails. As we noticed trees, shrubs, and blossoming plants we tried to identify them. I picked bouquets of wildflowers to take home with me as well. If we saw a bird we hadn't seen before we looked it up in our Audubon reference guide when we got home. We had access to the river as well. We put folding lawn chairs in the middle of it during late summer and sat there watching clouds float by as we looked toward the surrounding mountains. It was both tranquil and refreshing. We'd let the dogs take a dip in the water as well.

We had the Discovery Channel in our own back yard. There were anywhere from five to seven hummingbirds that visited us each summer. They were quite comical and extremely entertaining. We strategically placed two feeders and watched them continually bully each other off of them. At times, they chased each other around our yard and would buzz only inches from our heads, sounding like kamikaze pilots in battle.

Among many other bird species, Great Blue Herron frequented our land. They majestically flew overhead close enough that we could actually hear their wings swoosh while in flight, and then they disappeared over some trees and into a pond. Some nights just before dusk we watched deer eat apples from our trees and witnessed moose cross our field and enter a wallow nearby. Almost every summer evening we'd witness a pair of fox in action, wandering through tall grass in search of their next meal. We also noticed the occasional bear walking along the edge of our pasture eating wild strawberries and raspberries. Then they'd mosey into the woods headed toward the river at the far edge of our property.

On clear nights we stood in our yard and witnessed the most spectacular sky. At our house there aren't any street lights to block the pure illumination of the stars overhead. We were like two astronomy geeks captivated by its splendor and were able to identify some of the more popular constellations. One time as we stared into the night sky we saw a green, dot sized light traveling across it. Will mentioned that it could be the space shuttle. His inquisitive mind forced him to look online the next day. The website revealed a scheduled pass over our area, and that he was right. He constantly amazed me.

We enjoyed home cooked meals, abundant nature, reading, and weekly shows on public radio. On a very rare occasion we ate out, but I just preferred to eat my own cooking. I was used to eating healthy and restaurant fare didn't usually fit that bill. We discovered some finer dining establishments and splurged for special occasions such as anniversaries and birthdays.

In the cooler weather of autumn, we planned hikes in the White Mountains. Whether we were on a new trail or a familiar favorite of ours they were always exhilarating. We embraced God's creations in nature while we hiked with our dogs. The only sounds we could hear there were the jingle of dog collar tags, backpacks bouncing up and down on our backs with each step we took, our footsteps on beaten down dirt paths, our rhythmic breathing, and the sound of rushing water in the streams we crossed over. It was a therapeutic spa for us, and I believe that was the main attraction when it came to that activity.

We packed our lunches for the day and carried them with us to eat at the summit while enjoying the view. We even had special backpacks for our dogs and they carried their own water and snacks in them. We'd meet people along the trail curious about our dogs carrying such packs and they would stop us and inquire about them. Our journeys took us away from all the work and helped us to maintain balance in our life.

In winter, we'd resume our dog sledding routine along the trails that Will kept groomed at our house. We'd harness up the dogs, hook up to the gangline, and sled right from our back yard gate.

Some elementary school teachers in the region asked us to do a sort of show and tell for their students with our sled dogs. We agreed, and teamed up together to give the kids an education. We took our four dogs, their harnesses, the gangline and sled for visual aids as we spoke. We also had some video coverage I had taken while sitting in the sled basket one time, while Will was driving it with our dogs. We showed the kids everything we had and gave a good speech on the subject. They soaked up the information we fed them like sponges. Their faces expressed fascination for the sport presented to them up close and personal. We felt fulfilled and pleased to be able to offer such a gift to them.

We lived in one of America's best playgrounds in New Hampshire, and enjoyed the simplicity of it all. We didn't have access to cable in our village and we never missed it. We read books or listened to them in audio format for evening entertainment instead. Eventually, we developed an expansive video library and watched movies in the evening, once the living room remodeling project was completed.

Our peers could not understand how we evaded the strong hold of television. We were drawn to the woods of New Hampshire, and with that we enjoyed the great outdoors. We worked hard each season to maintain our land and walked our dogs daily. We knew about the expression; "all work and no play makes Johnny a dull boy," so we made sure to take time off too.

Intelligence, Integrity And Politics

———————— ⌒⌒⌒ ————————

Will was involved in many volunteer efforts to pass some lonely days while I was in Massachusetts working. In short time he was on many committees, helping with bingo, military veterans, and military youth. He worked to raise funds to send children of parents deployed in Iraq during the war to 4-H summer camps. With all his community efforts he became passionately active in politics as well. As I mentioned before, the man had a brain that remembered anything that entered into it and he always amazed me.

He began a library of biographies about our forefathers, books on more current presidents and politicians, going green on a large scale that would spin most heads, as well as writings on Mother Theresa. He began working on a blog and a newsletter, playing volunteer watchdog of our state and federal politicians. He commended the ones who performed well, and then put others in the "woodshed" for doing something against the best interest of the public who elected them. He was most certainly not afraid to put the truth in writing. He wanted to reach the average citizen and inform them of what was happening in the political arena.

He became so involved and passionate about state politics he decided to run for state representative in 2004. He attempted a grass roots campaign trying to broaden political awareness in local communities of his district. He went door to door to get his name into households, handed out hundreds of business cards, and gave his honest opinion to all he encountered. He even approached people in any diner where we'd be having a cup of coffee, and start up a conversation ending it with an education.

His honesty magnetically attracted people of all walks of life to him to hear what he had to say. He willingly took questions and answered them all to the best of his knowledge. If he didn't have an immediate answer he took their phone number and promised to get the facts and get that information to them. Will was a man of his word and great integrity and always followed through.

The campaign was an interesting adventure to say the least. I'd go with him to some functions, but the itinerary was too hectic for me. I couldn't keep up with it all with my work schedule. He won many hearts and made some enemies along the trail. He honestly answered anything asked of him and wasn't bashful about giving his two cents worth, which would be his demise at times. He was frustrated with the fact that people were so uneducated and unwilling to learn the truth about their elected officials. Will did not win the race that year, but he did do pretty well in the vote count considering he was an unknown. He was proud of that accomplishment, dusted himself off and prepared to run again in two years.

With that campaign effort Will met and supported many politicians. Through that, we received a surprise invitation to the upcoming Governors Inaugural Ball in February 2005. We were excited and discussed the prospects of attending, but weren't sure we wanted to spend the money. We were living on one income at the time. After a few days, the thought of attending the ball began to sink in and we reconsidered going to the event. We decided it may be the only time we got to do something like that so we returned the RSVP with a check.

I was so excited, but I didn't have anything appropriate to wear to such an occasion. I needed a gown. While I was working in Massachusetts I decided to take a stroll through the Lord and Taylor department store at the mall. I knew they had sales with deeply, slashed prices on formal attire after New Years Eve by past experience. I was determined I could find something without spending a fortune there.

The sale rack had amazing dresses with discounted price tags to match, but nothing was my size. I thought of buying something too big and having it altered. I didn't have time for that; the ball was in about two weeks. I wandered around and browsed the evening gown department a while longer. I had difficulty deciding on anything because of sticker shock. I struggled with the thought of spending too much money on a dress I may never wear again. I was not used to paying full price for much of anything other than groceries.

My gut instinct pushed me to go ahead and just select a few gowns, take them to the dressing room without looking at the tag, try them on, and then decide. With that strategy, if I loved it I wouldn't care so much about the price. I followed through with my plan, gathered several gowns, tried them on and fell in love with one. I swallowed, took a deep, cleansing breath, and looked at the tag. It was actually marked less than I expected. I knew Will would love the dress too, and if he were with me he'd persuade me to buy it.

I had never bought a gown so elegant before other than my wedding dress, and I was floating happily as if I was preparing for the prom. The dress was perfect for the black tie event. It was black and strapless, which was very daring for me. The skirt portion was like that of a ballet dancer, but long to my ankle with layers upon layers of black tulle with rhinestones affixed sporadically over it. The top portion matched, but with less layers of tulle folded in creases across the bodice. The dress sparkled as the light hit it and I felt like Cinderella going to the ball. Fortunately, I already had several jewelry pieces to embellish the outfit with, as well as a pair of shiny, black, patent leather pumps that all went perfectly with it.

When I tried the dress on to show Will, he could not believe his eyes. He had an incredible way of speaking to me with his eyes. I could just see him falling in love all over again, if that was possible, with me in his sights. We went to his closet and selected the perfect suit, shirt, and tie, to wear to the ball and we made a very handsome couple that evening. After so many years of marriage, I was finally comfortable with dressing up and being stunning.

Will and I were elegantly dressed for the party and off we went for the one hour drive to get there. We hired Will's nephew to watch our four dogs, instructed him how to operate the wood stove, (our only source of heat) and prepared a list of emergency phone numbers for him.

Special occasions such as the ball sparked deep, loving feelings we had for each other, and took us into our romantic, imaginary world. Our profound love for one another was oozing out of us that night. I could feel it inside my veins running through my body and it made me feel like I was sparkling. I loved Will with all my heart, but on those special evenings it was magnified. I think it was because I was out with my knight in shining armor, and I could honorably flaunt him just like he liked to display me to the world.

The evening was romantic and filled with the thrill of life on the flip side of the coin we weren't accustomed to. There was a cocktail hour prior to the party and we mingled with the other guests until we were all invited to go to the dining area. It was a magnificent ball room, intricately decorated for the holiday season, with white linens and chandeliers grand enough for the president and first lady. The meal was exquisite and was served by wait staff wearing crisp uniforms and white gloves.

A band took the stage and began to rock the house with their 1970's funk and rock genre. They were composed of several horns, with guitars, drums, and a keyboard, a male lead vocalist with three female backup singers. They were not only fun to listen to, but entertaining as well. We knew two of the members which made watching them perform more fun. Will and I danced some and then we did what he liked to call "work the room." He needed to stay in the political loop for his plans to campaign again in two years.

That night, I met the governor and his wife, as well as many other people in the world of politics that I had only heard about through Will's conversations with me. All the introductions reminded me of my first family gatherings with Will way back when. I met so many people, shook so many hands, and heard so many names my head was spinning. I knew I wouldn't remember the overwhelming amount of information, but nonetheless, I smiled and expressed my gratitude for meeting them all. I excelled in the art of schmoozing, I would have made a great politicians wife.

The evening wound down and we decided to take the early out, since we knew we had a bit of a trek to travel home, and it was snowing. As we picked up our coats, I took a deep breath to absorb the richness of the evening one last time. It was midnight and Cinderella was about to lose her glass slipper.

We drove home in a serious snow storm with intense caution at about twenty-five miles per hour. I was feeling on top of the world even with the stress of driving home in bad conditions, refusing to wake up from my dream. I knew in my mind I'd store the memories from that gala event for many years to come, especially since I was with Will, the love of my life. Will and I reflected on and savored the memories imprinted in our minds from the ball for weeks to come.

My husband continued his efforts in politics and campaigned again for an elected position in New Hampshire state government. While still in the loop we received an invitation to another Governor's Inaugural Ball in February 2007. We attended the party and felt the same enchantment as the first one.

Even though we loved the simplicity in our life we were grateful to have the opportunity to experience such upscale parties. I can't really explain why the desire to do such things was there, but it somehow felt rewarding for the hard work we did.

Our Simple Little Life

It was winter and life had resumed to what we called normal. We lived in the northern tier of New Hampshire, and that always meant plenty of snow and cold sometimes subzero temperatures. Between careers and all the snow removal we faced almost daily, we stayed busy, but still somehow managed to find time to escape. Will and I never really suffered from cabin fever because we enjoyed the outdoors year round.

In winter we just wore extra layers and did some light dog sledding or snow shoeing. In order to use the trails on our land we had to groom them. We didn't own a snowmobile, but we did have a four-wheeler. However, it didn't make the trails wide enough without dragging something behind it. We didn't have an implement for the job, so I came up with the idea of letting Will pull me behind the four-wheeler on a child's plastic sled. We attached the sled with something similar to water skiing rope, I climbed on, and we went zooming around the trail system. After a couple of wipeouts I mastered my mount on the sled. I sat up on my knees making it possible not only to steer better, but also stay on the sled. The successful experiment woke my child within from winter hibernation and it was truly exhilarating.

When we needed a dose of civilization we'd load the dogs into the truck and head to Littleton, "the big city", Will used to call it, which was about forty minutes away from our house. We'd usually poke into the little stores downtown and especially the local book store.

I enjoyed a good book, but Will was constantly reading. I don't think I ever saw anyone read as much as he did. He was like a professor and his brain absorbed everything like a sponge. It soaked up information taken from the books and gave him tremendous knowledge on many subjects. I called him *Mr. Encyclopedia* because he had so much stored in that pretty little head of his. He was able to quote historical information with very little effort, he was brilliant. We also discovered that our local libraries had used book sales and we accumulated hundreds of books, and ended up with an incredible library of our own.

Inevitably, while we were still in town we'd include a stop at Dunkin Donuts for a donut and coffee, Will loved his coffee, or at McDonalds for a quick bite. Will always ordered the same meal there; fillet-o-fish, quarter-pounder with fries, and two apple pies for a dollar, we'd share the pies. As I mentioned before, he was a witty fellow and when he ordered the apple pies he used to make me laugh. He'd say, "Two apple pies for a daaaaallerrrr," stretching out the word dollar at the drive up window, sounding much like Dustin Hoffman's character in the movie *Rain Man*. He wasn't poking fun by any means. He just liked to be different and perhaps give a little joy to someone's life; I think especially mine, which he did unknowingly in hundreds of little ways. I think that may have been his purpose in life; trying to make people happy, because he was so good at it.

Spring was usually short. Either winter lingered or summer came early, and we spent most of it preparing for summer duties. Either way we endured what the locals call mud season. We equipped ourselves with rubber dairy boots from a local Agway store. They went up almost to our knees and kept us clean and dry. Those boots were such a simple accessory, but aided us in so many ways. We not only wore them for chores, but to walk the dogs along our trails as well.

We had a vegetable garden, several acres of grass to keep cut, and wood to gather by June to split for winter heating. Once the wood was dry we had to haul it to the shed near the house and stack it for easy access. Our trails required annual maintenance as well. That mostly involved clipping out saplings and dangling branches brought down by winter winds. After that mowing was the only upkeep required.

Will maneuvered the tractor and had a habit of inadvertently cutting down the wild, low-bush blueberries. They were less than a foot tall and grew in the middle of the hay field. To avoid the mishap I staked the section off during mowing season. I picked berries during late summer and canned jam, made pies, and then froze some for future recipes and treats. We didn't have access to water outside the house, so we also set up rain barrels under the roof gutters. We filled watering cans to irrigate the vegetables and our patch of high bush blueberries. The chores continued through summer and autumn, we had a routine and always had something to do on the homestead.

It sounds like a hard life, but Will and I enjoyed the work, it was therapeutic somehow and we felt productive. We made sure that with all our efforts we would reap rewards though. Our compensation was designated weekends away from chore duties.

We thoroughly enjoyed the simple, little life that we had dreamed of living for many years. We jumped several hurdles and hit many brick walls achieving our goal, but once we did we acquired joy and peace with it. Our friends and family from Massachusetts weren't quite sure they understood the attraction. I think they were still being beckoned by the haunting call of urban living, filled with malls, traffic and too many people. The longer we were away from that hectic environment the harder it was for us to survive visits there. When we drove home from any trips we took south, we noticed a special phenomenon. Upon entering Franconia Notch we felt a sense of calmness in our souls, it was like entering Shangri-La.

Even though life seemed so simple to those on the outside it was very fulfilling to us. We hadn't become Quakers, but we enjoyed a simpler lifestyle than our city friends. We had running water, electricity, and all the modern conveniences of society; we just found a new way of life, our life. It felt like it was pre-planned through the Universe for us, and we had reached our destiny. We had everything we needed, loved each other more than the air we breathed, and we were completely satisfied.

We had experienced the world of culture and were still able to catch a glimpse of the ritzy lifestyle when indeed we wanted to. We engaged in it for anniversaries and birthdays or other special occasions. Anytime we made plans for an extravagant date, we'd include all the whistles and bells to make them even more memorable, since they were infrequent. We enjoyed the planning stages of it, and also gave our palettes the taste they sporadically craved and were then content. We appreciated the reward and then became grounded again and went back to our uncluttered, simplistic life.

It didn't take special occasions for us to sense the rewards I describe; we were blessed to notice that just our life together itself offered such exuberance. Words alone cannot define our love in its complete truth. We intuitively knew we were meant to be together. I think our souls took over and allowed us to love each other and the life we created together immensely, no matter how difficult things could be at times.

Friends have told me our love was uncommon, only known by a rare few. Others have pointed out that they didn't even know we were married at all because we seemed like best friends. I knew we had something sacred and special, but did not realize the magnitude of it witnessed by others. I was grateful for the compliments.

Holiday Wonderment And Solitude

———— ⟨⟨⟩⟩ ————

The holiday season was approaching and just like every other year we planned a full dinner and celebration. We had the traditional turkey on Thanksgiving and for Christmas we had ham and a duck with all the courses including dessert. It was just like the early days of cabin holiday retreats except we used the formal china.

We extended the invitation to our "flat-lander" relatives, but they always declined our offer. We were used to being alone and decided to celebrate in complete solitude. It was already our routine. We really didn't mind that it was just the two of us and our dogs at all. One year we did have the pleasure of hosting a traditional Thanksgiving with family at our house. Will's brother, his wife, his two children, and their dog joined us in 2004.

The weather that year was peculiar, it actually snowed Thanksgiving morning. After we ate our meal and the kitchen was cleaned up, we went outside to play in the snow. We let our child like spirits guide us and built a giant snow man about six or seven feet tall. We dressed him up with a scarf and an heirloom, colorful, striped Polaroid hat. Will's traditional Christmas hat he had since childhood. We used charcoal for his eyes and smile, and then a big carrot for his nose. He was so attractive I gathered everyone and took photos using my camera and a tripod.

I got a perfect snapshot for our Christmas card of me and Will, and our four Siberian huskies in front of the snowman. Each year we took "family" photos of ourselves and our dogs and mailed them to family and friends. I also composed an annual letter. It gave a rundown on what happened in our lives that year and I enclosed it with our card. I tried to abandon that tradition once, but quickly started it up again due to all the cries for an encore. I just hadn't realized people looked so forward to receiving it.

Over the years we became quite accustomed to our holidays alone. However, it did upset Will at times that no one ever accepted our invitations. I made it my job to offer him soothing words to help him realize it was their choice not to come, and that they didn't know what they were missing. I reminded him that we almost moved to Montana, and if we had we would have never seen family.

A phrase I use all the time is, "It's all about choices." When you implement that into your daily thinking, it is surprising to discover how many choices we actually do make, and how they control the outcome of our day or life. There's that philosophical side of me again.

Christmas was due to arrive. Once again we extended the invitation to lure family to spend it with us, but no one took the bait. We'd be alone so we planned our menu accordingly, just as we had every other year. To do our gift shopping, we usually took a day trip to make our purchases, get a coffee, and enjoy each other and the fun the season offered. We did a little shopping online, but preferred the old fashioned way of going out to do it.

I always thought about my gifts ahead of time and prepared a shopping list. I was inspired by the inundation of catalogs that arrived in the mail that time of year. I'd browse through them for ideas while lounging at home sharing homemade cappuccino's with Will.

I listened carefully throughout the year and got many ideas that way. I could usually surprise my recipient by giving them just the item they wished for. They, including my husband, wondered how I knew. I'd look at them and smile in reply and then tell them I just heard their wish in passing. At that moment I also got great joy out of my accomplishment.

Christmas Eve arrived and Will was ready to push the rituals up a few hours each year so we could open gifts. He justified his ideas by insisting Christmas Eve was Christmas Eve no matter what time of day it was, and logically speaking he was right. I was always the one to spoil the fun and persuade him to wait until evening though. With some debate I convinced him we should wait until after our private, little holiday meal to kick off the celebration. I know he was only teasing me, but every year we played the same game with each other.

Each year we started the celebratory ritual off with cheese and crackers, and assorted dips while dinner was cooking. I made spaghetti topped with melted butter and olive oil, some garlic and a little bit of grated parmesan cheese, and some home made bread sticks. If I couldn't get lobsters we had shrimp cocktail. It wasn't the grand meal his family put together each year down in Massachusetts, but it was special for us, we weren't hard to please. We had taken heed to Henry David Thoreau's wise words; we simplified and went to the woods.

As with every Christmas Eve since I've known Will, he became the director for gift organization and delivery. After all our years together we still opened one at a time. It made me happy to watch Will open his and see the surprise or joy on his face afterward. His technique was like a mini parade for gift giving. After all the thought and effort that went into the selection of them it should be special.

Every year we gave each other a predictable gift of a television series on DVD that was a personal favorite. Mine was Will and Grace and Will loved Cheers. After we opened everything and it quieted down we usually began to watch one of the videos. At the same time we always indulged in a slice of home made pie with fresh whipped cream on it too.

On Christmas day I'd create a magnificent meal large enough to feed the entire neighborhood. Not intentionally, but it gave us abundant, delicious left-over food to pick on later. I enjoyed cooking as long as I knew what I wanted to make and had a menu planned, so it was all very easy. It was my gift to Will. I always did my best to make it special and I'd add a little love from my heart in the process. An Italian cook on PBS once said that was how she prepared her meals and I thought it was a great idea. Will was impressed by my creativity in the kitchen and he always expressed that as well as his gratitude to me. Our meal was fully satisfying both to the taste buds and to the soul.

The next holiday was New Years Eve, but we didn't usually do too much for it. We had grown out of our partying phase and preferred to stay home. We didn't want to be out among the crowds getting completely inebriated to a sickening level. We either had Chinese Food take-out or a small home cooked meal and watched videos instead. We didn't have cable or any television reception, so we didn't even have a lazy night watching the ball drop at midnight in Times Square in New York City. Nonetheless, we always enjoyed our night in.

In 2008 we did do something quite exciting for the holiday though. I noticed a newspaper advertisement regarding a New Years Eve celebration on a grand scale at a local Hotel Resort called the Mountain View Grand. We decided at Christmastime to reserve tickets for the party in lieu of buying expensive gifts. It was the first time we went to an organized party to ring in the New Year since we had known each other. We attended it dressed in tuxedo and gown, enjoyed a five-star meal, and we danced to live music. We were so thrilled we splurged. We had such a fabulous time that night that we decided to go again the following year, making it our new tradition.

New Years Eve meant another wedding anniversary was just around the corner. Will and I always discussed plans to celebrate and usually tried to keep them low key. We still celebrated the one in May and felt it was our true anniversary even though we eloped before it. It was so cold in January and we didn't feel like going out in bad weather. Instead, we usually indulged in a special meal and dessert at home.

Neither one of us drank alcohol so we'd have a toast with sparkling, white grape juice. I bought some non-alcoholic wine once, but it turned out to be a bad idea. It tasted so real that Will was concerned after being sober for so many years he could be tempted to drink again. I was glad he was honest with me. I told him it was perfectly fine and I never purchased it again. I didn't want anything around that could lure him into the darkness again. We had already been down that path and survived once. Like I said, our partying days were over anyway and we found other ways to have fun without self medicating with booze first.

We always loved having something to celebrate so we continued to include the anniversary of our elopement every year.

The Little Things

———— ✍ ————

I was always reading books trying to find ideas to make married life fun. Years ago I read one called; *1001 Ways to be Romantic*, by Gregory J.P. Godek. In it he has a suggestion of going out as a couple on a shopping spree on a budget. Will and I actually did that a few times. With twenty dollars in our pockets, we divided up and searched for as many trinket gifts we could find. We not only enjoyed the challenge, but had a lot of fun at the same time. We experienced joy seeking the treasures, giving them, and then sharing laughter upon opening them. Will's gifts to me usually reflected his good sense of humor and he was so proud of his compilations.

Over the years our married life became rich with many sentimental gestures toward each other. Some days I'd just stick a love note on the seat of Will's truck for him to find when he left the house. Other times I'd leave his favorite candy bar in the microwave oven for him to discover the next morning as he prepared his breakfast. I left hand written love notes on the bathroom mirror in red lipstick, sealed with a kiss too. Will returned the spontaneous surprises for me as well and I always felt the love emanating from them. I believe they helped keep the spark in our marriage higher than a mere flicker.

We had a chalkboard in the kitchen. At first I only used it to write the dinner menu for the day or the "to do" list items on it. Later, I began to write little love notes to Will on it. With that he began to copy, and returned the treat. I'd usually write a loving message on it to Will on Tuesday morning as I left for Massachusetts to go to work. When I returned on Friday I'd find a new one on the board from Will to me. I felt so honored with each sweet greeting. It made me realize he was thinking about me when I was gone.

The little things really do go a long way and that is why I feel like we had everything. We had each other and all the little gem gestures that came so naturally. They somehow confirmed how much we loved each other because we expressed it constantly without having to be asked. Sometimes, "I love you" seems to get worn out, as if it is said by force of habit. When the little offerings that cost absolutely nothing are added into the equation, love is grand.

Each year unfolded like every other one previous to it. We enjoyed our life, love, and amazing friendship together in the little village where we lived. We had anonymity when we wanted it, or we could be known by many as we walked through town. We continued to strive toward goals both together and individually, but we knew where to draw the line of independence. Just like a garden requires water to keep it alive, we had to nurture our marriage to keep the flame glowing. Even with all the maintenance requirements of our homestead, our jobs, and Will's life in politics and community efforts, we somehow managed to do that.

We spent a lot of time working on our land getting sweaty and dirty. It felt good to see things materialize into reality from all our efforts. We had our seasonal routines and our favorite pastimes. We continued to make time to play and it worked for us.

We truly lived a diversified life, grimy one day and in a tuxedo and gown another. We never had fortunes, but felt we had everything we needed. We enjoyed the true gift of camaraderie with our best friend, each other, in the unity of marriage throughout our life together.

Pride And Sweetness

———— ⌁ ————

In February 2008, I left my job in Massachusetts to be at home in New Hampshire full time. Will landed the job with the transformer company and started on March 1st. The transition of being home and out of work sort of made me crazy. I always had to be doing something. I had worked full time ever since I graduated from high school. Within about six weeks I found a job in an optical center. I enjoyed the interaction with patients again.

I was working retail hours and they were interfering with my responsibilities of my dogs. I ended up leaving my job after only three months. Will was relieved and told me he never wanted me to work in the first place. He was making enough money for us to live on and then some.

Our roles had reversed. Will had been looking for work for months. Will was working out of town all week and now I was at home taking care of our dogs and the property requirements. We never really thought about it, but now he was away like I had been before. With that, things were the same as far as our weekends together being so important. We continued to cherish that time together puttering around just the two of us. It was great.

I missed him during the week and was lonely with all the down time. We continued the routine of communicating through modern technology just as we had while I was working in Massachusetts. Will was elated to finally be the bread winner in our household. He felt he owed it to me somehow. I never looked at my working that way though.

He was so cute. Each Friday when he came home he brought me fresh cut flowers. On occasion he would surprise me with a t-shirt from a state he worked in. He didn't have money to spend that way for such a long time and it made him feel good to do it now. I never expected him to adorn me with gifts or anything. I was content with what I had. All I needed was for him to come home and be by my side as my partner in life. I let him enjoy his new financial status and allowed him to treat me like his queen. It made him so happy and I could see the boyish glow about him whenever he got home and surprised me with something.

He was in New York near Niagara Falls in May. He was told he should go see the natural wonder while he was so close. He decided he would wait and take me there so we could enjoy its magnificence together. It was the week of our 18th wedding anniversary and we talked on the phone as usual. He confessed that he had gone to a mall to pass some time and found me a gift. We had already discussed not doing gifts and just going out to dinner at an upscale restaurant to celebrate. He apologized and told me he just couldn't resist.

Now I knew he had a gift and I felt I had to reciprocate. I only had a couple of days. I scrambled because in order to find something I thought would be perfect, it meant I had to travel. In the past, Will had asked me to give him a photo of myself to take along with him while he worked. He told me he wanted it so he could display it in his hotel room. He said it would make him feel closer to me when he was so far away.

I decided a self portrait would be my grand gift to my husband. I had recently taken a photography course and had some studio equipment at my access. I picked the perfect outfit and put on some makeup and prepared for the shoot. I set everything up and took about fifty pictures using a tripod. It's not an easy task to line up a camera, focus it on a blank space, and then get into the frame in time for the shutter to open and capture an image. I finally felt like I accomplished what I was after. I downloaded the images to a computer disc and decided which

218

picture to process.   The next day I rushed to have my prize portrait printed and inserted it into a card for Will.

He came home on Friday night and due to his excitement couldn't keep the gift he bought concealed. He asked me if I wanted to open it then, but our anniversary wasn't until the next day. I agreed we could go ahead and exchange our gifts instead of waiting until tomorrow. He surprised me with a peridot ring, my birthstone. I didn't feel worthy of it and thought it was too expensive. I tried to accept the gift gracefully and kept my thoughts to myself. My husband was so proud of himself and his romantic abilities, and I didn't want to extinguish his joy. I felt grateful and put it on my finger.

I handed him his card. I wasn't sure my gift was quite as exquisite. He opened it and fell in love with it immediately. He was so glad I actually gave him a photo like that and asked me where I had it taken. I told him it was a self portrait and explained how I did it. I could have never had a stranger take pictures of me dressed so provocatively. He hugged me tightly, almost squeezing me with excitement and gratitude for the trinket gift I just gave to him.

I did tell him he couldn't show it to anyone I knew. I was embarrassed because it was a bit on the revealing side. He promised me he wouldn't. Then he proudly put it into a frame and left it out so he could look at it anytime he wanted.

He took it with him while he worked and did set it out on a table in his hotel room. He saw his sister a few days later and told him that I had given him the best gift he had ever gotten in his entire life. She asked what it was and he told her what I had given him. She asked if she could see it. He explained our promise and then called me to see if I would be okay with him sharing it with her.

Without much thought I told him no. He told me I could e-mail it to her later if I changed my mind. I told him I wouldn't do that either. I thought it could get passed on too easily and wondered where it would end up. He asked me again in the future and I finally said yes. As time went by the novelty wore off and no one brought it up, so he never ended up showing anyone after all.

He was so proud of his gift that we had it transferred to a painting canvas and boldly framed. I was a bit shy being with him as the framing professionals looked at it. I could only imagine what was going through their minds. I'm so conservative and wasn't enjoying that side of me being seen publicly. We placed our order and waited for the call to come pick it up when it was ready. I picked it up alone in September. Will never saw his prize.

I had my birthday in August and Will pulled off a grand surprise. I could tell he was very proud of himself too. Just like every Friday night, he pulled into the driveway with a loaded van. I went out and greeted him as he did for me for so many years. We'd hug and kiss and then bring his bags into the house. I was taking something upstairs and he called up to me from the kitchen. He asked me what I was doing. I told him, and then he asked me to come downstairs for a minute.

I went down and the kitchen lights were off. He had yet another surprise for the woman he loved so deeply. He had stopped on his way home near Boston and picked up a key lime dessert from the Cheesecake Factory. He had already inserted candles and lit them and I saw them glowing as I entered the room. I felt like a giddy child with that grand gesture. He presented it to me as he waved his hand over it like a spokes model selling something on an infomercial. I blew out the candles and then hugged him, and he held me like he did so well. He told me the surprise wasn't over. He handed me some flowers and a gift bag. In it were my favorite Lindt Truffles and some t-shirts from his travels. I was overjoyed by his efforts and felt that sparkle about myself that only Will could generate.

My actual birthday was the following day. We had already planned on going to North Conway to do our favorite things. We went for a Starbucks coffee fix and we strolled through the outlet stores. We also ventured to the village center and browsed through the shops there. We always had a fabulous time together wandering around and holding hands. My birthday was no different. He knew how to make me feel special and make me realize he cherished me.

We had recently received an invitation to Will's nieces wedding taking place on August 23rd. It required a trip to the Boston area and we had three large dogs that could not travel in the heat of summer. Will was going to attend the wedding alone. As time to respond to the invitation approached, I became eager to find a way to join him. I asked my mother if she would once again dog sit for us. She said she would be happy to. I planned to go pick her up and bring her to my house so she wouldn't have to make the three hour drive alone. The plans and the RSVP were all set.

The wedding was held outdoors in a gazebo facing the ocean at a yacht club near Boston. The day was perfect and sunny for such an event. A reception followed the ceremony immediately on the premises. Will and I enjoyed each others company immensely as we always had.

That day we saw family members we hadn't seen as a couple for close to ten years. Someone actually approached us during the reception and asked how long we had been married. Will told him, eighteen and three quarter years, being the funny man he was. The man walked away and we assumed that inquiry was because he thought we had divorced. We could understand the curiosity since we had not been seen together at family gatherings for so many years. We chuckled to ourselves, thinking if they only knew.

The wedding day, the bride and groom, and bridal party were all beautiful. Will and I had a wonderful time visiting with extended family members. At one point I sat and visited with Will's grandmother. We had gotten close over the years and I love her like my very own blood relative. I invited her to dance with her grandson, my husband Will, but she declined. She said she was too weak and didn't think she could stand up for a dance. She was in her early eighties. I told her Will was strong and tall, and could hold her up for a short dance.

I then told her the story about how I danced with Will's father at his brothers wedding twenty years ago, and how he did not live to see Will and my wedding. I begged her and told her she didn't know when she'd get the opportunity again. For some reason I really thought she needed to dance with him. I went to Will and told him about my request and that perhaps he ought to go ask her to dance. He did better than that. He went to the band and requested a song, and when they played it, he took his grandmother out onto the dance floor and had that dance. I had my camera so I snapped a couple of pictures for the photo albums, which ended up being priceless.

We had to drive back home that same day and began watching the clock, thinking about leaving soon. One of Will's nephews was engaged in a military drill weekend with the Army National Guard. He didn't attend the wedding, but told Will he would most likely be there later in the day. Just as we began to make our way around the room to say our goodbyes Will's nephew entered the hall. Our plans changed immediately so we could mingle more and visit with him.

Will gave him a couple of bucks so he could buy a drink at the cash bar. He was still dressed in his military uniform, and as he ordered his drink someone insisted on paying for it, in recognition of his military duty. It made Will so proud to see a civilian step up to the plate and honor his nephew, a soldier. It was *the icing on the cake* so to speak for Will that day.

The clock was ticking away and we soon decided to venture off. First we changed into some comfortable clothing for our long drive back to New Hampshire. During the trip home we talked about how we were so happy we got to go to the wedding together after all. We felt lucky that we saw so many of his relatives at that gathering, figuring it would be another ten years before we'd see them together as a couple again.

We returned home around nine o'clock in the evening. The dogs were excited to see us and my mother told me they behaved for her. We were tired from the hot sun, the day's events, and the eight hours of driving involved in getting to Massachusetts and back. We rested and watched something on a DVD, and then retired early for the evening.

The next morning, Will and I took our truck to the mechanic and dropped it off for a brake job. Afterward, I took my mother home via the same route Will and I traveled just the day before. I planned to return home the same day. I wanted to spend time with Will before he had to go to work on Monday.

I arrived home to an eager lover and a sweet note left on our kitchen chalkboard that read, "Welcome home my love of my life, who I would marry 10 times over again." I felt the enchanted message vibrate into my heart as I read it.

That evening we enjoyed dinner together just as we did any other Sunday, not knowing it would be our last. As always Will thanked me for the meal and told me it was delicious. Monday came and Will loaded up his van for the work week that morning. He already had his schedule, and packed clothing and supplies accordingly. On his way to work he took me to the repair shop and we waited together to pick up our truck. We were flooded with emotions from recent events over the past few weeks.

Hind sight is always twenty-twenty and I wish now that I had asked him to insist on taking the week off from work. He put in the request. It wasn't his fault they forgot about it and scheduled him to work anyway. I have always told myself our departure time from this life is predestined, like punching the time clock at the end of the day at work. But now, I somehow wanted to think my husband would still be here had he stayed home as we planned.

The day he was killed I looked at the message he wrote to me on the chalkboard and I cried. I remembered how I almost washed it clear that very morning. I was so glad I hadn't done so. It's his final loving gesture and somehow validates his love for me. Something I need so badly now. This tragedy seems to keep the gears in my mind moving in search of a better ending.

That summer we went on one our best vacations ever, to Boston. We had the taste of vacationing in our mouths and wanted more. We began planning a trip to Bar Harbor, Maine for September that same year. We figured the crowds would be down then, and we could take walks with our dogs in cooler weather. Unfortunately, that trip never took place. Will didn't live long enough for it to happen.

Our wedding day, May 26, 1990, at the Hartwell House, Lexington,
Massachusetts.

Waiting for the limo after our wedding reception with Will's grandfather.

New York City, outside the Statue of Liberty, August 1988.

Our names carved in the sand at a secluded beach at Brewers Bay,
Tortolla, on our honeymoon.

Me and Ivan, my rock during prison years.

Last "family" photo with Ivan, August 2006, used in our Christmas
card that same year.

Hiking Lincoln Woods Trail along Kancamagus Highway, Lincoln, New Hampshire, autumn 2007.

Inaugural Ball for Governor Lynch, February 2007, at the Mount Washington Hotel, New Hampshire.

Spending the Economic Stimulus Package money on our final
vacation. Boston Public Gardens, August 2008.

At Thunder Hole, Acadia National Park, Mount Desert Island,
Maine, August 26, 2009.

Part Three

Life As I Knew It Is Gone

Since the discovery of my husband's death and the rituals and technicalities that followed, I am truly lost. I feel as if I am a stranger in a foreign country unfamiliar with the language and culture. My reason for living no longer exists. Life seems meaningless without Will and I am without purpose as I muddle along now. I question my strength to do this. I sit and cry drifting in sorrow never getting to know what could've been. A thought hits me, making me realize that I don't get to write the ending to my life's script, nor do I get to choose if or when to become a widow.

At times I think about how my husband would feel if he were the one left behind without me. I think God chose the right ending by taking Will first. I am not certain he could've endured this painful journey without reverting back to drinking, or making an attempt to end his life and join me. I have contemplated both, in order to ease or end my suffering. I feel better somehow thinking about the order in which things occurred in this situation are for the best. I hate being the one still here, but I truly wouldn't wish this pain on anyone.

The ashes Will requested to be released along the trails of our land were set free on his birthday in November, my "first" holiday since his death. As I walked the entire loop of our property I talked to Will and sprinkled some with each step I took. I reminisced in the memory of all the walks we took together there. I also drove our antique tractor, his

233

favorite toy, around our pasture and let the rest of them symbolically fly freely from my hand as I held it open up toward the sky. I was letting him go. Afterward, I made a German chocolate cake in his honor and wished him a happy birthday, and then ate cake without him. I don't know what compelled me to perform such painful rituals. Somehow they made me feel closer to the man I loved for so many years and still do with all my heart.

Christmas came and went with very little joy or appreciation of its grand meaning. I did manage to put up our Christmas tree, but mostly in honor of him. He loved the tree and I could really live without it. I felt if he was watching it would sadden him if I ignored the holiday. I cried as I hung the ornaments because we did it together, and we always talked about the origin of some of them. The anticipation of the holiday's arrival gave me such angst. I just wanted to fall asleep and never wake up again. I ended up getting so sick with bronchitis that it actually allowed it to slip past as if it never arrived. I felt good that it had gone.

On a good day while lost in my merry thoughts of the past the phone rings, and on occasion I rush to answer it thinking the caller is going to be Will. He called me several times a day while he was on the road just for small talk. When my husband was alive I was always ecstatic when the phone rang, thinking it could be him. Sometimes when I go out to do errands or whatever, upon my return home I see his truck in our driveway. For an instant I forget Will is gone and I get a rush of excitement that he got home before I did. I can't wait to go into our house to see him. That was my typical response while he was living. Part of me is still in denial mode and would love to wake up from my ongoing nightmare. I want to find him waiting for me in our house.

I pray to God as I cry, and ask Him what I ever did to deserve this. I have encountered many painful trials in my lifetime and this certainly is the absolute worst for me. I plead with God to take me home to be with Will in Heaven, but I don't hear an answer, nor do I get my wish. God answers in His own mysterious way blind to me for now.

Some days I can no longer keep the genie pent up in the bottle, and when the cork is released I go into a meltdown. One day about five months into this I was walking my dogs in the snow and collapsed from the pain in my heart. I was lying on my back on the snowy trail and cried uncontrollably. I screamed out to God, "Why did you take him from me?" I truly hope someday after this gut wrenching pain subsides, I finally get an answer.

I need Will to be here so badly to help me through my despair. He was always there for me before. He knew just how to pull me out of my glum depression periods I would sink into. I leaned on him for that because I felt safe with him and he allowed me to shut down. Most people who know me have never seen me in that dark place before. I was always the strong one. I had the ability to pull up the boot straps and do what had to be done. This time the darkness surrounding me is of a much larger magnitude and I feel helpless at times. I talk to him through my tears in hopes that he can hear me and somehow make everything okay now. I get stuck thinking I will never be alright or better, since there isn't anything that can bring him back to life. I feel as if half of me has died and is buried with him.

I lost twenty six pounds of weight from my already slender frame during the first few weeks of mourning. I've lost the delight in cooking or baking and presenting it. There is no voice coming from a smiling face telling me thank you for the meal or dessert and how yummy it was. I perform simple tasks each day that I performed out of necessity all along, but received joy doing them. I not only did them for myself, I did them for Will. Now when I do something as simple as make our bed it seems so unimportant. I catch myself carefully adjusting the blankets so there are equal amounts to keep each of us warm at night. The list of tasks is endless that once made me happy by doing for another and now find it a challenge to do for just myself.

I did all the manual chores normally in Will's portfolio around the homestead this year. Things I had never done before. I had to winterize the house for the brutally cold and snowy winters we endure. I split and stacked firewood for our only source of winter heat. I plowed and shoveled snow, cleared it off the roof, and took our dogs on their daily walks through our woods wearing snow shoes. I am not afraid of hard work and actually most of the time it is my friend. Working to sheer exhaustion has been my drug. It seemed as if the sadness was being released in the form of sweat coming out of every pore in my body, rather than in tears. I can only compare it to what joggers experience when they run and their stress melts away.

I have my normal appetite back, but with all the manual labor I have taken on I have only gained four pounds. I look at my thin body in the mirror and I see the changes it has made. It appears less frail, revealing an almost masculine muscle tone now. I have massive biceps and no longer have "lunch lady arms," and joke about being Mrs. Universe within my circle of friends. I laugh to myself and think if Will could see me now he would make an endearing remark about my new physique. He always told me how beautiful I was and that he loved my body, (one I didn't like so much) trying to stroke my self image so that I wouldn't be so inhibited.

I find that I am not willing to do anything extravagant without Will now. I had opportunities in the early months of his death to attend formal parties, but could not make myself go. I felt somehow in my heart it would be dishonorable to my husband. I suppose I'm not ready to accept that he is gone from this world even though I feel so alone in it now.

I still live my life in Will's honor even though he is no longer here, but it's what gets me through these uncharted, murky waters. He helped me come out my cocoon of dormancy and become a butterfly soaring in happiness.

I have slowly gone through my husbands belongings he no longer needs. It is strange to me to see boxes of trinkets once sentimental to him. They have become mere things now and are meaningless junk to someone else. I have managed to sort through some of his clothes, but checked the pockets in hopes of finding some sort of message to cherish now that he is gone. I came across his tuxedo and suits. I held them to my face and cried, realizing at that moment our Cinderella glimpses in life were over. I fell into a depression, crying uncontrollably and put those items back into the storage chests to deal with on another day.

It took me several attempts over as many months to make sense of any of it. I probably wouldn't have pushed so hard to do it, but I couldn't stand the disarray of the room. I also determined the task is so difficult that I will also go through my own things and downsize. I don't want to leave the same heart wrenching project for those I leave behind someday.

His library of books filled with a wealth of knowledge collects dust now, but I am unable to part with those mere things either. I found his old military fatigue jacket he used to wear, especially when we dated. I took it out of the box and it hangs on the back of my desk chair. I wear it as I write my memoirs. It makes me feel close to him as if he is holding me inside of the coat.

I find myself doing several little, quirky things that those who have not lost cannot understand. I have begun to select who I share with too. There are so many willing to judge. They also unknowingly throw harsh words my way. When they hurt me I just breathe and tell myself, "They know not what they say," thinking of Jesus when He said, "They know not what they do."

In February, during another attempt to gather Will's things, I discovered a cardboard box labeled, "Will's photos and letters." It was filled with pictures from his days in the Air Force. I laughed as I looked through them, noticing they resembled those of a teenager's sleepover.

There were also several dozen letters postmarked from England dating back to March 1988. I felt like I was prying reading them until suddenly, I came upon one mentioning my name. I finally found the prize I was searching for in Will's empty pockets. They were in reply to his mentioning that he had found "the one." The authors sounded ecstatic that he found the girl of his dreams. Those messages sent happy shivers up my spine. I was experiencing extreme joy in the discovery of what was written in those letters only three months after we met.

He had that box packed away for all the years I had known him and never revealed the contents to me. Every time we moved, we took it with us. By not knowing what I would find in there, I received a gift from my husband.

Spring arrived and I thought of all the chores the two of us did together. As a team we cleared remnants of winter away and at the same time prepared for summer. The mundane work occupies my mind and keeps my thoughts of Will alive.

With the arrival of the new season I encountered new tasks we did together, and was distressed about doing them alone. We spent afternoons on our back deck listening to the peepers and frogs. We watched all the birds returning for the warm season while sharing a cup of coffee and conversation. I stand there now as if he is here with me and I soak up the wonderfulness of those times. The memories bring me both pain and joy. Now that I have a few months of what I call recovery under my belt, I am able to accept those moments more regularly without going into complete tearful breakdowns.

It has been several months since my beloved husband tragically died upon accidental death. I still cry at least once a day, especially at night. Some days it seems all I do is cry for no apparent reason. I say goodnight to Will as I look at his photo on the bedside table and then I go to bed. Lying there, I say my prayers and try to give gratitude at the same time, although I don't always feel so grateful. I go on and speak aloud to Will as if he is hovering in the room somehow, blind to my eyes. I want so badly to give up everything and join him. Thoughts run through my head frequently of just how to end my life here and be with him on the Other Side. In my mournful state I am able to justify my death being easier for others to endure and accept. I imagine it couldn't be as miserable as the suffering I feel deep inside me from losing Will.

The wounds penetrating my soul from grief are still very raw and open and I can't envision ever healing. The good news is that my therapist tells me what I feel is normal and that there is no time line for grieving. I haven't had to walk in my darkness completely alone. My family members and friends have come to my aid during this time of deep despair. Early on and for many months they were there when I picked up the phone or sent e-mails almost every day. I also attend a grief support group, which I must say has been beneficial.

Directly after my husband died someone mentioned that option and I really didn't think it was for me. I never wore my heart out on my sleeve in the past and wasn't sure I could now. By mid November I was reaching out for it and discovered I was on a road traveled by many others. We meet and we all share stories, tears and laughs, and leave feeling less alone in the world. Between that and therapy I find small rays of light that give me hope that I can survive this. Although, I still fall into the deep lows of my roller coaster ride and wonder if I actually will, let alone enjoy living again. One day I'm up and another I'm down which makes this journey just so darn hard.

I continue to hear old expressions of how, "It is better to have loved and lost than never to have loved at all" or, "Time heals all wounds." As a widow I prefer not to hear those phrases. I can't imagine they are meant to be comforting, because they're not.

Well wishers also try to comfort me by telling me I will find someone else and marry again. I want to scream and tell them to keep their thoughts and remarks to themselves. They haven't walked the path I walk now. How could anyone know this kind of pain unless they have also lived it?

I was married to my soul mate, my best friend, the love of my life. If I knew there was a chance to find Will by going door to door with his size eleven shoe and trying it on every foot in the kingdom, just like in the fairytale, I would. I know he is gone from this life forever though.

People tell me I should sell our house and move away from the memories. Will made this house our home with his hands out of love for me. We found peace in the woods of our property. I can't abandon that gift. Besides, anywhere I go my heart will follow and that is where the memories are engraved. My soul is at home here and I will stay.

At about the seven month mark of Will's death, someone questioned why I was still crying myself to sleep at night. I explained how I feel as if I have been cheated or robbed. I no longer have the little things my husband offered to me in simple conversation or just his presence. I lay down at night and I no longer have the "goodnight my love," or the hug, or cuddle. I don't get to ask "how was your day," nor is it asked of me. I don't get to plan the day with Will tomorrow or the upcoming weekend. He understood me and my quirks. When I was down he brought me up or at least made me feel safe, by holding me and telling me, "I love you my honey, and every thing will be okay."

I need him and he is not here to do that for me now, which makes this all the more difficult. I lay there alone and just wish he could somehow show himself in my realm and give me the predictions of the future, but he can't. Some nights I just plain hope I do die of a broken heart and never wake up in the morning, if such a thing is possible.

Now I am alone and will have to find myself and live for just me when I am up for it. The inevitable changes will come one day at a time whether I want them to or not, since I cannot stop time from coming. I am an independent woman. However, at the same time I merged to be one with my husband and lived for him, for us. I loved, honored, and respected him, and was loved, honored, and respected by him. We had the perfect partnership.

Even going out with friends doesn't fill the void. It occupies my time and I enjoy the friendship, but it is like a double edged sword. I can have fun, but am saddened at the same time because Will isn't here to share in it with me. Perhaps it will just take some practice.

It is a strange feeling to lose someone so close to you. I feel like a part of me is missing, I feel so incomplete now. Memories of all my years being married to him flood my mind constantly. They keep me stuck in the past where it's comfortable and it's all I know. Those thoughts indicate our magical life did indeed exist. At this stage of my grief they are all I want, unless, somehow Will could rematerialize and come back to me and our humble, little life, but that's doubtful.

The present and future roll past me like breezes on my face having no meaning at all. I will take my life here on earth as long as I must. I would prefer being on the Other Side with my departed soul mate. I know we will be reunited again some day when my journey comes to an end. For now, I feel as if I can't wait for potentially another forty years and wish I was going sooner rather than later.

Visits And Coincidences

I believe in the metaphysical world and have had people sense Will's spirit here with me. I can't hear him or see him, but thoughts of him rush at me for no apparent reason. It is said that occurs when he is here with me in spirit. As a young girl I could hear my mother calling me as if she wanted me to come home at supper time. Sometimes I was a hundred miles away and it would've been impossible to hear her. I couldn't stop the voice so I'd call her to see if she was alright or looking for me. She always told me she was just thinking about me.

Since my husbands death I have experienced several visits through my dreams which were so vivid and lifelike. My first experience was about two weeks after he died and I will never forget it. It happened while I was just falling to sleep or just waking up, not in a deep sleep and not dreaming. I sensed someone standing beside my side of the bed. I was lying on my back and I felt a hand cradle the back of my neck. It gently lifted my head off my pillow and tenderly kissed me on the lips for what seemed like several seconds. I was then carefully lowered back to my pillow.

I woke up immediately and felt like Will had come to say goodbye. I later shared the story with my brother and he said, perhaps Will instead came to say hello. I was more excited about his interpretation and decided it indeed was hello and not goodbye.

Since then, I have had a few more very vivid dream visits. I have also experienced a sighting of my husband in a store as if he was walking this earth with me again.

About five months after Will passed away I began to experience some electronic malfunctions with my computer printer. I use it so infrequently that I leave it turned off when it is not in use to conserve electricity. One night I woke up in the wee hours of the morning to a buzzing sound and got up to locate its origin. I wandered around the house thinking it was coming from smoke alarms, but they were all fine.

The sound continued and I followed it. I was led to the office where the computer is. The printer was running and the ink jet was lining up as if preparing to print a document. The rollers were turning as if to feed paper through the machine. It was going haywire and it wouldn't stop. I hit buttons to see if I could turn it off, but it had a mind of its own. Finally, I hit the fax button on top of the unit and the window illuminated the words, "line busy." I don't even have the fax option connected. It made me wonder if perhaps a message was trying to come through from the Other Side. I know that sounds crazy, but that's what was going through my head.

The machine finally stopped going berserk and I hit print just to see what would happen. It did nothing because there was no power to it. I turned the power on and hit print again, but it only produced a blank piece of paper. After that night it continued to become possessed and start its ritual weekly. All I could attribute it to was that Will was trying to let me know he was with me. It gave me peace to know that.

I began journaling one month after my husband died so I could privately vent. I used that tool in the past and found relief by silently releasing my words during painful periods in my life. It was as if I was going to a therapist. I began writing this book in December 2008. After about eight weeks into it I got an e-mail from Will's cousin. She told me she was dreaming about him every night. In it, he told her he wanted me to keep writing and that he would speak to me through my words. She didn't know I was already working on this book. She had been having the same dream consecutively while I wrote. Once she gave me the message the recurring dream stopped.

With these "coincidences" I have been tugged toward the need to feel a connection. In April I sought out communication from the Other Side through reliable psychic mediums. It has helped me gain some peace knowing my husband is not only alright, but he is with me when I need him to be.

These mediums were not fed any information other than occasionally my husband's first name. With that, they told me how he died and that he died instantly. They told me he was communicating to me through electronics, flickering lights, song lyrics and license plates, and that he is here with me constantly. Also that he is sorry he had to go suddenly, but he will wait for me forever. Shortly after those readings I did see a license plate and it said; ILW84U – I'll wait for you…

The second one I saw told me that I was writing a book, this one, and that it would be very powerful and heal many people. She told me Will was telling her about our two weddings, and she couldn't have known about that. She confirmed many things revealed at my first reading as well. I was shaking from the rush of adrenaline pumping through me as I left. I was overwhelmed by the completely accurate information she had given me. I was excited and it gave me hope that I will be alright, and that writing this book must be my purpose in life now. I needed one and now I may have found it.

I don't know how a woman I have never met could know so much about this book. After I left I couldn't stop thinking about what she told me about it. She knew the format of the writing and that it was written in three parts. I was only in the editing stage of things. She knew that parts one and three would be the healing portions of the book. She told me my husband was telling her that part two was my love story with him. She hit the nail on the head.

With that, I have had positive thinking toward the success of this project. Initially, I wrote to shed the multi layers of grieving. My journal was my escape to release my dark feelings of despair. Writing about the happy memories brought me to a better place. Since the book has begun to materialize, I have had requests for a copy from people in eight states in America and two foreign countries. I have to believe in its power to heal. I think my current purpose is to help others by openly sharing my journey.

I heard about a radio show that hosts a psychic medium-intuitive who does phone readings on the air. I called and dialed for three hours and never got through. I tried the following weekend and still wasn't getting through. I looked at a photo of my husband on our mantel and asked him to make the phone ring because I needed it so badly.

On the second dial attempt I was connected to the show. I knew somehow Will made it happen. In that reading, I was told God took Will before he felt anything when the accident occurred. His soul contract was cut short due to it. She told me Will and I were soul mates. Our love was multi-faceted and we intuitively knew when to offer each other a pick me up. I know Will did that for me quite frequently. She confirmed that my computer printer is not possessed. It is Will's energy causing it to go berserk. I already knew that, but it was nice to have it validated.

I was so intrigued by the three minute reading that I wanted more. I discovered that she did longer phone readings by appointment as well. I needed more questions answered so I booked one.

In June she did that for me. Not only did Will come through for her, but his father did as well. She told me that was unusual. I told her I had been asking Will to let me know if he was with his dad. She said, that explained it and was exactly why he came through, he wanted to answer for himself.

She said we both had strong energies and that when he and I met; it was in the middle of a conversation. We had no beginning because we had loved in past lives. That explained my immediate comfort with him the night we met. Through her he told me to let go of any guilt regarding his death. There is no shoulda, coulda, woulda, and I couldn't have changed things.

The subjects that came up during our session helped relieve me of some of my anxieties. I had been playing the scenario out in my mind. I thought we could have made things different and he'd still be alive, he was supposed to be home that week. I was impressed that she also knew about the writing of this book, its format and content. When I asked her if Will was okay with it all, he told her absolutely yes, and that truth is truth. He told her I am not able to tell a lie and that I blush when I try. I confirmed that information was true.

Many of my questions were answered with that call. It comforted me and allowed me to know I'm not crazy when I sense him in my thoughts.

Lost And Broken

I'm heading toward the one year mark and still fight the feelings of despair and wanting to die. I loved Will so deeply and I think I was more attached to him than a child to a puppy. That must be why it is so painful to let go. I feel frustrated because I always had my life together for the most part. If I didn't, I could take a deep breath, come up with a strategy, and fix it.

I have a bit of an engineering mind, and strong, worker-bee determination to make everything better. However, I can't seem to fix this thing called grief. I can usually put on a good front though when I keep myself quite busy.

There is no manual on how to do this or survive it. It truly is individual and in a category of its own. I want the easy button or the crystal ball to tell me how to deal with this. I try to rely on my inner self, my gut instinct, for guidance that was so true to me in the past. It seems to be on vacation or curled up in the corner crying like I want to be now. I hope one day the guide within my heart will get up, dust herself off and come back to the partnership, and give me a little nudge like the ones Will gave me whenever I was depressed.

We are constantly told not to stop living. Neither our loved one, nor God would want us to. I know that, but I can't seem to find the overdrive gear and make myself go forward yet. I try to do things and feel extremely awkward if it is something I typically did with my husband.

Will and I talked about our funeral wishes candidly. We told each other we'd want the other to find someone and remarry and enjoy life again. I told him then and believe it now that I doubt if I would ever remarry, he was the only one for me. He told me he couldn't imagine doing so either for the same reason. I don't know what the future holds for me. I do know how wonderful Will was and the life we shared was extraordinary, and I would compare anything beyond it to it. I think I had a once in a lifetime gift in loving and being loved by Will.

I saw Bob Barker on the Bonnie Hunt talk show this year and he talked about how he lost his wife, the love of his life, twenty-seven years ago. He continues to wear his wedding band and says he'll never remarry either. Perhaps when one loves another so strongly, that is the only chance to come along. I feel like Mr. Barker and that I will finally find comfort in my new purpose, whatever it may be, and live for it with passion.

I am grateful for my strength although sometimes shrouded, for it will help me push through to fulfill God's ultimate plan. I have my work cut out for me because it would simply be easier to stand in line for a cyanide cocktail and end this horrible pain. My writing has helped the tears surface, and cleanse the bleeding wounds of my heart that I have suffered during this chapter of my life. I feel as if I have crossed some hurdles and have fewer bad days now.

It is definitely like a roller coaster ride just as my therapist told me. The high points on the ride go by quickly, then you zoom down into the lows and they seem to drag on for days at times. I have realized I cannot fight it and I just let the toxins from grief seep out through my tear ducts. In a million years I would never have been able to describe this pain or understand it until now.

Today I am thankful for therapy, support groups, and good friends willing to let me cry as they silently hand me a tissue for my tears. Like any times of turmoil you discover who your real friends are. I have also found peace in reading many books by those who have lost and about after death communications, stories by famous psychic mediums, the Bible, and a daily meditations book for grief. I'm glad I can talk to my dogs while they kiss me to make my pain go away. I also talk to thin air, releasing the bottled up steam accumulating daily and haven't been accused of being schizophrenic. I find joy in my relationship with my computer keyboard. I have spent dozens of hours writing this book, journaling, and sending hundreds of e-mails allowing me to passionately spill my guts of deep sorrow.

I have been seeing a psychologist twice a month since January. At first, I cried on the way to my appointments, during them, and on the way home. I felt pretty beat up on those days. I kept going because I knew therapy can have that kind of intensity.

I am glad I stuck with it. I have been able to spill my deepest thoughts to her. I have even shared that I have spoken to psychics. She never judges or makes a face to make me feel uneasy. She always listens and interjects at the right time.

One day she asked if I put a photo album together in memory of Will. I was surprised I hadn't already thought of it. I had made scrapbooks for my two dogs that passed away. It made sense and I did just that. I cried yet another river of tears making it, but they were medicinal. I look at it now, and remember who and what we were, and how we evolved over all our years together. It's a terrific keepsake for me now.

For awhile I wasn't really sure my sessions were helping me or causing me more anxiety. I had some aha moments on occasion, but I didn't feel the heroic, happy ending to my sadness I was looking for. Finally, in the eleventh month of grieving, my therapist listened and then spoke more than usual. She offered many useful tools for my journey.

She was able to tell me who I was and what my personality traits and qualities were. I was mesmerized by what she picked up on during my many tears. I guess she was paying attention. With that revelation, she has helped me to see warning flags when they come up and what to do with them. I'm still a work in progress, but I think that is because I am human. I'm not an expert... Each time I am a step closer to wanting to grasp life and hold on instead of following through on my suicidal thoughts.

The therapist I see is based with Catholic Charities. I love how she can hear my experiences and then compare them to biblical stories. It helps me remember this is a lesson and I am God's servant. I came up with an equation in April and expressed my thoughts to the psychologist. I put it like this: "Loss equals grief, which equals rebirth or soul growth, which equals instrument of God to do work He intended." Then I said, "Grieving is my illness transforming me through suffering."

I had been seeing her for five months and by June I was feeling kind of spry. I asked her if she thought I was finished with my need to see her. She told me she recommended I stay with it for at least the first year of loss. She then told me the second year can sometimes be more difficult and to consider continuing my therapy through that period.

I still have days where I find myself wandering around my house aimlessly. I wake up having great intentions of accomplishing something for the day, but get absolutely nothing done. My life is similar to the weather. Some days the sun is brightly shining, and others it's foggy or rainy and all I can do is go with it.

My goal with this book is to share, and hopefully help others realize they are not going crazy during their time of grief. They need to do whatever makes them feel better, even if it means crying for three days like I sometimes do.

I know I have sat down and gone through cards and photos that I knew would make me cry before I started, but did it anyway. I still wear my husband's jacket and it hugs me when I need one the most. I cry in the car when I hear our song or a song I have never heard before, but the lyrics resonate into my heart. Grief is a monster that only you can know during your journey. Anyone who has lost on the same level can share and offer some hope. Each person will still find their own experience is unique because we are all so different.

My husband and I had this pure, simple, indescribable, effortless love for each other. We knew what the other was thinking most of the time and were synchronized like the gears of a Swiss clock. It was just the two of us, and we relied on each other and did everything together. Once we moved to New Hampshire no one else influenced our decisions and choices. He was literally my other half and now he's gone. It wasn't supposed to happen like this; somehow we really thought we would die together.

For the longest time I thought it was impossible for anyone to understand the intensity of my pain. I felt like I was the only widow on the planet for weeks. I thought *my* love for *my* husband was so extraordinary that no one else could possibly fathom how badly I was hurting.

I am lucky I can share my most intimate thoughts with a couple of people. By testing the waters I have discovered who I can trust to listen with a loving ear, offer a soft shoulder to cry on, and a hug anytime I need one. It seems sharing has helped me the most and I can typically be very private at times.

It is very painful to discuss feelings of sorrow and despair. As I do, my chest tightens around my heart and my stomach ties into knots. I forced myself to bleed tears and am beginning to heal my broken self in itty-bitty pieces. I am told as I do this work, one day all the memories I hold so dear will not make me cry each time I reflect on them.

Today I still get trapped in my thoughts of all the wonderful things we shared in our life together. I continue to ask why this happened and still have no answer. We always shared a special relationship, but somehow our last summer together was extraordinary. It is bittersweet. We were on top of the world in the five weeks following the trip to Boston in July.

As I think about our last months together I recall so many magical moments. It makes me feel like the departure was unfolding before my eyes. I believe God had His hand in it and gave me a gift in disguise. The memories that conjure images to my mind of my husband smiling and being the loving soul he was are now a blessing and a curse. They make me happy on good days, but I cry on others. They have become the tools I need to survive this tragedy.

Redefining Myself

Even though I have good days more frequently, I still cry every night when I crawl into bed wishing he was still here. I reach over and touch his pillow as I talk to him wondering if he can hear me. There are days I wonder why I am still here and cannot be with my soul mate here or there. It is difficult to explain to those who have not lost someone they love so deeply. Someone recently said some very wise words regarding losing a husband or wife. She said, "No one knows until it happens to them." Those words say it all. I really could not have known this journey and the pain that comes with it until I lived it. No one can.

Since Will died, friends keep telling me they admire my strength and courage. Even people that knew me before Will, tell me I possessed those traits of bravery before I met him. I don't feel so strong and courageous these days. I'm still looking for a way to be organized again, and find a routine, and to have more joy than sadness.

Grief is multi faceted. There are hundreds of words in the English language that describe the misery of it. I find I have to be reminded that I have permission to feel all those emotions that come with it. I prefer to pretend that everything is alright. That I have dusted myself off, and gotten up onto the horse again, and am ready to ride with bandages on my bumps and bruises. I have deep drive to prove I am okay, but with that I feel tired and overwhelmed, broken, lost, hopeless, without passion or purpose, and oh so sad.

Mending my broken self seems like so much work and that the result will never be what I hope, so I sometimes crash and give up on it all. It seems easier to just stay in bed and wither away. Will was my reason for living. He helped me hold myself together anytime I was on the verge of breaking. He praised me and encouraged me to blossom. Now, I don't have my biggest fan here to inspire me. Others try to come to my aid, but the connection isn't there. I do not feel the same free comfort the way I did with Will. I feel like I have had to give up my addiction and so badly want my fix. Will was that for me.

I have been trying to be around people more. However, my calendar became crowded with too many engagements. That led to a small meltdown in the woods as I begged God to stop my anxiety. I discovered I had to retreat back to a more private life and find myself. When Will was here with me he was my circle of friends. We did everything together so I wasn't used to being with people so much. Without realizing it, I tried to jump in with both feet a bit too soon. I was overdoing it and giving so much of myself that I was feeling overwhelmed and anxious. I wanted to be put out of my misery and asked God to just take me. I wanted out of the class I was thrown into for a reason only known by Him.

As if grief isn't painful enough I have felt compelled to watch romantic, tear jerker movies. They bring my life with Will to the surface. I cry in the realization of the absence of the great friendship we had. I have watched my wedding video dozens of times in the past year too. I feel joy watching it over and over again because it was such a happy day. I see the love throughout it and realize I am not imagining what we shared. I am grateful I have that.

On May 26th I went out with my mother, she thought it would be good to get me out of the house. It was the nine month mark of Will's death. We had lunch and did a little shopping. I went to check on my dogs in the truck to be sure they were still in the shade, and if not I would move them. I did relocate the truck to a shady area and on my way back into the mall I saw a Zales jewelry store.

I walked into it and within moments the sales woman asked if I was looking for anything special. I don't actually know why I went into that store that day and I answered the woman by telling her I wasn't sure. I then told her it was my wedding anniversary. As she began to congratulate me I interrupted her and told her my husband passed away. The words just came from my mouth without a thought about it. She apologized and I think she was stunned. We continued to talk as I browsed through the cases filled with things that sparkled. I told her I was thinking about getting something symbolic to remember him by.

She pointed out some necklaces and bracelets. I explained that I don't really wear jewelry and thought a ring was my best option. I scanned the inventory as the sales woman made suggestions, until she mentioned Will's birthstone. I asked what exactly it was for the month of November, and she told me citrine. She led me to a case and a ring immediately captured my eye. It was citrine and diamonds set in white gold. I pointed it out and jokingly made a remark of being attracted to the most expensive thing. She told me that citrines aren't too pricey and she looked at the sales tag. As I tried the ring on and watched the diamonds sparkle in the overhead lighting, only found in jewelry stores, she took out a calculator and reduced the price. There was a sale that day.

I didn't balk at the amount she quoted me. I normally would never have spent that kind of money on myself. For some reason I was completely at ease and never experienced my typical stomach butterflies during the transaction. I wear the gift my husband led me to on that day proudly on my right ring finger. I continue to wear my wedding band with his, which I had sized to fit me, on my left ring finger. The two bands signify all we shared together and I want to relish in it for eternity. I feel close to him as if his ring is a part of him that he left for me in the physical world.

That evening, which would have been my nineteenth anniversary, I watched my wedding video again. I drank wine from one of our toasting glasses and smiled through it until the end. I talked to him and thanked him for all the fun through our years together, as if he may have been here in spirit with me watching it too.

Trying to live, I signed up for a one day sewing class. It was for making an evening size bag out of a men's necktie. I frantically looked for one of Will's many ties, but realized I had given them to his cousin. I kept digging through boxes because I knew I hadn't given away certain items that brought sentimental memories to me. Low and behold I found one last tie. He wore it to his nieces wedding only three days before he died.

The morning of the class I awoke to the smell of toast cooking in my kitchen. I was alone in the house and even noticed the toaster was unplugged. I couldn't get beyond the aroma filling the first floor of my house. I smiled and laughed a little to myself, and then spoke to Will. (It's a good thing I don't live near the state mental hospital.) I asked him if he was making himself some breakfast. He ate toast, among other things every morning. I went outside to gather up my dogs so I could feed them. I came back into the house moments later and the toast smell had vanished.

I went to the course and was in the middle of creating an adorable little handbag out of his tie. I was sewing some pieces together and sensed someone standing behind me. I figured it was the instructor looking to see how I was doing. I turned around and no one was there. I instantly got a shiver up my spine and then smiled. My eyes must have had a glimmer to them; I sensed it was Will watching me create something so sweet out of his tie. He was a sentimental guy and would appreciate the gesture.

In the eleventh month of grieving my loss I had a day where I needed to go into my attic and clear a path. Something was pushing me to do it. Most of my husband's things were already in boxes and just stacked wherever they ended up, leaving a wake of chaos.

Being disorganized makes me feel uneasy, and the mess upstairs was bothering me. I contacted an organization that took clothing, sold it, and used the proceeds to aid the homeless in our area. They were accepting donations, especially men's clothing.

I began taking the boxes downstairs and loaded them into our truck. After I took the last box out I went upstairs to do more. I went through the bureau where I had placed all of his suits. Those were the

254

hardest for me to let go of. I remembered how handsome he looked in them. I was physically attracted to him most when he dressed up.

I hung each one up on a hook and re-checked the pockets. I came to a sport coat and did find several things in it. I held onto each item, precious to only me. I was elated by the discovery, but cried at the same time. It reminded me that he was gone. I told myself, if I can give up the other clothes then I can be a big girl and release my grip on the suits as well. I wiped away my tears, took a deep breath, pulled myself together, and brought the suits to the truck. I delivered everything that morning still feeling as if I wasn't ready to. I decided it was never going to be easy, so I just did it.

I placed his tuxedo and shoes, and his favorite Levi 501 button fly jeans, as well as many trinket items into a box. It is a time capsule of sorts. I can't let it all go just yet. Those things remind me of him and his grand presence and humor. Perhaps it is that I still have many more tears to shed and when I see them, I will cry.

Shortly afterward, I spoke to my husband's sister and told her about my recent accomplishment. She calmly told me Will would be proud of me. She said he would be so glad someone else could now use the things he no longer needed. She was absolutely right and it made me feel better somehow.

A few days later I went into the attic just to rearrange some things to organize the cleared area better. My niece calls me a neat freak. I suppose I would have to agree with her. Because of that trait I made yet another heart warming discovery. I found a yellow sticky note lying on the floor where the boxes were before I took them away. In my husbands handwriting it said; I love you!! Love your Honey. On the back side of the note he drew a crown and wrote Hallmark underneath it. I felt like it was a new note from him. I knew it wasn't, but it still gave me a warm and fuzzy feeling knowing he loved me so much. Only those of us that have lost someone so dear can understand that.

It is August now. My tears come without warning still. I am a wreck thinking it is soon going to be one year since my husband died. It doesn't seem possible. I hoped if a year didn't pass, it meant he wasn't really gone or that I stopped time. It feels as if this milestone makes it a concrete fact.

At this point I still cry when I hear our songs on the radio. I tend to daydream on longer road trips and replay my entire life with Will in my head. I took my first solo bike ride the other day, and while I was doing so I thought of our treks to Arlington together. We'd ride in our spandex gear and arrive to the torment of teasing from his relatives for sporting such attire. I smiled at the thought of it.

I notice all the high voltage transformers he serviced as I travel along roadways in our area. I think how easy it would be to jump the fence laced with warning signs to keep out and end my pain. I am instantly brought back to the idea that suicide won't bring me to him.

Currently, I feel like I am walking barefoot on a beach covered with broken seashells. I am asked why I am not open to letting another man into my heart. I explain to them, I am still madly in love with my dead husband. That's where I'm at.

Some people still wonder why I am not ready to put on the charming smile I always sported before Will died, with a flick of a switch and move on. What is move on exactly? What is letting go? I don't think we can truly ever let go. Our loved ones will always be there close in our heart.

I have taken some steps alone and am able to survive and live, but I am still sad and feel very lost. I express my desires to get on the bus to eternity, if only it came to my doorstep. I have lived a full life and have no regrets. I know if I had to say goodbye today I could. At least I have that comfort.

I had another dream recently that coincided with some of my recent thoughts -- and plans Will and I made last year. An e-mail arrived the next day from the woman who was in my dream with Will offering to take care of my pets. I deciphered the dream and took it serious. Everything was falling into place for me to go to Bar Harbor; the trip Will never got to take. I followed my gut instinct and am booked to stay there for the one year mark. No other dates were available. It's eerie how it all transpired, but I am not afraid of listening to the Universe and my dreams.

Year Of Firsts

$\mathcal{It}$ **is said during the first twelve months** after losing a loved one you experience the "year of firsts." It has been just over a year since Will died. The journey has been a tumultuous one, and feels as if I have been tossed around by the waves of an ocean.

Each traditional holiday, anniversary, or birthday brought me severe anxiety. Initially, I thought I could keep my cool and let the significant dates come and go gracefully. Upon their arrival I felt like I was in an obstacle course. Half way in it became quick sand and I could not turn back. I had to finish or sink. Somehow, something inside me went into auto pilot mode and pulled me through with a will to survive.

There were many what I would have considered unimportant firsts during the year as well. Too many to mention really, but here are some highlights. One day I was at our local Laundromat, something Will and I did twice a month. As I fed the washing machine quarter's tears formed and began to spill from my eyes. I can't tell you why something so simple would make me emotional. But, at that moment I immediately reflected to a time when we were there together talking as we started the machines.

Another first was going to Starbucks and having a cup of coffee without Will. I felt those physiological symptoms that come with fear or anxiety and choked back the tears. I remembered one of the last times we went there together. He had a red t-shirt on that I bought for him at a church bazaar. It said, *Mr. Wonderful* on it in white lettering. The barista looked at us and smiled. She then boldly asked me if he was Mr. Wonderful. I chuckled in delight and told her that he was indeed.

Even during voting season I felt those anxious feelings of loss once again. Will and I always discussed in great depth who to vote for and then went together to perform our civic duty. I bantered with him in my mind about the possibilities and wondered who he would have voted for with the primary results in. He would have been surprised to see the race would end up being between Mr. Obama and Mr. McCain. When he died Mrs. Clinton was still in the running.

In autumn it was strange walking in my woods among the trees displaying a kaleidoscope of color without him. I thought of our past conversations and excitement of walking together. It came to my mind that we weren't experiencing the season together this year, or any other one from now on.

In April I attended my first wake since Will died. It was another veteran funeral. I saw the body in an open casket draped with the American flag and my eyes welled up. Will's coffin was draped in the same manner. I left the room, I couldn't bear the pain. Shortly afterward, I excused myself and went home. I told myself and friends I will not go to anymore wakes, I will mail a card and explain myself instead. The memories of my husband's memorial rushed back at me like it was yesterday. That experience confirmed my wishes of not having a wake when I die.

I continue to walk my dogs every morning. We all need it. I reach the woods beyond my pasture, and I begin to have small talk with Will while I give commands to my excited dogs hot on the scent of wildlife. I usually cry during my conversations, but still feel the need to express myself. It makes perfect sense since he and I always shared everything when he was alive. It helps me sort things out. At times things seem intolerable and I let him know it, and tell him I wish I could come over to him.

I have clutter surrounding me, where everything usually has its own place. I begin to clear the messes, but lose my train of thought and end up putting it back where I got it. I am usually so organized and have found myself in need of a time management refresher course.

I go to the veteran's cemetery where some of Will's ashes are placed to rest. I know in my heart he isn't there, but whenever I'm in the area I still feel compelled to stop by. The visits are usually brief and I have my act together when I arrive. I stop and talk to him, and then I touch his bronze plaque and I begin to cry. I verbally explain my tears to him and hope he can understand my sadness even though I am trying so hard not to be. The emotions are out of my control and cause my insides to shake. With that, I have to say goodbye. I kiss the plaque and tell him I love him and get into my car and quietly leave.

Spring rolled into summer and grass at our homestead had to be cut. Every piece of equipment seemed to have died with Will. I had to charge batteries, clean carburetors, do some carpentry repairs to the walking bridges, and things of the like. I think back to all the times we worked together and all the things he taught me that have come in handy now. I am grateful.

June came and I planted our vegetable garden. I had all these aspirations and the weather was cool with morning frosts still so I kept putting things off. One day I got a feather in my cap and worked all afternoon to get everything set. Finally, the deed was done. However, there was no excitement in the anticipated harvest. I still feel so lost without him.

One day in July I went grocery shopping. I was putting the food away and suddenly as I placed some eggs in the refrigerator I started to cry. I could hear Will talking to me as he did when he was living. Something that seemed so trivial sparked my tears. Then later the same day I was washing my hair and cried again. The emotions come unannounced and for no apparent reason at all.

I went to see a play in a local theater during the summer. It was an enjoyable evening and I laughed and in the moment felt normal for a change. Afterward, I drove home and began to cry, missing Will. We went to plays and now it was too weird for me to do something we so casually enjoyed together without him. It threw me into an emotional wading pool of uncharted waters. It will take more time to complete my transformation induced by grief. It's not yet comfortable doing all the things we did together, alone or with another friend.

I still listen to Frank Sinatra and as I do I cry. Why do I bring on the tears? I don't know. It just seems to force my sadness to surface and is then released I suppose. I keep saying my tears are the waters that cleanse my soul.

Each time I sign off the computer I see the photo set up as my desktop. It's a photo of Will and me when we were in Boston just before he was killed. I talk to him before I switch to stand-by mode and tears fill my eyes. I am grateful for such a beautiful trip, all the love we shared, and the cares we left behind. It still seems impossible and is so hard to believe he is really gone.

I have had several weeks of crying starting the end of July. I didn't know what was wrong with me, but then had a realization. I think the tears came unconsciously with the one year mark approaching.

I also had my first birthday without my husband ten days before the one year mark. I had great support to get through it though. I kept busy and received many birthday cards from my family and close friends. I was also honored with a lovely birthday party. We enjoyed a fabulous meal and laughter together. The distraction kept me from plummeting into darkness.

I was presented with helium balloons and my inner child surfaced and turned on some more fun. I opened one and inhaled the gas inside and began speaking. The voice that came out of me was so silly I laughed. With that, the laughing was even sillier and I laughed even harder. Everyone at the party, including all the adults, joined in and we laughed so hard my cheeks were hurting. It was a perfect ending to a wonderful evening.

My friend told me it was good to see me smile. It felt good too, but in the back of my mind I was missing Will. Especially after we all became intoxicated with goofiness, because Will would certainly have joined in on the fun. I am sure he was there with me in spirit and got a good chuckle witnessing it all.

My computer printer continues to play out its ritual occasionally. I notice it is usually on particular nights. I know he stops in for a visit because one day this summer I was looking at our wedding pictures.

Ten minutes after I put them away the printer began its performance. I absolutely love it and do a happy dance every time it occurs. I talk to him as if he is in the room around me and thank him for the gift.

I have a ritual each evening still. I say goodnight to all my pets and when I enter my bedroom I see Will's photo on the bedside table. I pick it up and as I hold it against my chest as if to hug him I cry and say, "goodnight my love."

Some days my heart feels deep, stabbing pain with the memories that sometimes come without much thought. It feels as if it has been surgically mangled and left to heal without any suture or closure of my chest. Initially, I felt robbed and wished I had never met Will, nor married him. If I hadn't I wouldn't have known the pain of today. He was stolen from me by the same Universe I believed put us together in the first place.

Time has changed that. I have many moments of sadness, but they make me feel happy. I now realize that I am fortunate to have had the time I actually got with my husband.

I still struggle with questions wondering why I am being punished by the same God I loved and trusted. I thought I lived my life in accordance to His commandments. It seems so unfair. I know God didn't do this, but that it is part of my soul's journey for learning and growth. It's a tough pill to swallow, but it somehow eases my anger toward God.

I have miraculously survived the first year of grieving. I have had some good cheering in my corner. I have put into practice realizing my strengths and trying to be proud of my accomplishments. I know Will would be for sure.

As I head into year two I still have to drink from the cup of courage. I have to constantly be aware of my ability to beat up on myself and stop the brutality. My therapist is helping me with that. Even though I knew I couldn't just put my grief into a pretty little box and put it up on a shelf to be forgotten, I somehow wanted to. There are so many triggers and the pain hits and my tears still flow. I wonder if I will ever stop being so sad and broken hearted.

One Year At The Sea

I was beckoned to the sea. I had dreams and other occurrences that called me. They got the gears moving in the direction Will wanted to see me head toward. He was leading me to Bar Harbor.

I accepted my friends offer to watch my pets so I could go away on a vacation. It was too coincidental not to. I contemplated canceling because I was concerned about my cat and his diabetic needs.

One day as I was splitting wood I smelled the ocean air. It caught me off guard and I sniffed the piece of wood I had just cut. It smelled like wood pulp and I shrugged it off thinking I imagined it and went back to work. About five minutes later the scent presented itself again. I then realized there was something bigger at work and I followed the bait.

I went in the house later that day and I sought out lodging that would allow me to bring my cat. I spent what seemed like hours online checking website after website. They either didn't allow pets, they were out of my price range, or they were booked. The task almost seemed hopeless and I hit the last link at the site I was on.

It offered all the features I was looking for. It even had a bigger perk than I expected. It was located on the waters edge with a magnificent view and serenity. I was so excited and called to reserve the dates I had in mind. They were booked two of the weeks I chose and my heart felt heavy. The woman on the other end of the phone line then mentioned she had the last week of August available.

I really wanted to avoid that week since it was the one year mark. I didn't think I would be up for traveling then. I cringed and accepted the dates she offered and booked the cabin. After I did I became so excited about the trip and that so many factors were falling into place. I knew it was meant to be.

Will and I were supposed to go there a year ago. He was gently nudging me to go now. I believe he is helping to lead me to living more fully. All in good time though. It's not easy.

I made all the arrangements and took my mother and my cat for a four day getaway. I had never left my dogs before. I wasn't sure I would be relaxed enough about that if I was gone longer. As I said my goodbyes to my dogs the tears began to come and they kissed me. I gave myself a little pep talk and managed to pull away from the sad puppy-dog eyes and be on my way.

Tuesday, August 25th we made the six hour trek to our destination at Mount Desert Island, Maine. I rather enjoy long distance driving so it was easy enough for me to tackle. We encountered the final intersection about seven miles before the location of the cabins. A few minutes afterward I noticed the odometer reading revealing we had about a mile to go.

Suddenly, I came around a bend in the highway and I saw the ocean. The sight was breathtaking. In the distance I saw a landmark mentioned in the directions. The cabin was tucked in behind it. At that moment I experienced goose bumps all over my body realizing I was going to stay there. I was so excited and couldn't believe how fantastic the place was. It was right on the waters edge at Hull's Cove. I thanked Will for bringing me to such a beautiful place.

I checked in and we settled into the twelve by twelve cabin. I brought a framed photo of Will with me and placed it on the bedside table. He was there with me. I sat on the deck and got lost in the view of the ocean and the sounds from gulls. I could envision us being there together and imagine the conversation we'd have. I knew how much he would have loved it.

I ventured down to the water. The tide was just starting to go out. I picked sea shells and cried thinking of all the times I gathered them with Will. It was a special moment reflecting on the small talk and laughter we shared.

My aunt and uncle were visiting the area as well and we made plans to get together that same day. My itinerary also included time to be alone on the 26th so I could deal with my emotions of hitting the one year mark. I planned a bike ride in Acadia National Park.

The afternoon we arrived my aunt and uncle willingly chauffeured us around the town of Bar Harbor. They were veteran travelers to the area over the last twenty years. We went to dinner and then browsed around in the shops downtown.

I went on vacation with the intention of indulging in fresh seafood that I can't get at home. I wanted lobster and mussels. The restaurant we visited that first night offered a combination meal including both delights. I not only accomplished my goal of eating to my hearts content, I enjoyed homemade blueberry pie as well.

While we shopped I noticed little things that would have sparked Will's interest. I could hear his laugh and things he would have said in life. I smiled at the recollections.

That evening I sat in the cabin and noticed the photo I placed near the bed and cried. I couldn't believe a year had passed. I still miss him as much as I did in the beginning of all of this.

I woke up early the morning of the 26th. I actually barely slept due to being in a strange place and perhaps the anxiety of the whole one year mark thing. I took a peek out the sliding door to the deck to see what the sunrise prospects were. It was foggy so I decided to lie back on the bed and waited for time to slip away.

I was having anxiety, most likely from the anticipation of what would unfold on the day marking Will's death. I made my coffee and went outside to sit and get lost in my own mind for awhile.

Time was ticking away very slowly and I paced. I went back into the cabin trying to be quiet so I wouldn't wake my mother up. I sat in a chair and wrote out some postcards. I then looked at the digital clock and it was 7:00 a.m. At that point I realized Will died exactly one year ago. I did not plan to remember that, but I did. That time of the day never hit me before. I felt intense emotions flood through me and began to cry again. How was it possible that he was gone? I was still stuck on the fact that it wasn't supposed to happen to us.

I still needed to pass some time before I could feed my cat and give him his insulin injection. I wandered across the street to a post office I noticed the previous day so I could mail the post cards.

Again, I was hit by a Mac truck of feelings as I approached the building to innocently send off some mail. In an instant the moment of when I was notified that Will died came rushing at me. It really shocked me. I had to mentally and physically take a hold of the flash back and shake it off. I was ready to drop to my knees just as I had when I first got the news.

I had a session with my therapist just after I returned from my trip. She told me those experiences are much like post traumatic stress disorder. She said I will most likely endure those memories year after year. Also, each time it occurs it will be less painful and shocking.

Enough time had finally passed that I was able to take care of my cat. I could then be off and running to hit the carriage trails of Acadia National Park for my bike ride.

I arrived, parked the truck, and went to the visitor center to get information about a trail called Witch Hole. I had an older map and it looked like a short enough loop. I figured I could ride, have a good cry, talk to Will, and then have the rest of the day to try and enjoy myself. I discovered the trail was only five point six miles.

I went to the truck and unloaded my bike and gear. A man was standing outside his car with his bicycle and started conversation with me. He asked me where I lived in New Hampshire. He noticed my license plates. His were also from the same state, but he lived further south. I told him where I lived, but he hadn't heard of it. I explained it was in the White Mountains and then he had a better idea of its location.

We got to talking since his wife was off doing something as he waited for her. I mentioned I was there for the one year mark of my husband's death. We had a nice chat and in it the subject of this book came up as well. His wife returned and they both wished me luck on my journey and we parted on our bikes.

I entered the trail system and wondered if I had bitten off more than I could chew. I immediately encountered a long hill and felt my muscles burning from the intense push to pedal my way up it. As I hit the crest there were some marker signs at a fork in the trail and I navigated easily enough. I felt at ease to know things were marked so well.

A few minutes later I passed a woman going up another hill. She was walking her bike up it. I gave her a bit of verbal encouragement as I went by her. I met with flat trail again as well as another fork in it. I stopped to try to figure out which way to turn, but this time there was no marker for the trail I was on.

The woman I passed a few minutes ago arrived and stopped to rest. Her friend was there waiting for her. I asked them if they knew which way to go for Witch Hole. They offered me a look at their map and it revealed I could go either direction and still be on the loop.

The three of us began talking. I discovered one of them was a teacher and she was on a journey of grief as well. I also learned that she was from a town near the area where Will was killed. She had seen the article in a newspaper when it happened. We shared and she told me she knew we met for a reason. I believed her.

I took a right at that fork on the trail and ended up on an incredible adventure alone. It was the perfect way to start the one year mark. During my ride I noticed the scenery and the flora and fauna along the hills I rode up and down. I pondered on thoughts of walking them with my dogs and Will.

I stopped and listened to the wind blow through the trees around me as it and the sun touched my face. Suddenly, I was bombarded by sadness. I cried and spoke aloud telling Will, "I miss you so much."

Near the end of my trek I arrived to a plateau overlooking Hull's Cove. I stopped to take in the magnificence of it. I stood there in awe and realized how much my husband would have loved it too. It was bittersweet to enjoy it all without him. Somehow I knew he was beside me showing it all to me though. A dragon fly made an appearance then. There is a belief that our loved ones visit us in their form. I knew it was my husband's gift to me.

I had seen a psychic medium a week before the trip. She revealed to me that I was taking a trip to the sea. I confirmed it and told her it was along the coast of Maine. She told me Will was telling her about three things for me to do there. She said to go to Cadillac Mountain, take a trolley ride, and to watch for a presentation at an area where towering rocks jut out of the sea with foam around them. She didn't know I was going to Bar Harbor. Cadillac Mountain is there. It turned out there was also a trolley ride there too. There is a place called Thunder Hole which presented the rocks and foam that she described.

I listened to her instruction and I think the message in it all was to enjoy the splendor, try to live, and perhaps even laugh a little. The trolley was actually a tour of the highlights of the area. The guide gave me quite an education with his narration along the route. He was also witty in the world of political jokes. I thought of Will and how he would have laughed and completely agreed with him. I remembered our visit to the USS Cassin Young in Boston and how informative it was. This tour was the same in that regard.

We saw Thunder Hole and Cadillac Mountain on our route as well. We only had time for fifteen minute stops at each place though. There is so much to absorb that it only allowed a small sample of what each site offered.

My mom and I met up with our relatives around five o'clock and went back to the cabin. I took care of the cats needs and then we got sandwiches and went to the top of Cadillac Mountain. We ate them there as we watched the sun go down. It was amazing. The excursion was satisfying to my soul. I felt immense joy being there to witness God's creation.

The anniversary date was difficult, but being busy and having such incredible scenery to look at made it easier. The visual and audio stimulation made me focus on happy times with Will instead of the way I found out he died. I had already encountered that in the morning and certainly didn't want to spend the entire day that way.

The next day I awoke in the same manner as the previous one. I got up and began the morning activities. I put together a camp breakfast and took it outside to eat by the sea. The ocean creates calmness for me. I wasn't going to be near it for long and wanted to absorb all I could from it.

I have been accused of having a vivid imagination in the past. With it I was able to reflect once again on conversations with Will as we vacationed in cabins in the old days. All our yesterdays make me smile inside. I love getting lost in them.

I had a busy schedule for the final full day at the island in Maine. My aunt and uncle were once again willing to take me anywhere my heart desired. They knew all the exciting spots to see and the great things to do while we were there.

I really wanted to see Thunder Hole again. It's not a place you can spend fifteen minutes at and get the entire gist of it. They took me to that majestic place again. We got there while the crowds were thin. I wandered all over the towering rocks jutting up out of the ocean. They made me think of the formation of the earth.

I stood there taking it all in and became aware of the ocean smell. It was the same one I noticed while splitting wood a few weeks prior. It hadn't occurred yet on the trip. I knew I was where I was supposed to be. I then thanked Will for guiding me to such an extraordinary place.

I had my camera with me so I spent some time trying to capture some frame worthy photos. Once again I could hear Will asking me what was taking so long. I tend to try to crop the frame perfectly so I don't have to do it later in a dark room. I enjoy a laugh as I hear the silly things he used to say.

We continued the chauffeured tour along Ocean Drive and went to Otter Cliffs. You can walk out onto them, but from the road it looks like they drop off immediately. I ventured out fearlessly and observed the incredible view. I love the mountains where I live, but the ocean offers me serenity. I was lost in time and basking in the peace of it all.

My mother stood watching me from the road. I looked back for her to see if she was ready to leave, but she wasn't there. My aunt was nearby and I asked her where she went. She told me my mother couldn't watch me get so close to the edge. It was an optical illusion from where she was standing. I was far from it. She had heard my outbursts of wishing I could die in the past. She may have been worried I was going to actually jump.

I continued to stand there engaged in my curiosity of a lobsterman cruising to his traps. I was intrigued by the seagulls hovering above the boat following it to every stop. They were in tune with the sound of its engine and landed on the water even before he stopped. They were hoping to snag some bait from the many traps he was checking. I was imagining the life of that man as I watched him.

We continued the drive along the loop and visited Sieur de Monts and I found my way to a bench in the sun. I sat next to an elderly woman and we took up conversation. We began with the typical, "where are you from?"

Within minutes I was telling her I was there to fulfill a need to go there in honor of my husband. I explained what happened to him and she expressed her sorrow for me. She then shared her news with me. She had stage four cancer. She didn't know how much longer she had to live.

Her daughter brought her to see the area because she always wanted to visit it, but just never got around to it. We are all guilty of that in some form or another it seems.

When her daughter arrived to take her to their next destination, I took her hand and wished her good luck on her journey. She said, "Same to you, and may all your dreams come true." I sat alone then as the sun shined on my face warming me and sending me into a relaxed state. I felt tears slowly stream down my cheeks and I knew we met for a reason.

I had experienced some interesting feelings on the island. I could sense Will's presence there and when I did I felt at peace and grateful to have gotten to go there.

The last night during the trip I had dinner at Geddy's in downtown Bar Harbor. As I sat with my mother, my aunt, and uncle I shared the story about Will's red Mr. Wonderful shirt.

The décor of the restaurant was chaotic and had hundreds of old license plates scattered all over the walls. Some were just numbered and others were vanity style. We had fun translating the messages on them as we waited for our meals.

As we were leaving the establishment I saw one on the wall next to my shoulder. It read; MR1DFUL. It was Mr. Wonderful! I thought of Will immediately and the correlation to our conversation before dinner. I hadn't seen it as I entered. It wasn't until after we spoke of the shirt and the comments we heard when he wore it. Was it a message from the Other Side? Yes, perhaps it was…

The next morning meant it was time to go home. Before we had to leave I sat by the sea one last time and watched the tide go out. I talked to Will aloud and thanked him for bringing me to such a beautiful place. I saw the most amazing landscape, waters, sunrises and sunsets, and met some angels in the form of people during the trip.

I also pondered on another amazing point. The trip I tried to plan for other dates unsuccessfully, turned out to be flawless. We enjoyed clear days and nights with abundant sunshine and perfect temperatures. All of that and we were there between two major storms. A hurricane hit only two days before we arrived killing one person. Then a Nor' Easter struck the day after we left leaving six inches of rain in its wake. I have to believe there was something other than my own self in charge of it all.

I loaded up the truck, checked out and thanked our hosts, and off we went toward home. I was leaving a magical vacation. Half way home a thought crossed my mind. I couldn't have gone on the same trip a year ago. Even though I was missing Will and wishing he was with me, a year passing made it easier. With that, I realized that some healing has occurred. Even though it feels only slight, I became aware that I am on the right track.

One Stitch At A Time

My husband and I were bonded like an alloy of molten metals cast together making one. I could never imagine life without him, but here I am. How could something so fantastic be cut short? I will never know.

Life has a way of resuming even if you don't want to stay in the game. I have to continue to be strong and believe this is a productive part of my journey here. I struggle to fight back the tears when I think about finishing my story without my husband here beside me. He was the fuel for my spiritual fire.

I think the heart of my broken spirit is in need of a thousand stitches and the sewing has just begun. I need more time.

Until Eternity

"Good night Will. I love you, I miss you…"

Acknowledgments

First and foremost I thank Will for taking me by the hand and giving me the best years of my life. The many precious memories we created come to me and I reflect on them and smile. They ease my pain. Also for coming to me in spirit and gently nudging me out of the darkness.

I thank God, the Universe, my Guides and Angels for pointing me in a direction to find my new purpose after feeling so lost.

Thanks to Kellyann for listening to my story over lunches as we edited this work. Also for letting me pause while I read -- to let my tears flow. I thank Ladys Slipper Vintage (www.ladysslippervinatge.com) for the use of photographic materials for this project.

I thank Evelynne for her amazing artistic talent. Without you I would not have been able to produce the heart brought to me in my dreams.

I thank my family, whether through blood or marriage, for the encouragement and faith that I could make this book happen.

Recommended Reading

Warren, Rick. The Purpose Driven Life, Zondervan, 2002

Hood, Ann. Comfort: A Journey Through Grief, Norton, W. W. & Company, Inc., 2008

Guggenheim, Bill, Guggenheim, Judy. Hello from Heaven, Bantam Books, 1999

Edward, John. One Last Time: A Psychic Medium Talks to Those We Have Loved and Lost, Penguin Group, Inc., 2000

Edward, John. Crossing Over: The Stories Behind the Stories, Princess Books, 2002

Rothschild, Joel. Signals: An Inspiring Story of Life After Life, New World Library, 2001

Piper, Don. 90 Minutes in Heaven: A True Story of Death & Life, Baker Publishing Group, 2004

Didion, Joan. The Year of Magical Thinking, Knopf Doubleday Publishing Group, 2005

Whitmore Hickman, Martha. Healing After Loss: Daily Meditations for Working Through Grief, Harper Collins Publishers, 1994